Enterprise-Scale Agile Software Development

Enterprise-Scale Agile Software Development

James Schiel

CRC Press
Taylor & Francis Group
Boca Raton   London   New York

CRC Press is an imprint of the
Taylor & Francis Group, an **informa** business

AN AUERBACH BOOK

CRC Press
Taylor & Francis Group
6000 Broken Sound Parkway NW, Suite 300
Boca Raton, FL 33487-2742

First issued in paperback 2017

© 2010 by Taylor and Francis Group, LLC
CRC Press is an imprint of Taylor & Francis Group, an Informa business

No claim to original U.S. Government works

ISBN 13: 978-1-138-11409-8 (pbk)
ISBN 13: 978-1-4398-0321-9 (hbk)

Library of Congress Cataloging-in-Publication Data

Schiel, James.
   Enterprise-scale agile software development / James Schiel.
      p. cm. -- (Auerbach series on applied software engineering)
   Includes bibliographical references and index.
   ISBN 978-1-4398-0321-9 (hardcover : alk. paper)
    1. Agile software development. 2. Scrum (Computer software development) 3. eXtreme programming. I. Title. II. Series.

QA76.76.D47S2957 2009
005.1'1--dc22   2009037003

Visit the Taylor & Francis Web site at
http://www.taylorandfrancis.com

and the CRC Press Web site at
http://www.crcpress.com

Contents

SECTION II PLANNING THE TRANSITION

SECTION IV CREATING THE AGILE ORGANIZATION

Preface

I wrote this book for three reasons, and while I explain myself more fully in the introduction chapter, I want to clearly state those three reasons without all the technical jargon and semi-impressive phrases.

First, it has been a lifelong goal of mine to write a book. It was always a question regarding what. I'm a big science fiction fan, so I always thought my first (only?) book would be a sci-fi story. I was never certain it would happen. I didn't even know what to do first. I certainly enjoyed writing, so I figured that was a good start. Then I met Ken Schwaber. Then Mike Cohn. Then Esther Derby. All authors! Boy was I impressed! And then I realized that more than impressing me, these three people brought the concept home for me. These individuals, my friends, are just people—like me. Whether or not I was going to write depended not on fate, but action. I needed to start thinking about writing a book every day instead of hoping it would just happen to me. Lucky for me, circumstances provided me both the topic and the opportunity to write, and because I was always thinking about it, the opportunity didn't pass me by.

I recently enjoyed the opportunity to plan, guide, and coach a fourteen-hundred-person application development department from using a variety of development methods to using agile development and Scrum.* I quickly learned upon embarking on that journey that there was little available information that would help guide us toward a successful implementation in an organization with fourteen hundred developers and managers working in several development sites spread around the world. So, my second reason for this book was to make sure that others that find themselves in my shoes have something they can use to guide them.

Truthfully, I didn't have a third reason until I started reviewing the various cities I've visited while helping others adopt agile development through coaching and training. I've always enjoyed traveling, and thanks to Scrum, I've been to places I never thought I'd visit: from Vancouver, Toronto, and Ottawa, Canada;

---

* For the record, a number of good people were involved in this effort. If I tried to list them all, I would do someone the injustice of forgetting to mention them. Suffice it to say, they know who they are and I greatly appreciate their help and energy as we fought our way into new territory.

to Cambridge and London, UK; to Brussels, Amsterdam, Stockholm, Helsinki, Munich, and Nuremburg; to Mumbai and Bangalore, India; to New York City, Dallas, Anaheim, Los Angeles, Pensacola, and Portland, Oregon. I consider myself fortunate for having been given the opportunities I've enjoyed and visited the cities I've been to so far. All of this reminds me of something Ken Schwaber challenged all of us with at a Scrum gathering in Boston a few years ago—that to the extent that we and our organizations had benefitted from Scrum, we should pay it forward, give back. So, there's my third reason: this book is one of my attempts to give back to Scrum and agile development what I have gained from it.

Acknowledgments

Many authors say it, but now I have a firsthand understanding of what they mean when they say how "this book could not have been possible without the help of many, many people." There are many people that have been involved in this effort, both directly and indirectly, and I will likely miss many people I would want to thank, despite racking my brain for many hours to ensure that I don't miss anyone in this list. So here goes:

I owe my most profound thanks to my wife, Donna, and my children: Rebecca, Melanie, Jacob, and Rachel. While there were many people involved in the overall effort that resulted in the information between these covers, only my wife and children had to deal directly with my frequent frustrations trying to make unusual concepts clear in a most limiting medium: words. Only my wife and children had to watch "Daddy" typing away many evening and weekend hours. While I typed, they kept the house quiet and kept things moving without my help. Truly, without their patience, understanding, and support, I could not have finished the manuscript.

Next, of course, come the key people with whom I worked to achieve what was arguably the largest implementation of agile development and Scrum in the world (whether this is still true I cannot say). Collectively, we had little idea of what we were getting ourselves into when we started and, as I've joked in the past, if we had known, we might have lacked the intestinal fortitude to go through with it. However, I'm glad we did, and were I in the same situation again, I would do it all over again (although I think the information in this book would help me to do it better). So, I offer my thanks to the following: Daphne Thomas, Brian Barr, and Tom Miller for creating the environment that led to a full-scale transition to agile development; John DuClos, Mark Engel, and Chad Haggerty for being there from day one and never taking a step back from the edge; Lisa Margerum for understanding how crucial coaching, training, and education were to the transition and making it all happen; and Kiran Thakkar, Chirag Dadia, Mike Bria, and Nick Conti for taking up the agile/Scrum banner and championing it in their respective groups and departments—they made it happen in the trenches and I will never forget the crucial roles they played in the transition. And a special thanks to Laura Anderson and Nancy Dohmson for the steadfast examples they provided and, of course, for helping keep me sane when the desire to run away screaming was overwhelming.

Lastly, I extend my thanks to the many trainers and coaches in the agile and Scrum communities with whom I have worked, even if briefly, that helped me gain the unique understanding of agile development and Scrum that I have today. Of course, among them are Ken Schwaber, Mike Cohn, and Esther Derby for playing a big role in showing me how and why Scrum works; and Bob Martin, Kent Beck, James Grenning, Martine Devos, and J. B. Rainsberger for helping me understand even more clearly during those times when I just didn't get it.

Over the past five years, I've worked with so many people that I'm sure there are others whom I haven't mentioned that also played a part in this effort, and if I have indeed forgotten to mention you, please know that you have both my deepest appreciation for your help and my sincerest apologies for my oversight. Let me know and I'll be sure to mention you in volume 2, OK?

Biography

Jim Schiel is a Certified Scrum Trainer (CST) with a strong background in enterprise-level Scrum installations. Prior to starting Artisan Software Consulting, Schiel worked at a large, multi-national software development company for 23 years, where he worked initially as a developer, then as a manager for 16 years, and eventually playing an instrumental role in creating one of the largest Scrum installations in the world. As a business process engineer, he helped identify, document, and implement best practices for enterprise Agile Development.

Jim is now the owner and CEO of Artisan Software Development, a company with the founding belief that software development is as much an art form as an engineering practice and that the key to high quality and high productivity is in the developers, not in the processes with which we surround them. Jim travels around the world helping organizations realize the full potential of their developers through the use of Agile Development and Scrum.

Jim lives just outside Philadelphia, Pennsylvania with his wife, Donna, and four children.

Chapter 1

Introduction

I would rather have a good plan today than a perfect plan two weeks from now.

Gen. George S. Patton (1885–1945)

On the day that I began what eventually became a full-scale transition of a fourteen-hundred-person organization to agile development, I had absolutely no idea what I was getting myself into. To be certain, I have no regrets. I've met intelligent, fascinating, funny, and friendly people who welcomed me into their group—what shall I call them? agilists?[1]—without prejudice or prevarication. At the same time, had I any idea what I was in for when I gave my management that first presentation on Scrum, I might have been a little less willing to charge headlong into the agile world.

So there I was, unwarned and unprepared: "where angels fear to tread …" and the like. Lacking solid information about how to do a large-scale transition, we plowed ahead, trusting in our knowledge of the organization and the unwavering support of both management and the developers. Four years later, somewhat wiser and a tad wary, the transition has gone well. From new project management practices to new requirements management, new ways of getting customers involved in development, and new ways for developers to work; from human resource policy changes to remarkable improvements in product quality—I've learned a lot. Along with the team that was strategic to guiding the transition, we made some good decisions and some bad ones. During it all, I found myself frequently wishing for a resource I could use that would at least give me a clue whether we were headed in the right direction. That is the genesis of this book.

I don't claim that this book will tell you everything you need to know about guiding a transition to agile development. Within its pages, however, you will find a good place to start. Some of what you will find within these chapters will work for you as written; much will need modification to work in your situation. Some may not work for you at all. However, this book will give you much to think about when creating and executing your transition plan and will be very useful in helping you make sure that you've thought of and made plans for many of the possible situations, risks, and contingencies.

Web Site

Because information about successful (and unsuccessful) enterprise agile transitions is always evolving, I've created a web site that accompanies this book: http://www. bigagiledevelopment.com. At this site, you'll be able to find additional information regarding many of the chapters in this book, sample presentations to support the training, and sample policies and documents to support the regulatory information provided in this book. Your contributions to the site and feedback on how to improve this book will be much appreciated.

About This Book

As previously mentioned, the purpose of this book is to be a reference source for organizations attempting to convert their transitional development practices to agile development. Contrary to being a step-by-step guide, this book is organized into chapters that provide the material in the order that you're likely (though not definitely) going to need. This book is *not* intended to be a "body of knowledge" type book that standardizes agile and Scrum practices. Agile development is about people, not prescription. The intent of this book is to offer guidance and a tool kit. Read it, take ideas from it, and pick what works for you.

This is not the software development version of the "great American novel." It is not organized to be read from cover to cover and, indeed, may be a reasonable remedy for insomnia should you decide to read it cover to cover.

The content in this book is based on the use of Scrum[2] as an organizational framework and on many Extreme Programming (XP)[3] practices used to define how software is written and tested. I recognize that there are many other frameworks and practices that can be considered, but I recommend the model represented by the combination of Scrum and XP for nearly all organizations.

I've also included information in this book regarding good development practices that are based on the International Organization for Standardization's ISO 9001 standard, which contains the requirements for the creation of a quality management system that helps to ensure consistent production quality. While many of you will not need the controls contained in such rigorous regulations, I urge you not to discount practices that will most certainly help you create consistently high-quality software in a cost-efficient manner.

A Balancing Act

Often, during the course of the book, we will discuss a topic that has a number of different possible answers. Rather than tell you that one answer is "better" or "more right" than another, I will instead try to call out those practices along with their potential positive and negative outcomes so that you can decide which will work best in your unique situation. Consider all alternatives thoroughly before you make a decision.

Audience

Agile transitions are, not surprisingly, a collaborative effort of product managers, trainers, coaches, management, executive management, human resources experts, quality control, and transition team leads as well as Scrum masters,[4] product owners,[5] developers, analysts, architects, writers, testers, etc. To keep it simple, this book is written from the perspective of someone guiding or leading a transition and attempts to address many of that individual's concerns by providing possible solutions at best and, at least, a heads up as to what problems will need to be addressed.

There also are items discussed throughout this book that will have legal or regulatory significance. In the case of these matters, it is advised that legal counsel as well as labor law experts and regulatory specialists be involved in the activities of the transition team in order to ensure that no laws are broken or practices put in place that would not pass a regulatory audit. As everyone's situation varies depending on the industry, the project, the country of manufacture, and the country in which the product is sold, the organization must take it upon themselves to ensure that all matters of legal or regulatory significance are properly addressed.

Success Factors

I debated whether or not to put this section in the introduction or in the section that follows, "Setting the Stage for a Transition." Obviously, this section won the argument. The deciding factor was simple: if you don't have the key success factors in place before you begin the transition, *plan to get them as the first steps of your transition!* We'll talk about all of these items in detail later in another section. The key success factors to a successful transition to agile development are:

1. *Executive management support and involvement*: Several aspects of the agile transition need executive management support to get off the ground. These include, but are not limited to, purchasing computing environments to support Scrum teams and continuous integration and testing, modifying the work environment to support team rooms instead of independent offices and cubicles, understanding and accepting the new reporting and estimating mechanisms used in agile development, and working with the sales and marketing as well as customer support functions of the organization to support the level of customer involvement prevalent in an agile development organization.

2. *Early successes*: There will be many in the organization ready to say things like "Oh, that won't work here"[6] and "Agile development really screwed *that* up!" The reality is that not everything is going to go perfectly the first time and you are going to experience a lot of difficulty throughout the transition. In fact, agile development is all about trying the best solution you have at the time and improving it as you go forward and gain more experience. In order to keep the initial momentum of a transition going, plan for early successes by not trying to address the most complex or riskiest problems. Consider a pilot project to work out some of the unique kinks in your organization before continuing on to something bigger and more critical. And remember, phrases like "That won't work here" are usually just cover stories for an organizational dysfunction that, if corrected, would make life better for everyone.

3. *Automated testing*: Agile development demands that you be able to add code to your product in small slices of functionality and then be able to ensure that the product, by and large, still works as intended. This is a crucial part of the XP practice of *continuous integration and testing* and helps to encourage both the frequent introduction of new code to the product and *test-driven development*.[7] All of these practices are crucial to ensuring that Scrum teams are providing completed functionality at the end of their sprints.

4. *Management support and involvement*: Managers play a key role in an agile transition. They are with the development teams helping make the day-to-day decisions that either enable agile development or allow the organization to make one compromise after another until the agile transition slowly fades away.

5. *Developer[8] support and involvement*: As much as management support is required to get the transition off the ground, developers also have to make it work. Agile development, and particularly Scrum, requires developers to do what is "right" to create high-quality software for their customers. In my experience, there isn't a product development method more so than agile development that *needs* every developer to act in the best interests of the product. Without the commitment of the developers, no agile practices can be successfully implemented.

6. *Discipline*: Contrary to widely held opinions, agile development does not suggest anarchic development (coding without planning, design, or documentation). It does, however, suggest a willingness to move forward with

a development project recognizing that software development is filled with uncertainty. In fact, a number of writings on agile development suggest that there is a unique balance of order and chaos required in software development that agile development recognizes and leverages. Think of it this way—you've gone on vacation to the Grand Canyon[9] in Arizona. As long as you're several feet away from the rim of the canyon, you feel comfortable walking or running as necessary. As you walk closer to the edge, excitement grows, but your caution increases as well. Agile development is all about getting right to the edge of the canyon without falling in—you get the excitement of being right on the edge of infinity, while, at the same time, you practice significant discipline to keep from becoming a permanent feature of the canyon floor. Without discipline, agile development becomes either too chaotic or too ordered[10]—in either case, the benefits that agile development provides (frequent delivery, high quality, innovative thinking, customer satisfaction[11]) cannot be fully realized.

7. *Patience*: By patience, I mean that an organization has to be willing to give the transition to agile development time to have a positive effect. While you may begin to see morale improve fairly early, improvements in software quality could take considerably longer. The cultural changes that accompany the agile way of building software applications *could take years to become an integral part of the organization.*

8. *Willingness to make mistakes*: Are you willing to make mistakes? There exists a mantra in agile development: "Fail fast, fail often." We learn much more from our mistakes than from our successes. Of course, we inspect, we adapt, and we frequently use retrospection to make sure that if we're going to fail, we get it over with in a hurry. Doing so allows us to get back on our feet and try again.

Suggested Readings

There are a number of good books and Internet-based resources that I would recommend to anyone involved in an agile transition or that finds himself or herself on an agile development team. I've avoided repeating the content of these books herein. These books and resources are:

Schwaber, Ken, and Beedle, Mike. 2001. *Agile Software Development Using Scrum.* Upper Saddle River, NJ: Prentice Hall.

Schwaber, Ken. 2007. *The Enterprise and Scrum.* Redmond, WA: Microsoft Press.

Cohn, Mike. 2005. *Agile Estimating and Planning.* Upper Saddle River, NJ: Prentice Hall.

Cohn, Mike. 2004. *User Stories Applied.* Upper Saddle River, NJ: Addison-Wesley Professional.

Beck, Kent, and Andres, Cynthia. 2004. *Extreme Programming Explained.* Upper Saddle River, NJ: Addison-Wesley Professional.

Feathers, Michael. 2004. *Working Effectively with Legacy Code.* Upper Saddle River, NJ: Prentice Hall.

Derby, Esther, and Larsen, Diana. 2006. *Agile Retrospectives: Making Good Teams Great.* Dallas, TX: Pragmatic Bookshelf.

Endnotes

1. I've also heard the term *agilistas* to describe those who evangelize agile development. My problem is that I hear *agilista* and I envision someone with a sombrero and a gun belt. Maybe it's just me?
2. For more information on Scrum, go to http://www.controlchaos.com and http://www.scrumalliance.org.
3. Extreme Programming is a discipline of software development based on values of simplicity, communication, feedback, and courage. For more information on Extreme Programming, go to http://www.xprogramming.com.
4. The Scrum master is responsible for making sure a Scrum team lives by the values and practices of Scrum. The Scrum master protects the team by making sure they do not overcommit themselves and he facilitates the daily Scrum (http://www.mountaingoatsoftware.com/scrummaster).
5. The product owner (typically someone from a marketing role or a key user in internal development) prioritizes the product backlog (http://www.mountaingoatsoftware.com/product_owner).
6. The phrase "Oh, that won't work here" is probably the most damaging phrase you can hear during the course of an agile transition. It is a clear indicator of an organizational deficiency. Here's the bottom line on that thinking: agile development has been used in organizations that are small or large, co-located or global, regulated and nonregulated. XP projects have been run successfully since the mid-1990s, and Scrum has been used since the early 1990s. There are thousands of successful projects as proof. The person speaking this phrase is really saying "Oh, I don't want to do that" or "It's not worth my effort to push the organization enough to change." And, by the way, the second most damaging phrase is "That's not agile," but we'll discuss this another time.
7. Test-driven development (TDD) is a software development technique consisting of short iterations where new test cases covering the desired improvement or new functionality are written first, then the production code necessary to pass the tests is implemented, and finally the software is refactored to accommodate changes. This helps to ensure that the tests enforce the design and not the code.
8. I want to clarify that when I say *developer*, I mean all of the people that are involved in the creation of the product. That includes the coders we usually think of when we say *developers*, as well as the analysts, testers, designers, database architects, system architects, writers, etc. During the course of this book, I will try to use *coders* when I mean coders and *developers* when I mean everyone involved in building the product.

9. For those of you unfamiliar with the Grand Canyon, it's an absolutely beautiful location in the southwestern United States. In some locations, the canyon is over fifteen hundred meters deep and is estimated at 5 or 6 million years in age. For more information, see http://www.nps.gov/grca/.

10. Dee Hock, founder and former CEO of the VISA credit card corporation, described the harmonious confluence of chaos and order as *chaordic*. See http://en.wikipedia.org/wiki/Chaordic for more information.

11. Find the principles behind the Agile Manifesto at http://www.agilemanifesto.com/principles.htm.

Chapter 2

Why Agile?

The first and most basic question to ask before you embark on a transition to agile development is: Why?

Why do you want to do this? If you are in a business, there's only one practical reason to do this. You want to improve your bottom line. You want to make more money. For those of you I just disappointed by my being so Machiavellian about my reasoning, I apologize. However, I haven't yet run into an organization that wants to transition to agile development to develop better-quality products even if they happen to lose money in the process. Except for government agencies and the Detroit-based auto manufacturing industry, no organization does anything that doesn't somehow help ensure the organization's continued existence. In fact, in several years of consulting, I've only found one organization that was already happy with their software quality, but wanted to transition to agile development anyway just to see if things could get better (and they found that agile development worked better for them too!).

Therefore, the question is: Can transitioning to agile development help you make more money? With but a few exceptions, my answer to this is always a resounding yes. But before we talk about reasons for going ahead with the transition, let's discuss some of the reasons why many feel they should not.

Myths about Agile Development

As with many other misunderstood concepts, agile development has garnered a number of nasty myths about it that stem from misunderstandings about agile development or poorly considered theories of why it failed in many organizations. Let's deal with some of those myths now, before diving into discussions of what agile development can do for you.

1. *Myth 1: Agile development does little planning.* This myth barely has a speck of reality in it, and that speck is that agile development does minimal up-front planning. In fact, agile development proposes just enough up-front planning to get the project started. From that point forward, planning is done at various levels as frequently as every day. Agile development, as evidenced in the Agile Manifesto, puts more value in expecting and embracing change than in creating detailed plans to deal with or control change. Think of it as just-in-time inventory management. This concept, which reduces cost and waste by closely monitoring inventory levels and customer purchasing trends and taking delivery of new inventory "just in time," has been championed by some of the largest retail chains in the world, including Wal-Mart Stores, Inc. Agile development works the same way. If you plan too far ahead in too much detail, you end up wasting time changing your plans when the prevailing circumstances change without warning. However, if you create long-range, high-level plans at the beginning of the project and supplement them with short-range, highly detailed plans on a daily, weekly, and monthly basis, you waste very little effort in planning.

2. *Myth 2: Agile development does little analysis.* As with planning, agile development reduces waste by doing just enough analysis on any given feature to reveal previously unknown details, risks, and requirements to support better and better estimation and more effective planning. As with just-in-time planning, doing the analysis throughout the project reduces the waste caused by features being changed or removed from the project during the course of the project.

3. *Myth 3: Agile developers don't write documentation.* As has already been pointed out in the description of the previous myths, agile development looks to reduce waste by not spending time and effort doing things that are very likely to change. Similarly, agile developers will write documentation only when the documentation is proven to have some kind of value to the organization. Putting it another way, I often coach my agile development teams to see if the documentation that they have been writing has an audience, that is, someone who wants to read it. For particularly long or detailed documents, we review every section of the document to ensure that someone actually plans to read and use it. If there's a reader, and they can't use any other documentation already produced by the development team, we write it. This is also true for documents that are created primarily (or solely) for compliance with a standard or regulation. Certainly, even documents that appear to have no other purpose than to satisfy a regulation have at least one very important reader: the auditor.

4. *Myth 4: Agile development "squeezes" roles out of the organization.* This one always puzzles me. In general, I hear complaints that agile development forces everyone to work in teams and, regardless of role or job title, to work on any tasks. This, I'm told, obscures role definitions (which, frankly, is not always a bad thing). Agile development, however, does no such thing. Agile

development creates development teams based on the skills needed to complete the assigned work. I usually see that handled by making sure that each team has a certain number of testers, analysts, coders, and so on. But all of these are, in fact (if a little vaguely stated), roles. If agile development can be accused of anything with regard to roles, it's in the focus on the success of the team. It most certainly has happened that team members not used to writing documentation, writing and executing tests, or creating reports have been asked to work outside their "role definition" in order to ensure that the team is successful.

5. *Myth 5: Agile development can't provide accurate project schedules to support organizational planning.* This concern comes up when a company transitioning to agile development asks for locked-in delivery dates and a locked-in feature list at the beginning of a project. In most instances, an agile coach or Scrum master will respond that he or she can either lock in the feature list or the delivery date, but not both. That's generally when the real shouting begins. More importantly, consider most, if not all, of the waterfall-based development projects that you've taken part in or watched from afar. How many of those fixed-scope/fixed-date projects ended as projected without changes to the included features or the staffing (usually by forced overtime)? How many of them sported project schedules that were perfect and didn't require significant changes at least once every hour or so?

Every project, whether agile or otherwise, balances the three key properties of people (or resources), time, and scope (what features/defects will be included in the release). It has long been agreed that you can't change any one of these properties without having an impact on at least one other (often both). For example, want to add new features (that's the scope property)? You'll have to add resources (people) to get the same amount done in the same time, or you'll have to add more time to get it all done with the same resources. This concept predates agile development and is part of basic project management (agile or otherwise). So, when Scrum masters say they can either lock in the date (leaving resources or scope subject to change) or lock in the scope (leaving resources and cost subject to change), they're just practicing good project management. Organizations have, for many years, attempted to lock in both date and scope without allowing changes to resources—this usually means the resources are going to be working lots of overtime and either or both the project scope and project timeframes are going to change at the last minute.

Waterfall projects have attempted for years to do enough up-front planning, analysis, and design to ensure that the project schedule is not only accurate, but capable of handling unexpected surprises. The reality, however, has been well documented in several studies: most application development projects are either cancelled outright or completed overbudget or overschedule and with fewer features than originally planned. The sad truth is that, despite the attempt to predict the problems that will occur, unexpected changes and uncertainty are a natural part of software development. Still, those of us who have managed waterfall projects know that while the project schedules and work estimates are created with apparent precision (often to the fraction of an hour), the precision is merely a mirage and our schedules are more than likely out-of-date as soon as we publish them to the organization. Agile projects don't create detailed plans up front because we know they are inaccurate and expensive to create—not enough information can be unearthed in order to create a precise schedule.

What does all this mean? The inability to produce accurate project schedules early in the project is a symptom of the uncertainty that is intrinsic in software development. Agile development doesn't attempt to reflect simulated precision in the project schedule. Relying on project schedules to be precise and then trying to squeeze more work out of your developers because the project schedule says they should be able to do it will require overtime to get the work done, and the work is done at the risk of reduced quality and lowered developer morale.

In fact, agile development does support organizational planning in a manner more effective than most development approaches. Here's how:

1. Agile development projects don't build features in phases. Rather, features are started and completed based on their priority. This means that agile projects deliver functionality sooner, and you will recover more completed functionality from an agile project that you have to change, cancel, or extend. When cancelled, waterfall projects usually provide lots of completed documentation, but little in the area of completed functionality.
2. Agile development projects can be easily planned to finish by a certain date with fixed resources. The variable, of course, is the scope, which can also be easily managed by modifying the priority of the features to get higher-value features earlier. You can more easily modify an agile project to get more or less functionality by adding or removing iterations from the project. This makes the cost of the project easily controllable by the organization's management.

Reasons to Stay Away from Agile

With all that said, why do organizations resist the transition to agile development?

I've heard many reasons why organizations don't try or try but quickly back away from agile development. It boils down to this:

■ It's too disruptive and too hard.
■ It won't work for us because we're too big/complex/regulated/distributed (fill in your reason here).

Let's be honest—these are understandable concerns. Transitioning to agile development is hard and it can be very disruptive. In fact, my major motivation in writing this book is to help you reduce the disruption and make it a little easier by giving you a path and some options that should work to get your transition well under way. If you aren't prepared to accept some disruption and some difficulty, to make significant changes to your organization and your organizational culture, you should stay away from agile development for now. As was already mentioned in Success Factors in the Introduction, management and development support are key elements of a successful transition.

As for the second belief that agile development "won't work for us," I often see this as a result of two different factors. The first factor is simple misunderstanding of agile development. Terms like *Scrum*, *sprint*, *planning game*, and *extreme* tend to drive even the most liberal of executive management into hiding. Who could blame them? We in agile development create terms like these to ensure that those who use agile methods clearly understand that these methods are very different from business as usual. However, that tactic seems to backfire when you try to sell Extreme Programming to the CEO of a financial institution. The second factor is simply that to start a transition to agile development, you have to see that a significant portion of the organization's policies, procedures, and practices as they relate to application development are actually attempts to make organization dysfunctions hurt less. An organization that isn't ready to accept the premise that a large majority of their existing structure needs to change is probably not ready to begin an agile transition.

Now, having talked about all the reasons why organizations won't try agile development or why they end their transitional efforts after experiencing difficulties, let's explore how an organization can benefit from agile development.

How Your Organization Will Benefit from Agile

Improved Software Quality

I have seen agile development benefit organizations in a number of different ways. First and foremost, software quality is always improved by the concepts ingrained in agile development. The continuous testing of an application, rather than waiting for the testing phase of a project to see if it all works together, is one of the most effective practices that agile development provides to an organization. I have witnessed integration efforts that took months, only to be followed by projects that included continuous integration and testing that eliminated any special time during the project when the only thing happening was integration. This is also reflected in the practice of test-driven development, where the code and its associated tests are not only kept current and working, but the tests are written before the code and are driven by the design, rather than being driven by the completed code.

"DONEness" is a major consideration in agile development and a major factor in the creation of high-quality code. Getting every feature to a predefined and widely agreed upon state of completion helps to ensure that the feature does what the customer wants it to do.

Improved Organizational Commitment

Related to the quality of the software is the commitment of the development organization and, quite possibly, the entire business organization. During my time as a developer or as a manager, there were many projects that we worked on for months on end just to deliver software as part of a larger project, and if we were lucky, we saw some snippets about how much the customer liked the new version. Sometimes, customers might even come in themselves and tell us how much they liked the software (but they never gave Too glowing a report—I suspect that it was like giving a hotel a perfect 10 on a survey; you always wanted to leave room for improvement). It was hard to stay motivated on projects like these and, more importantly, it was easy to never feel much in the way of ownership (shared or otherwise).

Whether the project went well or didn't, any potential positive feedback was so far in the future that it was easy to abandon one project to go work on another that either was using the latest technology or was the beginning of the "next great product." On the other hand, agile development, with its short iterations and sprint reviews, gave the developers that worked for me (and, truth be told, me as well) something to look forward to at the end of the sprint. Of the three possible answers we could get for any completed backlog item ("fantastic," "great but would be better with changes," and "not what I wanted"), two of them were at least positive and the third ("not what I wanted") was fairly easy to protect against by simply improving the product owner's contact with the team. Constructive feedback on a frequent basis keeps the development teams charged and engaged with the project.

Reduced Waste

Agile development also carries with it a strong aversion to waste, particularly waste caused by rework. As a portion of the Agile Manifesto suggests, "[We value] responding to change over following a plan." This appears in agile development in many ways, but is most particularly demonstrated in a principle borrowed from Lean manufacturing that suggests deferring decisions until the last reasonable moment. These decisions include allowing ourselves to probe deep enough into our prospective features to do appropriate planning, but not so deep that when a feature is removed from the project or significantly changed, we've wasted a lot of time on extensive analysis that now has to be thrown away or redone. The same thinking can be found in an agile development team's approach to writing documentation— they write just enough documentation to satisfy their internal customers (users, support, marketing, etc.) and their external customers.

Agile development's approach to requirements management is also a study in doing just enough to satisfy the current needs. Stakeholder requests (requests for new or changed functionality coming from the product's users) are rewritten as backlog items. Backlog items are historically written on index cards both to facilitate easy planning and to ensure that teams do not collect more information about a feature than they could easily fit on the card. As the project progresses, backlog items are analyzed and estimated; large, complex items are split into smaller items that are, in turn, analyzed and estimated. Each item exists in a state that has just enough analysis done on it to support ongoing planning. By the time an item is ready for a sprint, it may have been sliced down several times, accumulating more information and losing complexity during each pass through the ongoing analysis effort. In this manner, changes to backlog items can be introduced without too significant an impact on the analysis that has already been completed. Clearly, however, an item changed early in the project will result in much less rework than, for example, an item changed immediately before it is to be taken into a sprint and built.

Improved Customer Relationships

One of the strengths of agile development is pointed out in another line from the Agile Manifesto: "[We value] customer collaboration over contract negotiation." In other words, those of us who have embraced agile development have grown tired of the days where we use contracts as a wedge to force the customer to accept what we've built or pay more when they make changes from the initial specification. While we all recognize that there's a time and a place for good-faith contract negotiations, agile development makes a case for getting our customers closely involved in the development effort itself. Even small moves in this direction can be eye-opening and, in fact, may even be perceived as a product differentiator in markets where the competition is fierce. In one company, customers that represented various market segments of the company's flagship product were flown to the corporate headquarters to review the significant features that were planned for upcoming versions of the product. Over the course of three days, every major feature was reviewed and discussed. Experts from the company came in to define and clarify the features and the customers asked questions until they were comfortable they understood the premise. In addition, the customers were asked to do a high-level prioritization of the backlog; this prioritization would play a large part in the actual content of (at least) the next release of the product. At the close of the workshop, customers were asked to provide an evaluation of the session. In nearly every instance, the response was that the workshop was a long-overdue exercise that should be repeated a few times a year. The customers felt more connected to the decisions being made and even, in some cases, played a role in de-prioritizing features that had previously been considered to be a high priority.

Similarly, customers are considered to be the subject matter experts in how a feature will be used in the finished product. Therefore, while customers don't drive what a Scrum team works on (what a team builds is defined by the prioritization of the product backlog and how much the team is able to commit to), they can have a significant impact on how the feature actually works. In addition, those same customers can make suggestions for improvement that can be passed to the product owner and be added and prioritized on the product backlog immediately. In this way, a customer can actually suggest new possibilities and potentially see those possibilities become reality in a short space of time.

Customers that feel more connected to your prioritization decisions and feel more a part of how your product is built become satisfied and committed customers.

Summary

Organizations transition to agile development for the simple reason that it helps to improve the bottom line. However, there are a number of myths and concerns about agile development that often cause organizations to back away from agile development or to somehow adulterate agile development practices before even trying them as defined. These myths state that agile does too little planning and analysis, doesn't produce the necessary documentation, forces homogenization of roles on the development groups, and can't provide enough information to support organizational planning. The myths are easily debunked as misstatements and misinterpretations of agile practices—agile analysis and planning is done in a "just enough" manner that is spread across an entire project and does not occur just in the beginning phase of the project. The myth that agile developers do not write documentation is simply an untruth, though we do try very hard not to write documentation that no one needs. Similarly, role homogenization is a gross misinterpretation of the expectation in an agile development team that everyone works together to get the job done—even outside their typical responsibilities. The final myth states that agile development does not provide enough information in the project schedule to support organization planning. The truth here is that while the detailed schedules built from waterfall projects provide the illusion of precision, agile projects provide significantly more flexibility to the organization by being able to be easily ended or extended based on the organization's plans and needs.

In addition, many organizations see an agile transition as too hard and too disruptive, or that agile simply won't work because of complexities unique to a specific organization. Without doubt, a transition from more traditional methods to agile development will indeed be both hard and disruptive, and while some of the difficulty and disruption can be mitigated by learning from previous efforts (and using this book, of course), the organization unwilling to accept some difficulty and disruption probably shouldn't attempt agile development. Those concerned that agile development can't work in an organization that is too complex are often really just saying that they've already spent a lot of time building a detailed and complex organization and they don't want to make significant changes in order to bring in agile development. What this means to any successful transition plan is that the current organization must be continuously examined to determine how agile development practices can be introduced while preserving the best parts of the organization and keeping the overall work disruption to a minimum.

Finally, of course, here are the reasons why an organization would want to transition to agile development:

1. Improvements in software quality that come from a number of agile development principles, not the least of which is the collaborative nature of agile development teams.
2. Increased organizational commitment to the product development effort, which comes from the frequent feedback that results from reviewing every sprint. This provides more continuity in development and increases the possibility of productivity improvements from innovation and overall experience with the software.
3. Reductions in waste are always desirable and agile development helps to reduce waste by doing the right amount of work at the right time, so as to minimize the risk that unexpected changes later in the project don't result in significant rework for the development teams.
4. Improved customer relationships that come from the direct involvement of the customer in prioritization decisions as well as helping the development teams build the right feature that works the way the customer does.

In the end, whether you decide to transition to agile development or not depends on your commitment to doing it right and your tolerance for being exposed to, dealing with, and solving organizational dysfunctions. You'll need both commitment and tolerance in good supply to successfully complete a transition to agile development.

SETTING THE STAGE FOR A TRANSITION

One of the most crucial aspects of the agile transition is preparation. As with software development, the transitioning of the organization to agile development can have a good start, but there is a considerable degree of uncertainty in the approach. Therefore, just like software development, we'll also handle the transition in an agile manner. We'll get our high-level plans laid out and then seek out more detail as we move forward. However, as we're starting with an organization that is not yet agile, there's a lot of up-front discussion on team organization, transition concepts, and expectations required in order to get the transition started. Later sections of this book will discuss topics and tasks related to managing the ongoing transition and operational management of the agile organization. In this section of the book, however, we'll discuss many of the topics that need to be discussed and tasks that need to be completed in order to get the transition started. Those topics are:

- *Concepts*: Just like a sprint goal, the transition needs a place to go. The section on concepts helps you set your goal for the transition. How far do you want to go? What do you want to accomplish? At what point do you decide that the transition is finished and the organization can learn effectively on its own without a guiding transition team?
- *Barriers*: What in your organization is going to get in the way of a successful transition, and what are you going to do about it? This section will walk you through identifying the potential barriers so that you can make plans to deal with them at an appropriate time.

■ *Management in an agile environment*: The success of your transition is in the hands of the managers that pay the bills. Like everyone else in an agile transition, their job is significantly changed by agile development. What are the specific challenges that management will face? More importantly, will management commit to staying the course when your product development is under stress?

Chapter 3

Transitional Concepts

This chapter focuses on a variety of concepts and principles that you should be familiar with before beginning the agile transition. While a lot of it may seem like a lot of technical mumbo jumbo, understanding what all of it means will be critical to putting together an effective transitional backlog and guiding your developers and managers through what will most likely be the most substantial cultural change of their professional careers.

Read the following sections carefully. At the end of the chapter, we'll start building your transition backlog and get this ride started. First, however, let's get you somewhat acquainted with agile development.

What Is Agile Development?

Since this book is not intended to teach you all there is know about agile development, I'll keep the explanation short. I've recommended several very good books on the topic in the introduction to this book.

At a high level, the term *agile development* refers to a genre of application development techniques characterized by an adherence to what's currently known as the Agile Manifesto.[1] In short, these characteristics are:

1. Emphasis is placed on individuals and teams doing the right thing, rather than trying to prescribe the entire development activity with high-ceremony process and overweight quality management programs.
2. Focus is on working software, not documentation that describes software. Teams are required to be able to demonstrate working software throughout the project.

3. Rather than keeping them at the "end" of the software development activity (when it is finally delivered to them), customers are highly valued participants in the development process, providing perspective as the eventual purchasers and users of the software product.
4. Planning and estimation activities are not done only at the beginning of the project. They are done at different levels of granularity throughout the project. This allows the project to easily absorb change while avoiding significant waste.

Agile projects can use quality management systems to help ensure the infusion of quality during the development process and to comply with various government regulations. Documentation is still created during agile projects, and enough planning is done at the beginning of the agile project to create a reasonable projection as to when the project might be finished. But agile projects put their emphasis on individuals and teams, working software, collaboration with customers, and the assumption of change (which then leads to planning that is considerably more change tolerant than most waterfall-based projects).

This book is written with an assumption that you will employ a combination of Scrum and Extreme Programming (XP) practices to implement your agile development environment. You can, of course, implement DSDM[1] or FDD[2], only Scrum or only XP, or perhaps even some other method that will be discovered sometime in the future. As long as that method is considered an agile method, it will abide by the characteristics listed above and should still work well with the content and direction of this book (with some changes in terminology, probably).

Workflow

First, let's begin with how work flows through an agile project, as illustrated in Figure 3.1.

Requirements for a product come from several sources: customers and the marketplace, specific business strategies, regulatory requirements, internal requests, and technical needs. All of these items merge together into the product backlog where they undergo an initial evaluation by the product owner followed by prioritization of each item relative to the rest of the backlog.

Product Backlog

An item on the product backlog is, not surprisingly, called a *product backlog item* (PBI). These items provide information about:

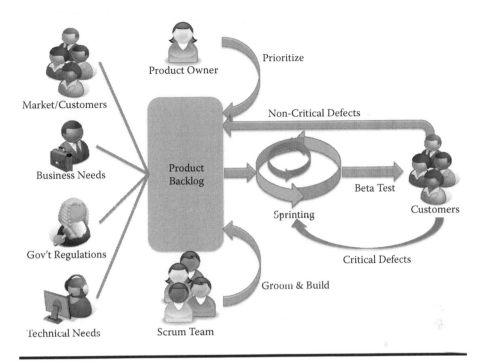

Figure 3.1   The basic workflow of a product backlog item.

1. New things that the product needs to do or improvements to what it does today (features)
2. Corrections to fix mistakes in the product (defects)
3. Changes to correct technical deficiencies or keep the product technically current (technical debt)

Prioritization

The prioritization of the product backlog is largely a subjective exercise done on an ongoing basis by the product owner. While an item's cost (i.e., the effort estimate), risk, and customer value have a significant impact on the prioritization, the product owner also has to weigh the competing needs of the product vision, the business plan, his customers, the government, and the technical debt incurred by the product. While this seems straightforward, most product owners use the cost/risk/value attributes as guides, but not as the final decision maker in any prioritization.

Grooming

Using a prioritized backlog, the product owner and the Scrum teams work together to analyze the highest-priority items. As feature and technical debt PBIs are sliced into smaller and smaller items, they become less complex, easier to estimate, and usually contain less risk. Many teams, while they slice items down into smaller ones, often record what they've discussed about each item in a separate document, on a wiki, or on paper, so that when it comes time to work on the item in a sprint, everything they've discussed about the item is right at hand. Grooming of the product backlog begins when the project begins and ends as the project ends. The product backlog is always a work in progress.

Defects on the product backlog may sometimes be left exactly as they are until the defect is assigned to a sprint. In some cases, however, where the defect is quite large or difficult to solve, product backlog grooming will include research on defects in order to rewrite the item as an actionable change. For example, assume that a product backlog item reads as follows:

> The inventory search function hangs when the user searches for two items with the same manufacturer.

Like most defects added to the product backlog, this item tells us what the user doesn't like, but it isn't "actionable" in its current state. In other words, we need to change it into something we can estimate and do during the project. After some research, we may discover that the problem lies in a locked table caused while accessing the database. So, we might rewrite the PBI as follows:

> Change the inventory search function so that the second query on the same manufacturer does not result in a table lock.

Notice that we aren't trying to write the solution into the backlog item, just the problem. Research on solutions can wait until sprint planning or even during the sprint. We don't need to know how to fix it during grooming; we simply want to know what to fix.

Sprinting

Once a product backlog item has made it to the top of the product backlog and there's a Scrum team ready to work on it, the item moves into a Scrum and is added to the sprint backlog for that team's sprint. At this point, all of the remaining analysis and design on the item is completed. Tests and code are written to satisfy the item's acceptance criteria and hopefully, by the end of the sprint, the completed story is demonstrated to the product owner and approved to be a part of the product. If the item does not pass sprint review, it is returned to the product backlog, where it will likely (but not definitely) be picked up and finished by the same team in the next sprint.

Beta Test

At beta test, we deliver the completed product to a small number of customers. At this point in the project, we're looking for any configuration anomalies in the product that were not caught during the development effort. When the software proves that it can work effectively in a real customer environment, it is generally released to the market. This effort can be, but need not be, sprint based.

Defects

Throughout the development process, we are taking steps to find and remove defects as much as possible. Within the sprint, unit, acceptance, and functional level tests are run continuously to ensure that code changes are not breaking previously existing functionality and are fulfilling the acceptance criteria of the features being built. However, should a defect be found during the sprint, the developer usually makes it his or her top priority to solve the defect immediately (to the exclusion of all else). In cases when the defect either (1) is a very low priority or (2) was caused by another Scrum team or (3) was caused in a previous sprint, the defect may be added to the product backlog instead, to be prioritized by the product owner and solved at a later time.

Defects may also be found at the customer site during the beta testing period. Just like defects found during the sprint, defects discovered at the customer site are evaluated for priority. Those defects that warrant an immediate solution are pushed directly to the responsible Scrum team (the team, depending on the complexity of the defect and the effort to create and test a solution, may need to work with the product owner to reset their sprint goals) or are added to the product backlog and prioritized with the rest of the items on the backlog.

Workflow Summary

The overall workflow, from need to finished product, is intended to give you the beginnings of a framework upon which most of your transition can be built. The rest of this chapter will be spent discussing some of the challenges that you will face while transitioning to this framework. In the next two chapters, we'll discuss some of the organizational and people-oriented barriers to agility, and then we'll delve into management and the types of behavioral changes that will be needed in order for your transition to be a success.

The Product Backlog

Unless you're starting agile development with a completely new product, you already have a list of requirements for your current development effort. When the

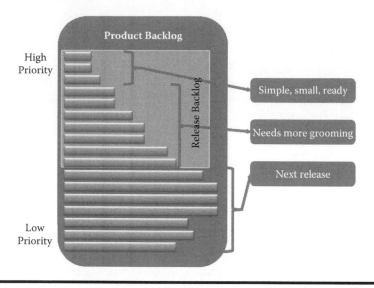

Figure 3.2   The product backlog and the grooming condition of the backlog items.

transition is complete, you will need to have a product backlog (see Figure 3.2) that satisfies the following criteria:

1. It is written in a manner that can be groomed by your product owner and Scrum teams.
2. It is in a constant state of reprioritization led by the product owner.
3. It is in a continuous state of emergence as new items are added, large items are sliced into smaller items, and other items are completed or simply removed.
4. It is reflective of the product owner's vision and direction for the product.
5. The highest-priority items on the list are broken down into items or steps that can be completed by two or three people in less than a week.
6. It is visible to the entire organization.

The highest-priority items on the product backlog are often said to be a part of the release backlog, which is to say that those items are part of the current release plan. Items nearest the top of the backlog are generally the smallest on the product backlog, having been previously analyzed by the Scrum teams and sliced into smaller and smaller units of work that are less and less complex. These smallest items are said to be sprint-sized, Scrum-sized, or more generally, right-sized. That is, they are small enough to be quickly broken down into tasks and built by a Scrum team.

As you further explore items with a lower priority, you will find that these items are generally larger and more complex. Some, in fact, may be nonactionable items (items which, as written, do not describe "something to do" to the product). Defects are an example of nonactionable PBIs. The further down in priority you go, the bigger and less defined (on average) the items get.

Eventually, you will reach the portion of the backlog that describes content that will likely be in a future release of the product. Looking further, you will discover items that either (1) are not actually prioritized but are simply sitting in a general "bucket" of items, (2) are waiting to be evaluated by the product owner for prioritization, or (3) will likely never be built.

So what does all this mean? Let's go deeper …

Written in a Manner That Can Be Groomed …

As discussed before, grooming is something agile organizations do to product backlogs in order to get the backlog items ready for development. Grooming teases out important details without getting Scrum teams mired in endless, low-value discussions too early in the development cycle. What this means, however, is that creating your product backlog isn't as easy as dumping your requirements repository into a new list and saying "ta da!"

For example, let's take one of the most common types of requirements:

> The system shall support a customer last name of no longer than thirty characters.

Nice, huh? The problem with these types of requirements (often known as detailed requirements) is that they describe a very small portion of the overall application. Worse, I can't really estimate this requirement because I can't tell if the customer last name appears on one screen or one hundred screens. The same is true for databases. Will I find this data element in one table or ten? Twenty? I can't use or even make plans from this requirement because I really don't know what it means.

How about this one?

> The vehicle shall have four wheels, two attached at opposite ends of two axels.

What are we talking about? A car? A golf cart? How about a wagon?

Before we go any deeper into this problem, let's lay out the parts of a typical user story. While there is no standard structure for a user story, many of them contain some or all of this information:

1. *Story headline or description*: This is a short sentence that tells you what the story is about.
2. *Value estimate*: This can be done in many different kinds of units as long as they remain consistent through the project or multiple projects. While

valuation makes the most sense in dollars, any consistent standard of measure works fine. Often the value is broken into two different kinds of estimates:

    a. *Benefit*: What's the value to the organization (i.e., to our customers) for including this item in the product? This helps to measure the relative value of this item compared to that of other items.

    b. *Penalty*: What's the potential penalty for not including this item in the product? This helps to elicit the need for regulatory requirements and technical debt items in the product. Low-penalty items basically have to depend on their benefit in order to have a chance to get near the top of the product backlog. On the other hand, an item with a high penalty for not getting done (can't sell the product in the United States or Europe without it, could go to jail without it in the product, etc.) will find it's way at the top of the backlog rather quickly.

3. *Complexity estimate*: Usually done in points, the complexity estimate is an estimate of the complexity of the story.

4. *Risk estimate*: The risk estimate measures the risk inherent in building a story. This is often very helpful in the product owner's prioritization efforts.

5. *Acceptance criteria*: These short sentences (or fragments) tell you what needs to be true before the story can be considered finished.

6. *Priority*: This is often expressed in the relative position of the story on a list with the rest of the stories, rather than as a number (e.g., 1st, 2nd, 514th).

So, having explained a little bit about user stories, let's go back to the first requirement: the system shall support a customer last name of no longer than thirty characters. Now, by itself, that detailed requirement really tells us very little, but what if we took a step back to look at why we have this requirement. What we're likely to discover is that the last name requirement is just one of several detailed requirements that are all referring to a "parent" requirement of sorts. As you can see in Figure 3.3, there is an overarching requirement for the system to support customer registration. That requirement has subordinate requirements (a name and a home address), and those have further subordinate detailed requirements.

Putting all of these items on the product backlog would be very ineffective. As mentioned before, we can't estimate "The customer's last name shall be up to thirty characters in length."

However, what we *can* do with these shows the real power of user stories in agile development. So, let's turn these requirements into user stories in two easy steps:

Step 1: Rephrase feature requirements as user stories. Using the example in Figure 3.3, the highest-level requirement that we can rephrase would be:

The system shall support customer registration.

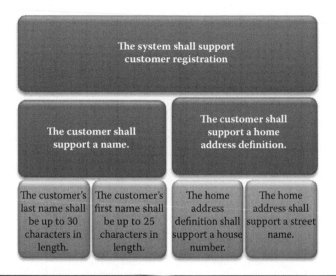

Figure 3.3 Customer requirements.

First, who *needs* the system to support customer registration (and be careful, because there might be a couple groups of users who actually need this)? Without going into too much depth, it's pretty clear that there might be two groups of users who want to do this: the customers themselves and the salespeople who use these registrations. This, of course, leads us to our next question: What do the groups of users really want to do and why?

In the case of the customer users, they might want to register their names and addresses to get more information about whatever it is our product is helping us to sell. In the case of the salespeople users, they probably want customer contact information so they can follow up with the customers and see what they can sell them. From this, we can derive two user stories (I added story IDs, as shown in Figure 3.4, just to ease the discussion later on).

Story 1: As a customer, I want to be able to register my name and address so that I can get more information about this company's products.

Story 2: As a sales manager, I want my customers to register themselves so I can use their information to contact them for potential sales opportunities.

Figure 3.4 Creating user stories.

Step 2: Rewrite detailed requirements as acceptance criteria. When it comes right down to it, detailed requirements don't tell you anything about your product's features. What they really do is tell you what your product's features need to be able handle or support. With user stories, detailed requirements aren't subordinate to the stories: *they actually become part of the user stories.* Let me show you what I mean.

Let's take story 1 ("As a customer ..."). In Figure 3.3, there were two subordinate stories to the registration: the customer had to be able to register their name (1) and home address (2). As you can see in story 1, we've already rolled both of those requirements into the story, so let's just concentrate on the bottom-most requirements:

1. The customer's last name shall be up to thirty characters in length.
2. The customer's first name shall be up to twenty-five characters in length.
3. The home address definition shall support a house number.
4. The home address shall support a street name.

These really don't tell us about product functionality (as I mentioned earlier); they are really about the criteria that the product functionality needs to support. So, we can really just roll these up under the user story that they refer to, as illustrated in Figure 3.5.

Now, isn't that better? All of that stuff that was on the original list of requirements is really just background information for the really important stuff: what we want our product to do!

Sometimes, however, the detailed requirements are a little tougher to make work. It isn't always a simple transformation to acceptance criteria. For example, let's try these:

■ The system shall support accepted standards for credit card purchase transactions.
■ The system shall be written using the current version of Sun-based Java as of January 1, 2009.
■ All interaction with the external customer will take place in less than five seconds at least 90% of the time.

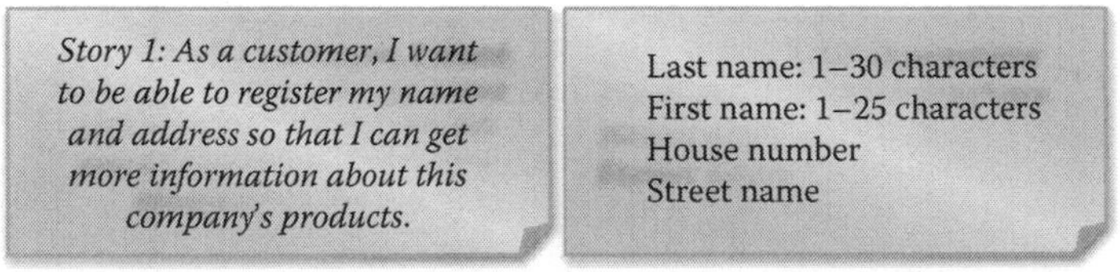

> *Story 1: As a customer, I want to be able to register my name and address so that I can get more information about this company's products.*

> Last name: 1–30 characters
> First name: 1–25 characters
> House number
> Street name

Figure 3.5   Adding acceptance criteria to the user story.

These detailed requirements are actually nonfunctional requirements—requirements that describe a product characteristic instead of a product capability. Requirements of this nature are generally not assignable to a small number of stories (like the length of the customer's last name). Instead, you may want to consider creating a separate list of nonfunctional acceptance tests for the entire project or product against which every story must be verified before the story can be considered complete. In other words, having finished story 1, you would still want to look at the nonfunctional acceptance criteria. For example, does story 1 satisfy the requirement that:

- *Accepted standards for credit card purchases are supported?* Technically, this requirement doesn't apply to story 1 because there is no credit card purchase included in the story.
- *The code be written in the proper version of Java?* We can add this to the acceptance criteria for the story, to ensure that the proper version of Java is used when the story is actually built.
- *All interaction with the external customer will take place in less than five seconds at least 90% of the time?* We'll need to add this performance requirement to the story's acceptance criteria and then make sure that we write tests that help verify this requirement.

Then we would continue down the rest of the nonfunctional acceptance test criteria until we were satisfied that they were all either nonapplicable or passed.

Under Constant Reprioritization and Continually Emergent

The product backlog, by definition, is an emergent artifact. It is under constant reprioritization managed by the product owner and driven by:

- Changing business requirements (including a willingness to take on risks in product development)
- Customer demands
- Government regulation
- Changes in technology
- Changes in development team staffing
- Project schedules

There is no typical product backlog size. Depending on the complexity and the maturity of your product, your backlog could be five hundred items long or fifty thousand items long. Regardless of size, however, product backlogs are usually organized in a similar manner—the highest-priority items on top, the

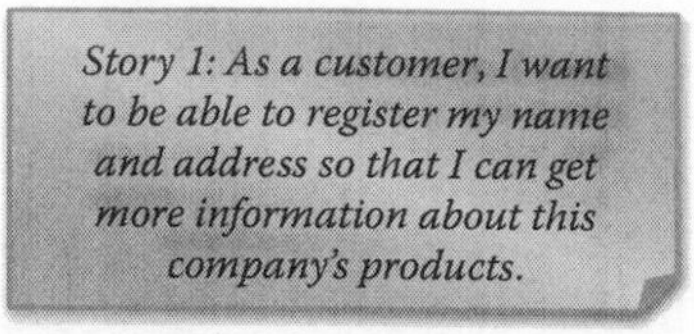

> *Story 1: As a customer, I want to be able to register my name and address so that I can get more information about this company's products.*

Figure 3.6 Looking at story 1 again.

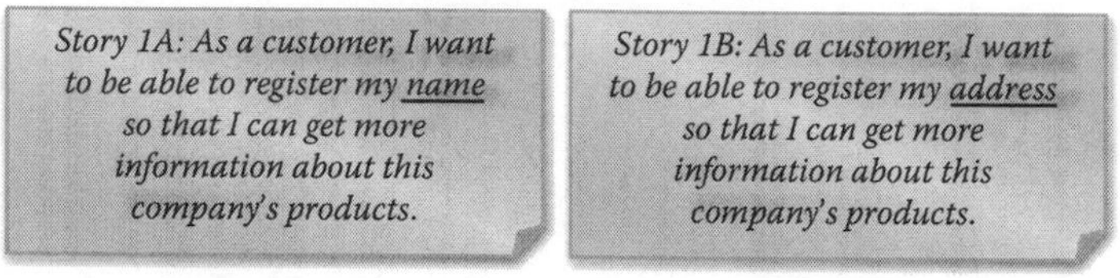

> *Story 1A: As a customer, I want to be able to register my name so that I can get more information about this company's products.*

> *Story 1B: As a customer, I want to be able to register my address so that I can get more information about this company's products.*

Figure 3.7 Slicing story 1 into two pieces.

lowest-priority items on the bottom. Additionally, as items move closer and closer to the top of the backlog, they are sliced by Scrum teams into smaller and smaller items.

Slicing, sometimes called *sashimi*, is the practice of taking a story and reducing it in size and complexity by converting the same story into two or more smaller ones. Let's go back to story 1, mentioned above (see Figure 3.6).

In this story, there is a clear way to slice around the data being collected during the registration. In other words, I could slice the story and come up with the two listed in Figure 3.7.

These two stories are simpler than their parent, easier to estimate than their parent, entail less risk than before, and when completed, accomplish the same thing as the original story 1.

Endnotes

1. Dynamic Systems Development Model (DSDM) is an iterative development model that provides role and process descriptions for all stages of product development. For more information, see http://www.dsdm.org.
2. Feature-Driven Development (FDD) is an iterative development model that specifies product development in five activities: develop the overall model, build the feature list, plan by feature, design by feature, and build by feature. For more information, see http://www.featuredrivendevelopment.com.
3. Beck, Kent, Beedle, Mike, van Bennekum, Arie, and Cockburn, Alistair. 2001. *Manifesto for Agile Software Development.* http://www.agilemanifesto.org (accessed January 22, 2009).

Chapter 4

Transition Barriers

There are a number of possible barriers that could hinder or block the progress of an agile transition. The identification and mitigation of these barriers will need to be a part of the transition plan and may possibly take up a significant portion of the team's time during the transition. Should you be able to avoid most of these barriers during your transition, consider yourself very fortunate. Most of you, though, will deal with a considerable number of these barriers. We won't be discussing solutions to these barriers, however. That'll come later in the book. At the end of this chapter, however, we'll start your transition backlog by considering each of these items.

To keep it simple, I've grouped the barriers into two categories: people and organizational.

People Barriers

People barriers are barriers that are caused by the people in the organization. They usually concern the misuse of people in the organization, and they are often the most difficult to solve.

People barriers include:

- *Wolving*: This is what happens when one or more people on a Scrum team are taken away from the team during the sprint to work on something more that is considered to be an emergency or simply more important. Usually when this happens, it involves one or more people that the team cannot spare to lose. Everyone else on the Scrum team is upset when the makeup of the team is changed during the sprint. The team may lose a day or even find they are unable to complete the sprint. No matter what the impact, it is extremely difficult for the team to do as good a job with one or more missing team members as they could have done with them. Certainly, it is possible that the team may complete most or all of their sprint goals, but remember that they met their commitments while short-staffed. Be prepared for issues (e.g., defects) that may plague the team for the next couple months, if not longer. Just as likely, be prepared for the team to go to the product owner and renegotiate their backlog commitment. Remember, the team made a commitment to the product owner of a certain amount of work during sprint planning. That commitment was based on each team member's known availability. When that changed, so did their commitment.

■ *Resource slicing*: Managers often seem to blur the distinction between the positions that we have in our organization and the people that fill those positions. On paper, you can easily allocate the time that a position is supposed to spend on one or more projects, and the numbers always add up to 100% (e.g., 50% on project 1 and 50% on project 2 = 100%). However, when you ask a developer to work on multiple projects at the same time, that developer incurs delays caused by:

 – Saving what he or she was working on, physically and mentally
 – Clearing his or her space to allow for something else
 – Checking emails and having conversations (as long as he or she is between tasks, why not?)
 – Frustration caused by having to switch from task to task
 – Remembering where he or she was on the other project
 – Realizing he or she forgot some details about where he or she was on the other project and having to re-create the work/intelligence

There have been many studies that conclusively show that context switching is very expensive. In fact, in Gerald Weinberg's book *Quality Software Management: Systems Thinking*,[1] he proposes a rule of thumb based on past experiences: when you add a second project to your developer's plate, he or she loses 20% of his or her productivity. With the third project, add another 20%.

■ *Teams not accountable for results*: The Scrum framework creates a clear delineation between responsibilities in the building of a product. Whereas the product owner takes responsibility for building the right product, the Scrum teams take responsibility for building the product right. Scrum teams are accountable for following the Scrum framework, the team's and the organization's accepted development practices, and abiding by the team's and the organization's definition of DONEness. When a Scrum team makes a commitment to their product owner at sprint planning, the team does everything reasonable to achieve their goals or to alert the product owner immediately if any portion of their sprint goal is in danger of not being properly completed by the end of the sprint, or if any portion of the sprint goal suddenly becomes considerably more expensive than was originally anticipated.

At sprint review, the product owner should feel justified in testing the team's completed backlog items by requesting to see test summaries, demonstrations of working product functionality, copies of updated documentation, models, artifacts, etc. It is the combination of building the right product and building the product right that creates a high-quality, high-value product.

■ *Chronic lateness to team meetings*: Some team members show their reluctance to work in a team environment by coming late to team meetings (including the daily Scrum meeting) or by missing them entirely. It's important for the team to address this problem together.

■ *Teams lack appropriate skills/"Not my job" syndrome*: By definition, Scrum teams are cross-functional and possess all of the skills needed to complete their portion of the product backlog. Teams often fall short of this need for two reasons: (1) because some of the more limited skill sets are not available (e.g., user-interface (UI) interaction designer, testers, technical writer, database architect, etc.) and (2) because some team members may have a "not my job" attitude about the roles that they agree to do. Designers may be unwilling to help write test scripts; coders may be unwilling to write customer documentation. While agile development will never suggest that everyone on the team should be able to cover everyone else's jobs, the team members have to be willing to stretch their duties in support of team, and thus organizational, success.

■ *Scrum master manages the team*: In instances where the Scrum master may not have been properly trained or coached, or has a particularly difficult team to work with, the Scrum master may resort to more direct command and control in order to accomplish the team's goals. In these teams, the Scrum master will often be setting the sprint planning master and might even go so far as to hand out task assignments from the sprint backlog. You will also see evidence in the daily Scrum meeting, where the team members are clearly reporting to the Scrum master, rather than talking to one another. Certainly, there are times when more direct management of a Scrum team is needed (particularly during team "storming" periods). However, when the Scrum master manages the team for longer than the situation requires, the team becomes dependent on the Scrum master, self-management and self-organization seldom occur, and the Scrum master becomes a bottleneck to progress, rather than a facilitator and a remover of obstacles.

■ *Teams are larger or smaller than the five- to nine-team-member recommendation*: The size of a Scrum team is recommended to be seven plus or minus two team members. Teams that are larger than this size tend to have too complex an infrastructure, making it difficult to make decisions and organize around the committed work. Teams that are smaller than this size find Scrum to be more ceremony than needed to complete the work. While you may wish to have teams with more than nine team members, or less than four, you will attain higher productivity within the recommended size.

■ *Teams do not self-manage or self-organize*: Scrum teams work best when they self-manage and self-organize. Put simply, teams that self-manage handle their own issues and conflicts, provide regular reports to business and product management, and manage their own work commitments during the sprint. Teams that self-organize determine their own approach to how they will meet their commitments. They determine who will work on what aspects of the sprint backlog. Teams that do not (or cannot) self-manage or self-organize force someone else to play that role in order to ensure that work gets done. Unfortunately for that individual, he or she also becomes a bottleneck for the team, as the team members have to go through him or her in order to get their work assignments.

■ *Teams improperly plan their sprint*: Many teams, due to inexperience or a feeling that they are somehow saving time, cut short the sprint planning meeting once the sprint backlog is completed. This allows them to hold one- or two-hour sprint planning meetings and then begin the actual coding right away. In this case, the team misses a prime opportunity during sprint planning to do some group design and take other useful steps to ensure that everyone has the information they need to work effectively during the sprint.

■ *Teams not co-located*: For various reasons, often related to where the organization's domain expertise is located or due to outsourcing for lower cost, teams are often split between two or more locations. This creates an inherently difficult situation, as the ability for the team to work closely together is diminished by their inability to quickly and easily communicate face-to-face and without preamble. In cases where this is unavoidable, every effort should be made to provide constant communication among the separated pieces of the team. However, be prepared for two possible outcomes:

1. Reduced production
2. More documentation required to produce the same results as a co-located team

Organizational Barriers

Organizational barriers are barriers that are caused by a number of factors common in organizations, including:

■ Quality management systems based on waterfall development strategies
■ Procurement processes based on tight cost control strategies
■ Product development based on command and control concepts

Examples of organizational barriers include:

■ *Processes that promote inefficient development*: Many organizations define productivity in ways that promote inefficient development. For example, some organizations measure progress in terms of thousands of lines of code (KLOCs) produced during a specific time period. Some organizations measure the effectiveness of quality assurance (QA) by the total number or priority of defects found during QA testing. Other organizations look at schedule compliance and earned value to determine productivity. Unfortunately, all of these methods (and many more) tend to create unwanted behaviors and cause inefficient development. In the case of KLOCs, developers will often choose more complex and code-intense solutions to problems in order to maximize the number of lines of code developed. Even more off target, many languages support line breaks in the middle of executable statements, and many line-counting routines miss this in their calculations. In the cases where the number and severity of opened defects are counted, such organizations usually find themselves dealing with unexpected avalanches of defects with exaggerated severities that detail every dimension of every aberration in every aspect of the tested product (e.g., four separate defects opened to log the failure of the application to work with VISA, MasterCard, Diner's Club, and American Express credit cards where one tracking entry would have served the same purpose). And while this might sound like exactly what an organization would want to produce a quality product, it ignores two drawbacks:

1. The development team will spend a considerable amount of their valuable time working their way through the defects, reevaluating severities, and combining logically duplicated defects.
2. The organization's focus is shifted from infusing quality during the development process to putting additional effort into the quality inspection process.

■ *Processes that promote waterfall development*: Many organizational processes define critical decision-making milestones along the lines of traditional waterfall development phases: concept, analysis, design, code, test, etc. It is impractical to map the end of analysis or the end of design to any point in the typical agile project, where these activities occur simultaneously during the entire course of the project.

■ *Management assumes fixed time, fixed scope*: Management is used to setting project deadlines and project scope while carefully controlling project staffing, based on the feature estimates, to minimize the overall cost of the development effort. Estimates are never a guarantee, though they are frequently used as such. This creates a very difficult situation for agile development, which recognizes that the development organization owns the work effort estimates and will produce what it can during the timeframe provided with limited opportunity for development acceleration. Following a fixed-time/fixed-scope approach, many features have to be built faster and with less care in order to satisfy the project schedule. This results in quality issues that are discovered later in the development cycle and further restrict the availability of the developers who are also responsible for solving defects found in the software.

■ *Product owner is not sufficiently available to the team*: The role of product owner in the agile development world is often the most difficult role to hold. The product owner is expected to create, maintain, and communicate the vision of product; to work frequently with business owners, management, stakeholders, and customers; to maintain the product backlog; and to support one or more Scrum teams in the realization of that product backlog. In all size organizations, this is a very difficult and very crucial role. As a result, many product owners often are not as available to their Scrum teams as the teams would like them to be. While you want to have sympathy for the product owner, the Scrum team will either develop the wrong thing or nothing when they lack product owner guidance.

■ *Quality assurance is separate from product development*: In more traditional organizations, the quality assurance department is kept independent of the product development department in order to avoid conflict-of-interest issues. In some cases, the separation of departments is often mandated by the organization's quality management system or other state or national regulation. The difficulty this presents to the agile organization, however, is that the separation of these departments optimizes for an organization that does most of its product testing after development. In agile development, we need an organization optimized for continuous testing, beginning during sprint planning and continuing until the product is finally considered generally available.

■ *Individually focused performance and reward structure*: Many organizations base their performance evaluation system (including the decision-making processes for promotions and raises) on individual performance plans. This method, while often effective, just as often creates agendas that are counterproductive to agile development teams. In order to maximize the productivity of the agile team, the primary goals and responsibilities of each team member have to be focused on supporting the team, not on spotlighting the individual. The agile manager, indeed the agile HR department, must find more effective means by which to incent their development team members.

■ *Development sprints are producing minimal, if any, customer value*: In the complex world of software engineering, it is very easy to lose focus on the end result of a project (particularly long-running projects). In the agile environment, this will evidence itself when teams begin completing sprints that produce little to no customer value. Now, this isn't to say that the team wasn't busy; however, agile projects focus on maximizing the customer value delivered at every stage of the project, and stopping the project when the incremental value delivered falls below management's tolerance. In a Scrum team, this is usually caused by an ineffective (or unavailable product owner), or some other influence that has the team focusing on low or no-value items that may or may not actually be on the product backlog.

■ *Teams lack resources to properly implement source code control and continuous integration and testing*: Transitions to agile development come at a cost that often exceeds management expectation or willingness to pay. This frequently leaves agile development teams doing Scrum (which is good), but unable to pursue additional Extreme Programming (XP) practices like test-driven development (TDD), automated testing, and continuous integration and testing. These practices will vastly improve Scrum team productivity, not to mention product quality and customer satisfaction.

Endnote

1. http://www.amazon.com/exec/obidos/ASIN/0932633226.

Chapter 5

Management in an Agile Environment

As challenging as it is for a developer to work in an environment where he or she is expected to self-organize and self-manage, it is often much more difficult for the manager. Trained to control, budget, and direct, the transition from command and control practices to agile development forces the traditionally trained manager to question some of the most basic precepts of his or her knowledge and expertise.

Many managers are accustomed to taking responsibility for a project, getting "the right people for the job," and then getting the job done by taking advantage of the skills on their staff and using organizational savvy to get the needed support from the rest of the organization. Budgets are carefully created and monitored. Information is passed from the corporate echelons to the staff, and status reports passed from the employees to the manager and beyond. Unexpected changes to project plans are quickly absorbed into the project planning, and the resulting changes are communicated to the staff to handle it. The challenge of the job comes from building and maintaining a good staff, and job satisfaction comes from completing projects on time and on budget.

Then agile development comes in and the manager's world gets some significant makeovers. Teams own how they build their products and are responsible for managing themselves. Product owners define what the teams will build and in what order. Managers no longer play a primary role planning how development work is to get done, nor do they have any authority to say who is going to do it. Unexpected changes to project plans are incorporated into the product backlog and managed by the Scrum team. From the perspective of the unsuspecting managers, everything that made them effective in their jobs disappears when agile development steps

41

in—although the reality is that the manager's job truly becomes more fulfilling, not less.

Getting Management Ready for the Transition

While there are numerous ways to arrange your organization, let's just focus on two: the bureaucratic organization and the matrixed organization. The bureaucratic organization is very straightforward—all nonmanagement employees report to a first line of management (often called first-line managers). These managers report to middle-level management, who in turn report to top-level management. Typically, because product development is so complex and difficult to manage, bureaucratic organizations usually have a very flat arrangement with many first-line managers, a much smaller set of middle-level managers, and just a small handful of top-level management (see Figure 5.1).

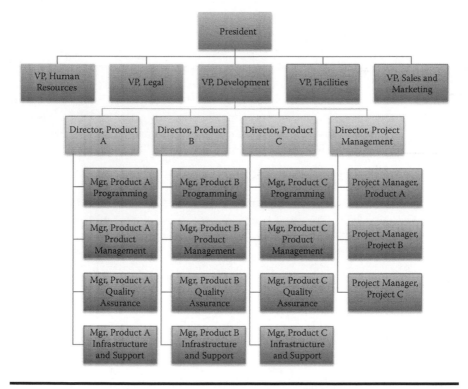

Figure 5.1 The bureaucratic organization. Vice presidents manage the major business functions. Reporting to the VP of product development are the directors. Each director manages the development of a specific project and has the staff needed across all disciplines (except, often, project management) to completely develop the product.

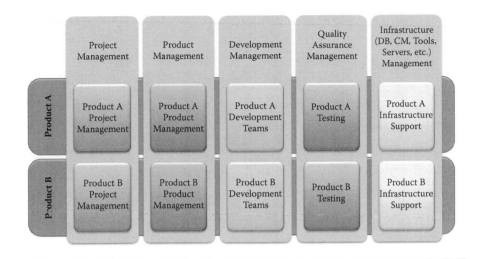

Figure 5.2   The matrixed organization.

Some organizations find that the bureaucratic arrangement is too slow to respond to change and attempt a more complicated matrixed organization that superimposes a project-oriented structure on top of a function-oriented structure (see Figure 5.2). In truth, however, even the matrixed organization, from the management perspective, is still frequently a bureaucratic arrangement. The managers of the products and the managers of the functions still report to middle-level management or are themselves middle-level managers reporting to top-level managers.

In both organizational styles (but more so in the bureaucratic arrangement), there is a tendency to direct training at the bottom-most and top-most layers of the organization. This is explained by the implementation modes of agile development: either bottom–up or top–down.

In a bottom–up implementation, a grassroots movement started by a small number of first-line managers or by development teams starts to experiment with agile methods. Driven by success, and often running "under the radar," the movement grows to include more and more teams until management begins to notice the improvement in one or all of software quality, cycle time, and time morale. At that point, if all goes well, the implementation is formalized with a team and a budget and a broader implementation begins.

In a top–down implementation, executive management becomes aware of agile development through colleagues, conferences, or their own reading and research. Recognizing the power of agile development, but also the collaborative aspect of agile, the executive then brings together a team that consists of lower-level management and senior developers and proposes a piloting approach that starts with one or two small teams and, depending on the success, grows to incorporate the rest of the organization as reasonably quickly as possible. Both instances are fairly similar. The most significant difference is that the grassroots aspect of the bottom–up approach is roughly equivalent to the piloting phase of the top–down approach.

At this point, an interesting split occurs. As training begins, it is clear that all of the employees that will be participating on a Scrum team will need proper training in Scrum and agile techniques. Likewise, the executive-level management that kicked off the project (either as a pilot in top–down or a full-scale implementation in bottom–up) requires that they receive proper training immediately. After all, it is they who will be explaining agile development to customers, executive peers in other companies, higher-level executives in their company, or even the board of directors of the company.

The formal implementation begins with a focus on employee education and a separate track for the executives. Often, as part of the kickoff of the project, the entire organization receives a general "This is agile" type presentation. Unfortunately, however, as the project progresses, it is not only common to neglect entire levels of management in the organization, but it is equally common to fail to address the needs of each level of management (see Figure 5.3).

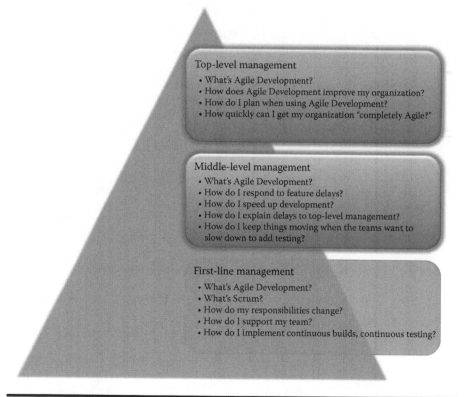

Figure 5.3   Management concerns at different levels.

More importantly, even in the most motivated organization, there is an unspoken tension between the layers of management that must be addressed as part of the organization's transition to agile development. Specifically, while top-level management plays a positive and effective role getting everyone on board for the transition, they are still communicating to their middle-layer management that *nothing can be delayed just because we started transitioning to agile development.* Similarly, first-line management is experiencing all of the day-to-day challenges that an agile transition will surface and will frequently look to the middle-layer manager to help resolve situations and explain delays to top-level management.

This puts middle management in a very poor situation: while trying to do their jobs and keep top-layer management satisfied, middle management must also find a way to not lose the faith of the developers in the organization that are scrutinizing every action against a personal understanding of whether the action is or isn't agile. More often than not, it's the pressure from above that wins. This results in directives that interfere with the progress of the agile transition. Some examples include:

1. Scrum masters are also developers and have tasks on the sprint backlog.
2. Many developers are on two, three, and sometimes even four projects simultaneously.
3. Teams are frequently affected when knowledgeable team members are taken away from the team during the sprint to deal with other matters.

The best solution for resolving the conflicts between different levels of management is to discuss roles and responsibilities across the management layers and to discuss how the organization will handle particular issues that may come up during the transition. It is a rare scenario when an organization can simply stop producing software while the agile transition proceeds; in this chapter, we will assume that everyone already has work to do when the transition begins.

An Effective Organizational Arrangement for Scrum Teams

Whether the organization is bureaucratic or matrixed, the key is whether or not the resources needed to complete the project are available under the control of a single organizational hierarchy. If not, and the resources are distributed across the organization, there will be perpetual difficulty—more difficult to align on product development, more difficult to align on development practices. As illustrated in Figure 5.4, one of the best organizational structures I've worked with doesn't really concern itself with anything above the first line of management.

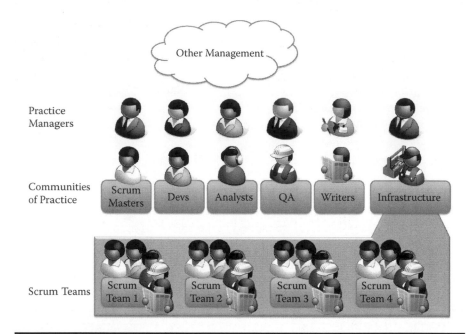

Figure 5.4   Aligning communities of practice to make Scrum teams.

Each of the practice managers is administratively responsible for up to fifteen individuals within a single practice, including staffing and budgeting and performance management responsibilities. A practice is defined as a specific area of expertise or discipline. Common practices (not all of which are shown in Figure 5.4) include:

■ Scrum masters
■ Product owners
■ Developers (coders)
■ Architects
■ Analysts/business analysts/product management
■ Testers/QAers
■ Technical writers
■ Infrastructure specialists

Each practice group, depending on its size, will have one or more managers who may report as peers with other practice managers to a VP or as a team to a director (where the directors of the various practices then report to a VP). Most communities should meet as a team at least once a month (the Scrum master and product owner communities should meet weekly, as their impediment clearing and product backlog work is more time sensitive). Each practice group or "community of practice" is responsible for the following:

1. *Improving the skills of the team*: Through weekly seminars taught by other practitioners, management, or someone from outside the team, the community is constantly working to improve their skills. This could include facilitation techniques for Scrum masters, story-writing classes for product owners, and new design patterns for architects. Another good way to improve skills is by selecting a small team of community members to attend a conference and then report back on what they learned.

2. *Furthering the development of their community*: Recognizing that there is always room for improvement, communities should always be looking for ways to improve the practice of their role. Product owners can look for better ways to prioritize backlogs and determine backlog value. Coders can evaluate code generators and create better coding standards and code review practices. Testers can find new ways to evaluate and determine test cases. The possibilities for study and improvement here are endless.

3. *Looking for ways to improve the organization*: Scrum masters are always dealing with team and organizational impediments. Likewise, each community of practice has similar opportunities to improve the organization by looking at what's negatively affecting their practice and advocating change. One-day cross-training seminars held on a quarterly basis provide an excellent opportunity for each community to discuss, in the presence of the other communities, what they've been working on, what they've accomplished, and what challenges they face in the coming year.

Communities of practice also make up the resource pool from which Scrum teams are created. The Scrum master community provides a Scrum master, the development community provides two or three developers, the analyst community provides one or two analysts, etc.

The advantage to this structure is that it is more flexible than the bureaucratic arrangement, but much less complex than a matrixed organization. Scrum teams are seeded from the communities of practice—team members report only to one manager, their practice manager, for administrative purposes. Each practice manager is assigned one or more Scrum teams as a management sponsor. The management sponsor provides needed support to the Scrum team. True to the concepts of Scrum, however, the Scrum team self-manages, working with the product owner to determine what they will be building.

When a new Scrum team is needed or new Scrum team members are needed, practice managers are responsible for working with the appropriate human resources or staffing personnel to initiate the interviewing process. A strong practice manager, however, will involve members of existing Scrum teams to supplement the interview process and ensure that the hired candidate has the best chance of fitting into the organization. We'll talk more about this, in detail, in the following section.

Hiring New Scrum Team Members

Hiring new Scrum team members can be an intense process, both for the organization and for the candidate. Careful attention must be paid as much to the candidate's technical skills (experience with various programming languages, experience developing applications, experience with certain types of development software or operating systems, writing skills, presentation skills, etc.) as to the candidate's "soft" skills (leadership ability, adaptability, teamwork orientation, customer orientation, willingness to challenge the status quo, etc.). In fact, I would suggest that the soft skills are considerably more important than the candidate's technical skills.

Is hiring for a candidate's ability to work on a team is more important than his or her ability to code Java? Yes, definitely. Why? Well, there are two reasons: First, developers, analysts, and testers got into the software engineering field not because they wanted to learn how to do one thing and do it for the rest of their lives. They entered software engineering because the field is always changing and maturing. We tread new ground every day. All things being equal, which job would you take— the one that allows you to do the same thing you've been doing for the past eight years, or the one that will have you working with the newest technology and the latest concepts? The latter position promises new stuff to learn almost every day.

The other reason you should give more weight to soft skills over technical skills is that software engineers (including developers, analysts, testers, etc.) are usually eager learners. They adapt quickly and adopt new concepts with an astounding rapidity. Hiring for technical skills they already possess is actually aiming pretty low. On the other hand, would you rather teach a developer a new programming language or teach them how to work well with others? Frankly, I'd choose the former any day of the week. Besides, I've never actually had to teach a developer a new language (except when I taught a programming language course at a local college); give developers the right tools and a week or so, and they'll make themselves instant experts.

In short, hiring for Scrum teams is much more about hiring motivated engineers (again, including analysts, developers, testers, etc.) that work well in team environments, and then making sure you give them enough time to pick up any technical skills that they need to learn. If they happen to have some previous experience in a similar language or development technique, that's a plus.

To put it another way, which would you prefer on one of your Scrum teams?

- The perfect developer with fifteen years of experience with the right development environments who alienates the entire Scrum team with his condescending attitude and desire to be left alone, leaving you handling complaints from team members, other managers, and even customers?
- A relative novice with some previous experience working on a development team who picks up new concepts rapidly and works well with the team, motivating the team to work smarter (not just harder) from time to time?

We've probably all seen similar examples of this problem on professional sports teams across the world: the star athlete who, from his rookie year, is clearly headed for the hall of fame, assuming he doesn't first get dropped from the team by his coach for making enemies of his teammates or for simply doing something stupid during the off-season and getting put in jail.

While often handled by management, the staffing of Scrum teams is best handled by joining the capabilities of human resources to provide initial screening (reviewing CVs/resumes, phone screens, etc.), and then both practice managers and Scrum team members to do in-house interviews. It is extremely important to include Scrum team members in the interview process—they will be the best at understanding if an individual will work well in a team. In fact, you might want to have people from a couple different teams involved in the interviewing process if possible; this will give you choices for placement on a team. Most importantly, it ensures the Scrum team that someone isn't going to be "forced" on them and keeps the teams involved in the decision process.

Depending on the number of Scrum teams for which you are hiring, you will want to describe the interview process with every team, to get their buy-in on the process, to suggest potential improvements in the process, and to go about determining how the team will provide resources to the interview process (again, not only keeping the teams involved in the hiring process, but making them decide which individuals on the team will act as their "proxy" in the decision-to-hire meeting).

On the day of one or more candidate interviews, you'll need to set up a series of short (20 to 30 minutes) meetings with each candidate. The candidate should meet with an HR representative first to make sure that the candidate is eligible to work in your country. Then, the candidate should attend three more 30-minute meetings, as follows (the order isn't important):

1. *Hiring practice manager*: Discuss the position with the candidate (making sure you describe how your organization practices agile development), answer any questions, etc.
2. *Soft skills*: This should be with one or two team members. Ask probing questions about teams that the candidate has worked on before, how the candidate has resolved conflicts, and personal likes and dislikes regarding the work environment. Will this candidate work well on a team? Can he or she handle constructive criticism offered by other team members? Will he or she share information? Will he or she take on tasks that no one else wants for the good of the team? Does he or she want to learn more?
3. *Hard (technical) skills*: This should be with one team member or a team member and another manager. Ask probing questions about the candidate's part experience. Be willing to test their knowledge with specific questions. Does this candidate have the basic skills needed to perform well in your organization?

Give the candidates a break from time to time, being sensitive that they may not be at their best after sixty or ninety minutes of potentially stressful questioning. At the same time, observe how they handle stress—do they lose control? Shorten their responses?

Having completed all of these meetings, get everyone that was involved in the interviews together for one more short meeting to discuss the outcome of the interviews. First, after making sure that everyone is clear on which candidate is being discussed and that no details of the discussion will go beyond the walls of the meeting room, invite anyone to speak any thoughts they feel are important with regard to the candidate—good or bad. Following this, everyone votes. A single no vote with a clear (and legal) reason to back it up is enough to deny the candidate a position in the organization—this is an important aspect of the interview process; it gives the Scrum teams the ability, with reasonable cause, to outright deny a candidate a position with the company. This, as mentioned earlier, keeps the team involved in the hiring process and ensures that they continue to be empowered and take some accountability for the staffing process. However, if the votes are all positive or mostly positive with no more than one or two "on the fence," the candidate is accepted and HR works with management in another discussion to determine salary and other details.

The Care and Feeding of Scrum Teams

Managers face an interesting dilemma in an agile environment—how to maintain organizational control while simultaneously allowing Scrum teams the freedom to self-manage as much as possible. A manager ill-prepared for this type of work environment may find himself or herself trying to be helpful by assisting a Scrum team in planning a sprint only to discover, too late, that the team already had an approach in mind, but deferred to the manager. Another manager changes team membership every sprint, hoping to cross-train as much as possible. A third, hoping to truly empower the team, waits for the team to resolve internal difficulties until it is too late and the team self-destructs.

W. Edwards Deming suggests that there are basically two mistakes a manager can make: They can react to an outcome as if it came from a common cause (i.e., something that is inherent in the defined process) when, in fact, it came from a special cause (i.e., something that is unexpected or unusual). Or, they can react to an outcome as if it came from a special cause when, in fact, it came from a common cause. We can simplify it further:

■ *Tampering*: The manager gets involved to fix things when the process is working as defined.
■ *Ignoring*: The manager avoids involvement, even though the process is out of control.

Some real-life examples of well-meaning management follow.

Tampering

- *A manager, who promoted Scrum within the organization, then proceeded to make all of the decisions for the Scrum teams.* If you don't allow your teams to self-manage and self-organize, you're basically telling them you don't trust them to do it right. Scrum failed in this organization within just a few weeks.
- *An organization decided to "grade" Scrum teams on completing the stories they agreed to do during the sprint.* Sounds reasonable, doesn't it? Unfortunately, this led the organization's Scrum teams to repeatedly undercommit during each sprint planning meeting. Why go out on a limb if being aggressive during a sprint means getting a "bad grade" if they aren't 100% finished by the end of the sprint.

Ignoring

- *A Scrum team, having difficulty with a team member, was encouraged by the functional manager to continue to work to resolve their own conflicts.* That's what we teach our Certified Scrum Masters—Scrum teams are supposed to resolve their own conflicts. However, it can easily get out of control. In this case, the manager did not act quickly enough and, rather than getting involved when the team was clearly over their heads, the most experienced team members were lost to transfers out of the team and out of the company.
- *A Scrum team entered its third sprint review without completing more than a small portion of their sprint goals.* The Scrum team never asked for help and the manager decided that the team simply needed some time to figure out their mistakes and correct them. When the product owner, frustrated with the lack of progress, finally unloaded his frustration on the functional manager, a quick investigation revealed that a senior team member, convinced that agile development couldn't work, had used his influence to redirect the team's efforts into lengthy analysis efforts of the entire product backlog, certain that coding should only proceed on small modifications and that detailed analysis efforts were required before building any new features.

What this suggests is that the best training that managers can receive regarding how to best "care and feed" their Scrum teams is the same training that their Scrum team members receive, though perhaps presented from the perspective of the manager instead of the team member.

Managers, for starters, need to understand how the agile methods (Scrum, test-driven development (TDD), pairing, etc.) work so that they can clearly discern between common causes (stuff that is supposed to happen from time to time) and special causes (unexpected stuff). Even then, however, they need to understand when to allow the team to handle special causes and when to step in and assist. In one organization, management allowed a Scrum team that was suffering with problems doing continuous integration to experience partial sprint failures over four consecutive sprints, learning from their mistakes, rather than stepping in and imposing their decisions on the team. There was legitimate concern that forcing continuous integration on these teams would have created skeptics that would constantly hinder the effort. Letting them fail and succeed on their own would create developers who would probably use continuous integration for the rest of their careers.

There are many managers who, during an organization's transition, simply get it. These managers create an effective fusion of management and leadership that works well in an agile development environment. They understand that the agile manager's new role involves some very clear responsibilities:

- Improve organizational performance
- Improve Scrum team performance
- Improve employee performance
- Support Scrum teams

Improve Organization Performance

Many Scrum masters maintain an organizational impediments list. The manager in the agile organization will be exposed to many additional impediments—often ones different than the ones faced by the Scrum master. These impediments are frequently caused by the organization itself and are not only beyond the scope of responsibility of the Scrum master, but must be addressed by the manager. Organizational impediments will appear in various forms:

- Ineffective organizational structures
- Ineffective development policies
- Counteragile management direction

In all cases, the manager will need to protect their Scrum teams as much as possible from the effects of these impediments while, at the same time, working with management and others throughout the organization to identify and enact solutions.

Improve Scrum Team Performance

Teams are, of course, responsible for their performance and the quality of their output. However, good managers will seek ways to challenge their Scrum teams to improve their performance by providing an overall direction and then assisting with improvements in team skills and team practices. This can include things like:

- Helping the team to locate training, seminars, or books that enable the team to acquire new, needed skills
- Working with the team to brainstorm changes to practices to fix issues noted by the team during a sprint retrospective
- Challenging the team to find ways to develop their product with less effort and higher quality
- Clearing the way for the purchase of a data projector, a projection screen, new hardware, or new software that the team believes will help them get their work done more effectively or with higher quality

In one case, a Scrum team found themselves with a dilemma because the team could complete items considerably faster than the manager and the business analyst could write new items much faster than the team's tester could validate the completed items. The team, with help from the manager, changed the team's development processes so that other team members would step in to assist whenever they recognized that process bottlenecks (writing the items or validating the software) threatened to leave the developers with nothing to do.

The skilled manager will accomplish all of this while ensuring that the team owns all of their improvements.

Improve Employee Performance

In any organization that makes continuous improvement a high priority, you will also find attention must be paid to individual career development. Even on a Scrum team, individual team members have individual needs. Employees are always interested in developing the skills that will allow them to move either laterally (from one position to another similar position) or upward (to more senior—and better paid— titles or potentially into management). Employees should be constantly challenged to do some work outside their comfort zone during a sprint (this can be accomplished simply by volunteering for sprint backlog tasks that the employee wouldn't normally take on). The wise manager is always aware of the career development plans of each of his or her employees (indeed, those plans should be documented and clear goals set, reviewed, and updated on a regular basis). Within the scope of those plans, the manager should always be looking for opportunities to allow employees to grow without disturbing the progress of the Scrum team.

When working with an employee on performance development and career development, consider a balanced plan that recognizes the employee's responsibilities to:

1. *Himself or herself (career/professional development)*: What responsibilities does the employee aspire to? What does he or she want to be doing in five years?
2. *The company (performance development)*: What goals does the employee have for the year that benefits both the employee and the company as a result of improved skills and improved performance?
3. *The Scrum team (product development)*: What goals does the Scrum team have (all employees on a Scrum team share the same goals)?

Regardless of the manner in which employee performance is connected to raises and promotions, a balanced performance plan, and attention to it throughout the year, helps to ensure that the individual employee feels valued by the organization and does not feel that his or her accomplishments are lost in the recognition of what the Scrum team accomplishes. A sample performance plan might look like the one in Figure 5.5.

Support Scrum Teams

While the Scrum master is, by default, responsible for removing obstacles within the Scrum team, there are many obstacles that he or she will be too busy to address or simply unable (due to lack of authority) to remove at all. For example, issues of budgeting, facilities management, procurement of materials, and staffing (including staff-related performance problems, filling an empty position, immigration, and work visa issues) must be handled by a manager with the proper authority.

More generally, however, Scrum masters can be overwhelmed by their responsibilities (particularly new Scrum masters or Scrum masters with potentially difficult teams). Management should not only always be standing by to aid the Scrum master when needed; they should already be aware of the issues that the team is dealing with so that they are prepared to help out when (if) the team or Scrum master asks or if no one asks but, in the manager's assessment, his or her involvement is critical.

Care and Feeding: Summary

A manager's first care for a Scrum team is to support the success of the Scrum team. To do this, he or she needs to continually look for opportunities to improve organizational performance, Scrum team performance, and individual employee performance while, at the same time, supporting Scrum teams to be successful. Managers have the added concern of balancing the needs of the organization with the needs of the Scrum team. Does it make more sense to help the team solve a problem or to let the team solve the problem themselves?

2008 Employee Performance Plan for Smith, Nancy J.

Current job title: Advanced programmer/analyst
Since: April 10, 2005
Reporting manager: Jones, Marsha M.
Title: Senior manager
Reporting period: February 1, 2008, for 12 months with quarterly reviews

I.   Career Development: High-Level Goals

Nancy wishes to satisfy all remaining requirements for promotion to senior programmer/analyst during the current year. Longer-term goals (3 years) are to move Nancy to a senior architectural position within her current product area.

II.   Performance Management: High-Level Goals

Product development work currently planned for the year will require some experience in J2EE and Java applet development. Nancy could also play a strong role in some of the analysis backlog items currently on the product backlog. Also, I would like to see Nancy more willing to be involved in pairing with other team members. (Nancy agrees that there were opportunites to do so that she specifically passed up this year that would have benefited her and her fellow team members.)

III.   Specific Performance Goals

- By April 1, 2008, Nancy will review the current organizational coding standards and devise an alternative method for building supportability into the code. This will also require her to work with current support teams to understand what makes code more supportable. Nancy will review her proposed modifications with the Scrum teams and support teams and, on approval, add her changes to the standards (career).
- By October 1, 2008, Nancy will mentor one new developer to be hired by the company to ensure that this developer is fully knowledgeable in Scrum, the XP practices used by the company, the product, and has a coach for programming problems that may come up during his or her first three months of employment. (career).
- By April 1, 2008, Nancy will volunteer to work on a backlog item that will allow her to build an applet. It is expected that she will do appropriate reading beforehand (performance).
- By July 1, 2008, Nancy will read two or more books on J2EE development and will have volunteered to work on backlog items that involve J2EE development (performance).
- Scrum team will maintain code coverage of 86% (as measured on December 15, 2007) or better on unit tests (team).
- Scrum team will continue to *not* deliver backlog items that do not meet the team's and the organization's definition of DONEness unless it is expressly requested by the PO and the development manager that DONEness items be skipped and a new backlog item opened to cover the skipped DONEness elements (team).

Figure 5.5   A sample balanced performance plan.

An analogy that I've heard used and find particularly apt is one where the manager is likened to a sheepdog. Just as the sheepdog keeps the sheep together, protects the sheep from wolves, and herds the sheep in the proper direction (to pasture in the morning, to a barn in the evening), managers have similar responsibilities. Managers help Scrum masters keep the team together and focused. It is expected that teams will resolve most of their own conflicts, but managers will sometimes need to either step in to help resolve the conflict, or give the employees the tools and skills they need to resolve the conflict themselves. Managers help protect the Scrum team from unnecessary or unexpected interruption caused by outside interference or *wolving*, where someone from the organization "steals" a team member to solve a critical problem elsewhere in the organization. Managers help provide support and direction, ensuring that the team has the information, resources, tools, and skills to get their job done.

PLANNING THE TRANSITION

In the first section of this book we laid out the basics of agile development. We asked questions about why an organization would want to take on agile development. In this section of the book, we will start with setting up agreements within the organization about the transition to agile development, and then move on to the transition team and the planning and execution of the transition. But first, let's talk a little about how we'll actually run the transition.

It is appropriate that the transition itself is run as an agile project. We will form the transition teams as Scrum teams, build our list of things to do in the form of a transition backlog, and execute the transition as a series of sprints. In addition to being an effective manner in which to manage the project, this approach has the benefit of getting your organization used to Scrum and backlog management faster by using it. The methods we will begin using in the transition planning and project execution will be the same ones that we'll use in an actual project once we actually create development Scrum teams. Therefore, our plan of action for beginning the transition will look like this:

1. Determine project goals: Quantify the goals of the project.
2. Create transition team: This team will drive the transition.
3. Set agreements: How will the organization support the project?
4. Create transition backlog: Define and prioritize the backlog; create the teams to address.

Once the transition backlog is created, your highest priorities will likely be the creation of:

1. The communication plan: Define how, and to whom, information about the transition will be communicated.
2. The budget: How much money do you expect to spend on software, hardware, training, etc.?
3. The training plan: Define what kind of training will be needed, for which roles, and how often.

The creation of these critical plans is outlined in the chapters that follow.

Chapter 6

Create the Transition Team

As we begin to discuss the elements that we will need to have in place to launch the transition, the most important priority is for the creation of the initial transition team. I suggest an initial team because the membership on the team at the end of the formal transition may be quite different from the team that we begin with. Early in the transition, we'll be focused on higher-level organizational issues—facilities changes, software and hardware purchases, development process changes, maybe even some organizational (reporting structure) changes. Later in the transition our focus will be on more detailed and technical matters. Regardless, however, the transition team should always be representative of as many areas and disciplines of your organization as possible. It is important to have managers (first line, middle management, and senior management) on the team, certainly, but you should also ensure that you have coders, architects, analysts, writers, and testers on the team as well. A transition to agile development has an organization-wide effect, and similarly, the team driving the transition must be representative of as many different views and needs within the organization as possible.

There are two approaches for the organization of the transition team depending much on the size of the organization. In a small to medium-sized organization (up to about 250 personnel), you may want to consider a single transition team that drives the transition. However, in a larger organization, you will likely want to consider creating subordinate teams that specialize in particular aspects of the overall transition, but take the actual executing details away from the core transition team. In the larger, more complex organizations, the transition team structure may look something like Figure 6.1.

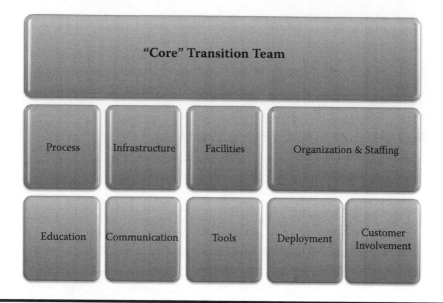

Figure 6.1   Complex transition team structure.

Where necessary, or in smaller organizations, you can reduce the number of subordinate teams by combining multiple purposes into similar teams. For example, you could have a single process and tools team (tools are generally, after all, automated extension of the defined development process). You can also combine infrastructure and deployment into a single team, as most deployment concerns are addressed by infrastructure. Any functions not handled by a subordinate team will need to be addressed by the core transition team. The result could look like the structure in Figure 6.2.

As you put together your transition team and any subordinate teams, consider the teams listed in Figure 6.1. These teams, whether or not you create them for your transition, handle various aspects of the transition that you will need to address. By understanding what the teams in Figure 6.1 are responsible for, you can be more certain that your teams have the membership that they need to handle the transition.

- *The core team*: This team drives the creation of project goals and measurement and routinely reports transition status to the organization; it is the coordination point for all subordinate teams and all transition backlog items that are not addressed by a subordinate team. When there are subordinate teams, a core team member acts as the product owner for a subordinate team; thus, the core team also manages the overall project and prioritizes the efforts of the subordinate teams.
- *Communications*: This team drives the creation and execution of the communication plan. It handles communication with other departments in

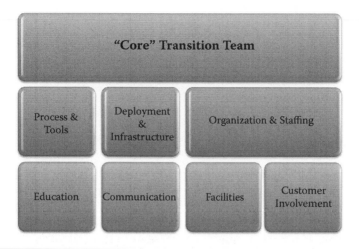

Figure 6.2   A simplified transition team structure.

the organization, ensuring that the broader organization is aware of the transition.

■ *Customer involvement*: This team will concern itself with the issues of getting customers involved with the agile development teams. What do the teams need to know and do? What do the customers need to know about their roles? What about intellectual property rights or confidential information? What happens when three, four, or even ten teams ask the same customer to get involved with their work?

■ *Deployment*: This team will concentrate on how to get software safely added to the main product code base and go from there to a customer environment.

■ *Education*: This team will deal with the creation and execution of the training plan.

■ *Facilities*: This team will deal with issues involving the modification of your organization's work environment in order to ensure that the development teams are working in open team rooms.

■ *Infrastructure*: This team will help manage the artifact configuration (including source code control) as well as handling the creation of new server environments for team-level and product-level testing.

■ *Organization and staffing*: This team will deal with possible changes in the organizational structure, changes in staffing procedure, and change in job descriptions and career paths caused by the transition to agile development.

■ *Process*: This team will help create documented practices based on changes caused by the agile transition and will work to ensure that applicable regulatory requirements are adhered to and that the new practices replace or are properly integrated with the existing practices.

- *Tools*: This team will help drive the selection of tools that are needed to support the agile transition. Once the tools are selected and installed, this team plays a significant role helping to ensure that the tools are properly integrated into the organization's practices.

The Transition Team Lead

While the transition teams are, for the most part, agile teams that self-organize around their work, we still take a lesson from Scrum, looking for a single individual with ultimate responsibility for the prioritization of the transition backlog and the vision of the agile transition. Your choice for the transition owner (i.e., the transition project's product owner) needs to be someone with a good understanding of the concepts of agile development and what the organization hopes to accomplish in undertaking this effort. The transition owner should be held accountable for achieving the transition project's goals, prioritizing the transition backlog, and using the transition team (or teams) to resolve any issues that surface during the project. The transition owner should also be a strong team leader and should excel at working with teams to gain consensus.

The Executive Sponsor

The transition team also needs an executive sponsor. The sponsor needs to be an individual who, by his or her involvement with the transition team:

- Demonstrates the organization's commitment to the agile transition. The executive sponsor should be the person from whom the rest of the organization first hears about the agile transition. They should be able to speak at a high level to the benefits of agile development and the transition plan. They should plan on repeating the message frequently to the organization and the stakeholders in order to demonstrate their commitment to the transition. The executive sponsor must be willing to state clear and unwavering commitment to the agile transition, explaining that there will be problems and mistakes, but there will also be success.
- Can defend any mistakes that the organization makes to corporate executive management. Corporate management, often removed from more than the basic details of the transition, may initially be quick to blame failures in agile development if the organization makes mistakes. The executive sponsor will be in the difficult position of having to explain the nature of the changes that agile development requires of an organization and will have to explain the fine line between the organization having difficulty making the change and how much benefit there will be after the change is successfully made.

■ Can authorize certain expenditures on behalf of the transition team. The transition team will be developing the initial budget for the transition plan as well as asking for resources necessary to execute the transition plan. Both will likely be significant requests and will require senior management approval before continuing anyway. In addition, when you are asking for resources to take part on the transition team (or teams), you will need some of the best people in the organization, not the ones that happen to be available. You may need your executive sponsor to help get the type of participation that you need.

Chapter 7

Define the Organizational Agreements

While it's important to get the employees excited and ready for the transition, it's equally important to make sure that the management staff is involved in the definition of the new rules of engagement. Starting the transition without helping them define their new roles invites confusion, frustration, and counterproductive decisions that will echo continuously throughout the organization.

So, step 1 is to define the ground rules. Get the agreement of the executive sponsor that the management team is going to hold a workshop[1] to discuss several critical issues common to agile transitions and come up with solutions that the organization is going to have to commit to.

If you can get all of your management together in a workshop, do so. Otherwise, get a representative group of managers together and make sure that everyone understands what the workshop is for and that the managers that attend will be setting operational policy for the organization. Start the workshop by making sure that everyone understands what agile development is and how Scrum teams work. It is extremely important that you emphasize the following points:

1. Product owners define the *what* of product. That is, they describe and prioritize what they want done based on the vision of the product and their role of maximizing the return on investment of what is developed.
2. Scrum teams define the *how* and *how long* of the product. No one else gets to estimate development work or gets to make changes to the estimates except for the developers. Scrum teams need support, but need control over the *how*.

3. Management ensures that the right people are employed by the organization, that they have or will attain the right tools/skills, and that management immediately addresses any obstacles encountered but not solvable by the team. Management sets the overall tone for the environment and is constantly looking for ways to improve productivity.

These points are important as they clearly delineate some of the truly fundamental responsibilities in a software development shop, and you can refer back to these points during the workshop while trying to work out some of the more difficult problems.

With the basic rules defined, you can continue the workshop by dividing the groups into teams that include management from every level (first line, middle level, and top level). Get them to discuss the following points and decide how each will be handled:

■ Being a Scrum master is a full-time job. Asking a Scrum master to be a Scrum master *and* to develop code or write documentation or tests limits their ability to be a strong Scrum master for your team. How will the organization deal with this? What is the organization willing to commit to? What is the organization willing to give up?

■ Scrum teams determine the effort estimates for the product backlog items on which they work. More importantly, they determine how much work they can reliably do during a sprint. No one else defines how much work a team will do during a sprint—that has to come from the team itself. How will the organization handle it when less is getting done during a sprint than was originally anticipated on the release plan?

■ Scrum teams work best when the team members are 100% dedicated to their teams. Studies have clearly demonstrated that attempting to work on multiple projects at the same time significantly reduces their effectiveness, quality, and productivity. Will the organization try to ensure that all team members are 100% dedicated? If not, what is the organization willing to commit to?

■ Scrum teams need to be allowed to work in an uninterrupted manner during the sprint. Pulling individuals off teams to address customer issues is not recommended. In fact, teams perform better (although there is still a loss of productivity) when customer issues are given to teams to figure out how to resolve rather than pulling someone away from the team. Will the organization agree that team membership must not be changed during the sprint? If not, what is the organization willing to commit to?

■ Agile development embraces the concept of sustainable pace. This means that teams accelerate to their greatest natural rhythm while working an optimal number of hours each week. Many organizations make up for schedule delays by forcing overtime on the development teams. Many studies report the same thing—developers can work reasonable overtime for approximately two weeks before their performance drops to preovertime levels and their software quality drops even further. How will the organization manage schedule delays? When overtime is seen as a possible solution, will it be for weeks or months on end, or just two weeks? What is the organization willing to commit to?

■ Agile development leverages the Lean development concept of deferring decisions until the last reasonable moment. This helps to ensure that the organization does not waste time on something until the odds of actually doing it are fairly high. This also means that feature and task estimates will be very roughly defined at the beginning of the project and will increase in precision as the project moves forward. In other development methods, a greater degree of precision is gained much earlier in the project by devoting considerably more time to analysis at the cost of actually producing working features. Can the organization agree to release planning and project status based on rough estimates? Can the organization deal with scope projections that may change each month as more features are completed and more is known about the ones that aren't? What is the organization willing to commit to?

If you have the people who can do it, put people knowledgeable in agile development on each team so that the managers can ask clarifying questions.

Give the groups an hour to work on these questions; you might even want to give them a short break during the discussions. At the end, bring everyone back together and pick one team to review a question and their decisions. Invite questions, different views, and other ideas from the other groups. Limit the discussion to between fifteen and thirty minutes to ensure that you cover all of the material. Then require the group to reach a final consensus on each question.

If you think it will be necessary to get help to get the management team to agree on something, schedule the executive sponsor to join the workshop either during the discussion or after all of the decisions have been documented. Remember, though, this isn't about the executive sponsor making the decisions. His or her function in the meeting will be to discourage long, drawn-out discussions about issues that really shouldn't be issues and to encourage the team to make decisions.

Finally, it may also be necessary to get everyone to agree to follow the policies during a probationary period, after which the policies and their results will be reviewed in another management workshop. If someone really has doubts about the policies and isn't satisfied with the outcome of the workshop, encourage him or her to follow the policies for now and, in the meantime, keep an open mind and keep thinking about a better solution. Periodic management review of policies and processes is a good idea anyway—get your organization thinking about this now.

The agenda for your workshop might look a little like Figure 7.1.

8:00am–8:30am –	Breakfast/coffee (fill their stomachs first!!)
8:30am–8:45am –	Welcome, review agenda
8:45am–9:00am –	Executive Sponsor welcome
9:00am–10:00am–	Review of Agile Development
10:00am–10:15am–	BREAK
10:15am–11:00am–	Review Questions for Group Discussion
11:00am–12:00pm–	Group Discussion
12:00pm–1:00pm–	LUNCH (best to provide it and keep everyone in or near the meeting room)
1:00pm–2:00pm –	Group Discussion
2:00pm–4:30pm –	Discuss Group Findings, Decide on Policies, Document
2:30pm–2:45pm –	BREAK
4:30pm–5:00pm –	Review outcomes, next steps, Adjourn

Figure 7.1   A sample agenda for the organizational agreements workshop.

Document the Agreements

The agreements should be documented and distributed throughout the organization as quickly as possible. Be as detailed and as precise as you possibly can. For example, the first of the ground rules should handle the question of full-time Scrum masters. A documented decision might look like this:

> As of April 4, 2008, the three current agile transition pilot teams will have dedicated trained Scrum masters. As the transition expands beyond the pilot, however, there will only be a maximum of eight full-time, dedicated Scrum masters. These Scrum masters may, when ready, handle up to three teams each. All teams that cannot be covered by a dedicated Scrum master will have to fill the role from their own staffing. Training will be provided in those instances.

So, from this decision, we know that, while some teams will have dedicated Scrum masters, other teams will not. As those teams take on the role of Scrum master, however, proper training will be provided to them. As the transition moves forward, keep an eye on the progress of teams with and without full-time, dedicated Scrum masters. If you see a good reason to revisit this decision in six months or a year, be prepared to back up your position with hard facts.

How these issues are addressed by management will tell you a lot about how successful your organization will be transitioning to agile development. Let's take a look at the rest of them:

Issue 1: Scrum teams determine the effort estimates for the product backlog items on which they work. This issue challenges the common practice of reducing development estimates, *estimate reduction*, in order to make the project schedule appear to be more in line with management expectation. When an organization engages in the practice of estimate reduction, they are actually recognizing the problem, but making the schedule look better anyway in order to defer the bad news, often in the hope that something else will happen that will make the schedule delay someone else's fault.

An organization ready to make a transition to agile will accept that developers own the product backlog item estimates but, at the same time, will be vigilant that the Scrum teams are not engaging in estimate inflation or padding, a common practice used to mitigate the effects of estimate reduction. Managers familiar with the technical aspects of product development should remain closely engaged in backlog grooming and backlog item estimation activities in order to encourage the teams to resist the old temptation to inflate their estimates. Basically, the agreement here needs to be that management promises not to reduce developer estimates while the developers agree to no longer inflate them. More than that, however, management and product management need to accept the estimates provided to them by development and resist the urge to reduce the estimates, except by the deliberate and systematic simplification of backlog items, in the hopes that simpler items will result in lower estimates.

Issue 2: Scrum teams work best when the team members are 100% dedicated to their teams. In organizations where there are multiple releases of multiple products and plenty of work to go around, there will be a constant desire to spread the most experienced personnel across multiple teams in the hopes that their experience will improve those teams' likelihood of success. Unfortunately, this practice often results in the senior personnel being ineffective for all their teams. Rather than helping multiple teams, multiple teams are hurt.

Scrum defines teams as being self-managing and self-organizing. What this means in terms of education is that the Scrum team is also at least partly responsible for identifying what skills they lack and for making plans to correct that lack, whether it's to get the proper training or to acquire the needed skills from another source. One effective solution is to build an educational policy for Scrum teams around the following points:

1. The organization holds continuous education as a high priority and will devote up to eight hours per month to ongoing education (seminars, reading, classes, etc.).
2. The typical duties of a senior developer will include training and coaching other developers in their area of expertise.
3. Senior developers that demonstrate expertise in an area that few have but many need are not assigned to Scrum teams. Instead, they take on an advisory role (expert consultation), assisting many teams, but not owning the individual tasks of any teams.
4. Senior developers that demonstrate expertise in an area that few have but many may have to temporarily join a single team (expertise infusion) to accomplish a specific goal and then disconnect from the team when they are finished.

In the end, your organization must look for ways to keep resources 100% dedicated to a single Scrum team, and your policies should enforce that goal. Widely needed skills or knowledge that are held by a very few people in the organization should be shared across the organization by expert consultation or temporary expertise infusion, rather than trying to have your most experienced personnel work on tasks for multiple teams at the same time.

Issue 3: Scrum teams need to be allowed to work in an uninterrupted manner during the sprint. Just as Scrum team members need to be 100% dedicated to a single team, the team also needs to be allowed to work in a relatively uninterrupted manner during a sprint. Teams develop rhythms that (in most cases) tend to allow them to become more and more productive as time goes on. In Bruce Tuckman's[2] team development model, it was recognized that there are four stages in team development:

- *Forming*: High dependence on leader for guidance and direction. Little agreement on team aims other than received from leader. Individual roles and responsibilities are unclear.
- *Storming*: Decisions don't come easily within group. Team members vie for position as they attempt to establish themselves in relation to other team members and the leader, who might receive challenges from team members. Clarity of purpose increases but plenty of uncertainties persist.
- *Norming*: Agreement and consensus largely forms among team members, who respond well to facilitation by leader. Roles and responsibilities are clear and accepted. Big decisions are made by group agreement. Smaller decisions may be delegated to individuals or small teams within group.
- *Performing*: The team is more strategically aware; the team knows clearly why it is doing what it is doing. The team has a shared vision and is able to stand on its own feet with no interference or participation from the leader. There is a focus on overachieving goals, and the team makes most of the decisions against criteria agreed to with the leader.

In this model, it is generally recognized that the performing stage is where you want your teams to be as much as possible. Unfortunately, it is also generally accepted that any changes to the team (membership, health of team members, organizational change, etc.) will cause a team to regress from whatever stage they are in to an earlier stage. Therefore, any changes to a team during a sprint can have a significant impact on the team's ability to meet the commitment made to the product owner at sprint planning.

In enabling Scrum, the organization *must* recognize that it is the Scrum team that is a key element in making agile development work. A strong, high-performing Scrum team can make up for an inexperienced product owner. However, even the best product owner cannot cover for a poor Scrum team. It is extremely important, therefore, that the decisions that the organization makes consider the need for stable Scrum teams of paramount importance.

At the same time, the "wolving" of a resource from a Scrum team is usually caused by an urgent customer issue that requires immediate attention and a rapid response. So, as always, there must be a balance of the needs of the team with the needs of the organization and the customer. One way to deal with this is to understand that, like padding estimates, organizations often seek out the *best* person to solve a problem instead of finding the most *practical* person to solve a problem. In other words, while there is always one person who can solve the problem faster than anybody else, there are also likely a number of people who are capable of solving the problem *quickly enough*.

Rather than pulling the *best resource* from the team to solve a problem, assign the problem to the *right* team and let them decide how best to solve the problem. They may request a consultation from the best resource, but the teams affected will work together to decide how they can solve the problem quickly while still managing their sprint planning commitment. Most importantly, the decision of how to solve the problem was never taken away from the team.

Issue 4: Agile development embraces the concept of "sustainable pace." The great myth of employee overtime is that it's pretty much the same as getting more resource for the same money (most developers these days are salaried and therefore not eligible for overtime). The problem with this myth is that we've been using the wrong metaphor. Let's try this one instead.

You're driving a car down a dark highway. You frequently have to steer your car to avoid rocks, potholes, and wildlife crossing the road. Visibility is poor, so you have to be very careful, as you'll have very little time to avoid these obstacles when they first appear on the road. If you're not careful, you could drive off the road and down an embankment or, worse, hit whatever appears on the road. Either way, once you do, your car will likely be ruined and you'll be stuck until you can fix the car or someone finds you. Since you've been doing this for a while now, you've gotten pretty good at it and you're able to maintain a respectable velocity of forty-five miles per hour.

Now, increase your velocity to seventy miles per hour. How about ninety miles per hour?

Getting worried? This is a more appropriate metaphor for what happens when overtime is forced for more than a few weeks at a time. The obstacles are the rocks, potholes, and wildlife. Your visibility is poor because it's hard in real life to see more than a few hours or a few days into the future with any real accuracy (sure, we can plan, but reality is often very different—just look at the nightly weather forecast). So, as the speed of the car is increased (that is, overtime is worked), the risk of plowing head-on into an obstacle increases. Sure, you're getting more done (that is, your velocity has increased), but the odds of hitting an obstacle with no warning increases too.

Studies show that developers can handle about two weeks of overtime before quality and productivity drop below the preovertime levels. Unit tests, normally required, will be skipped in order to get more code done. Documentation that is supposed to be updated will be left for "later, when we have more time." Functional- and acceptance-level testing will be saved until the end of the development effort and will often be considerably shortened in order to ensure that the project ends on time. The end result of this corner cutting is a reduction in quality that, not surprisingly, will reduce development productivity even further when your quality assurance department and your customers begin reporting defects and your developers take more and more time away from new feature development to fix the defects.

While this can be a difficult concept to embrace, unless your organization seriously wishes to accelerate development at the cost of reducing quality, an agreement must be reached among the management staff regarding the use of mandatory overtime.

Issue 5: Agile development leverages the Lean development concept of deferring decisions until the last reasonable moment. There are seven fundamental principles in Lean development that are leveraged by Scrum to improve development performance and product quality. These principles include eliminate waste and defer commitment. It is these principles that will potentially cause significant difficulty for those used to the illusion of precision that waterfall projects often provide.

According to the Agile Manifesto, agile developers prefer to embrace change as opposed to attempting to control change. We recognize that, while we could provide detailed estimates of features in the beginning of a project, there is a very high likelihood that information gained during the course of the project will either cause us to have to reestimate the feature, restate the feature, and then reestimate it, or remove the feature from the project entirely. Additionally, were you to plot the accuracy of an estimate against the effort expended to calculate that estimate, you would draw a curve of diminishing returns (in other words, spending more time doesn't necessarily return more and more information; at some fairly early point in the analysis effort, most of the knowable information has been discovered). Both these concepts being true, agile projects usually provide very high-level estimates of effort in early stages of the project. As the project progresses, estimates become more firm and precise until the development actually builds the feature.

As a result, agile projects remove waste from development by reducing the effort spent estimating features and defer commitment by delaying more precise estimates (and avoiding unwanted rework) until a point in the project just before the development team builds the feature. In the end, this allows agile projects to begin producing code earlier in the project while still doing a sufficient amount of analysis to ensure that the right product is built.

For those used to detailed project schedules early in the project, however, this aspect of agile development will be difficult to get used to and may result in demands to create and commit to detailed feature estimates at the beginning of the project. An organization planning to engage in agile development will need to determine how they will resolve the differences between the illusion of precision that waterfall projects provide and the clarity of imprecision demonstrated by agile projects.

Issue 6: Some developers will not successfully complete the transition. Unfortunately, this past history of agile transitions has shown that a small percentage of employees (estimates range from two to ten percent) will not be able to successfully complete the transition. Developers that prefer to work by themselves and not on a team, or that want their achievements to stand out and not be part of a larger team goal, are generally not good fits for a Scrum team. There are also developers that I like to call heroes. These developers are easily identified when they say something like, "It is easier to do it myself than to explain it to you." What's worse is that these developers often feel that they do perform well on a team; it is usually the team members that raise the issue of the hero developer's performance.

Whether the issue is raised by the employee or by the team, it is important for the organization to react quickly. In some cases, the issue can be solved with some education and team building. In others, it's just a matter of moving the employee to another team where he or she might perform better. In the most extreme, but hardly rare, instance, the employee may need to be discharged from the organization to find work elsewhere.

What's most important is that the organization be clear that developers are required to work on and with Scrum teams; the organization should *never* look to make special positions for employees to create their own environment outside the Scrum teams, no matter how important that employee may appear to be to the organization. Once the decision is made to employ agile development and form Scrum teams, the organization should not negotiate this for individual employees.

Issue 7: The organization may need to reset some customer expectations. When the transition to agile development begins, the organization is also recognizing that development will occur based on a product backlog and at a pace set by the Scrum teams. For this reason, it is possible that customer expectations for the delivery of certain features may need to be changed. If the organization is not willing to renegotiate some of these potentially unachievable goals, it will be very difficult to properly implement agile development and Scrum.

Endnotes

1. You can find supporting materials at http://www.bigagiledevelopment.com/organizationalagreements.
2. Tuckman, Bruce. "Developmental Sequence in Small Groups." *Psychological Bulletin* 63 (1965): 384–99. http://findarticles.com/p/articles/mi_qa3954/is_200104/ai_n8943663 (accessed November 10, 2008).

Chapter 8

Determine Transition Goals

This crucial (and often overlooked) activity helps to set the expectations for the project. How many products/groups/people will be involved? How long is the organization willing to wait before seeing productivity and quality gains? How much gain is the organization looking for, and how will those gains be measured? Unless these questions are asked and answered early in the project, the transition teams will have a difficult time answering questions that will come up again and again during the transition.

For example, without a clear idea of how the organization is planning to support continuous integration and testing (Is the organization planning to provide a working environment for each Scrum team? Will those environments be real or virtualized on centrally controlled servers? Will there be an infrastructure team responsible for the servers, or will each Scrum team be responsible for their own?), the transition team will be unable to make important decisions about training, coaching, and hardware purchases.

Knowing how many people will be involved in the transition and how fast the organization hopes to see returns from the transition is also critical information. Will the transition team have six months? One year? Two years? This will have a tremendous impact on how training is managed, how new teams are created, and the requirements of any software purchased in support of the transition. I see this step as similar to defining the product architecture before beginning feature development. Without a good idea of the underpinnings of the product, it is very difficult to proceed confidently.

With your goals identified, you are one step closer to being able to determine how you will monitor the transition and measure its progress.

Measuring and Monitoring the Transition

Any organization that spends time and resources on an agile transition will want to be able to measure the progress of the transition and what kind of effect the transition is having on the organization. We do this by observing certain outcomes of the transition and measuring those outcomes against our expectations. Assuming those expectations are the correct ones, we can quantitatively demonstrate the progress the organization is making and, even more importantly, can acquire a level of statistical control over the organization as it transitions.

Having said that, it is extremely important to be aware that any measurement of an organization *will* have an effect on that organization's behavior. The organization is going to act to improve the measurement in any way possible in an effort to achieve its goals. So, if you're going to measure an organization in some manner, follow these two rules:

1. Consider carefully whether a quantitative measurement is needed. Establishing any measurement is a calculated risk that could cause unwanted and detrimental behavior.
2. Use the goal/question/metric (GQM)[1] paradigm to ensure that your measurements are driven by the appropriate model, i.e., that your measurements will yield useful information that directly impacts your transition goals.

Let's talk about how to use the GQM paradigm to safely measure your organization. We'll start by going back to your original goals.

In most organizations, goals for an agile transition will focus on performance, quality, and costs. Except for the cost-related goals (which would have far too many variables to accurately exemplify in a simple case study), an organization's goals might look something like this:

1. Improve software development productivity by reducing software defects by 20% from the point of view of the corporation.
2. Improve software development performance by increasing the overall value of features by 30% from the point of view of the customer.

Contained within these two goals are the necessary elements for writing good measurements. We have the object being measured (software development productivity and software development performance), the object of interest (software defects and overall value of features), and the perspective of the object of interest (the corporation and the customer) to ensure that the measurements address the proper perspective.

Improved Productivity through Reduced Defects

In the case of the first goal (improve productivity by reducing software defects), the corporate perspective means that we're only going to concern ourselves with defects that are reported to the corporation either internally or by our customers. Defects reported by customers that are duplicates, customer error, or issues where the software is working as expected will not be included in this goal.[2] We also want to be able to measure a 20% reduction in monthly defect reports, so we need a starting point (i.e., a baseline) from which to measure. To establish this, we need either historical data that match what we plan to collect during the transition or a very good guess. Usually, historical data regarding defect reports aren't terribly difficult to get.

At its very simplest, then, we could decide to measure total defects reported internally or by the customer. Taken over a period of months, we could easily graph this as shown in Figure 8.1.

As you can see in the figure, total defects start around 230 and, over a two-year period, decline to approximately 180. This demonstrates a reduction in software defects of about 2.7 per month, or an overall reduction of (230 − 180)/230, or 21.7%. So, with this basic graph, we can prove that one of the goals of the transition was achieved. But let's look a little deeper.

From the perspective of the corporation, which is how this goal is written, we may discover that the corporation would like a little more information about the defect reports. For example, should the defect trend move upward, it would be a good idea to understand where the defects are being reported, that is, at what point in the development process. In an agile environment, we can separate defect reports into the following useful categories:

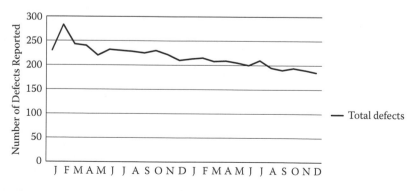

Figure 8.1 **Total defects measured over a 24-month period.**

1. Defects found during a project iteration (one important caveat here—defects found during an iteration that were caused by work that occurred in that iteration are fixed without being reported). What we are looking for here are defects that "escape" an iteration.
2. Defects found during final iteration of the project (the final iteration of an agile project is often, but not always, given over to final testing and putting the finishing touches on the release).
3. Defects found during beta testing.
4. Defects found for the first year after the product is considered generally available.

This view will give the corporation a clearer view of where defects are being found and, potentially, where those defects are coming from. If we take the same data from Figure 8.1 and break it down into these more precise categories, we might see something like Figure 8.2.

Figure 8.2 clearly shows the same total defects statistics as in Figure 8.1, but we can now clearly also see where in our development system the defects were discovered. For example, the "GA + 12 Months" line (which represents defects reported against software from general availability, when the software was generally available to consumers, through a period of 12 months) shows a trend of fewer and fewer defects being reported by our customers. Assuming that our customers have not suddenly decided to stop reporting defects, a decline in defects found by our customers is most certainly evidence of improved development productivity.

Another positive indication is displayed in the "During Beta" line. This line shows how many defects our beta customers are finding. As you can see in Figure 8.2, our fictitious corporation is releasing a beta version to our customers in April and May of both years. However, the defect spike seen in the second beta is much smaller than the first beta. So, what's getting to our customers is getting better, from the beta customers to the general consumers.

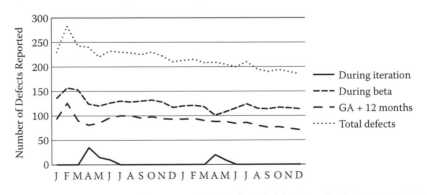

Figure 8.2 Defects reported broken down into categories.

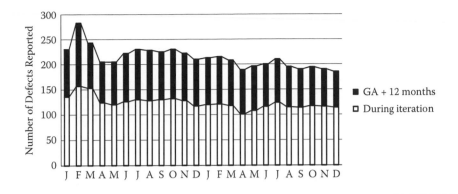

Figure 8.3 Defects found during development sprints and during the final or release iteration.

One final noteworthy point is the pattern drawn by the "During Iteration" and "GA + 12 Months" lines. These lines represent defects found during development iteration as opposed to those found at the customer site, respectively. If we are indeed improving the productivity of our development teams, we should be seeing the total number of defects drop and, at the same time, a greater percentage of defects during development, with a lesser percentage being reported by our customers. Take a look at just the defects found during development and the defects found at the customer site as a bar chart instead, as illustrated in Figure 8.3.

Figure 8.3 shows the relationship between defects found in the product during development iterations and those defects found after the product was released to the general consumer. In the first month of the transition, customer-reported defects made up 43% of the total defects reported that month. By the end of the two-year transition, customer-reported defects fell to 38% of the total defects, dropping from 94 in the first month to 71 in the last month.

Improved Performance through Increased Feature Value

We could also measure the second example goal through a similar process: "Improve software development performance by increasing the overall value of features by 30% from the point of view of the customer." The key with this goal is to determine the value of every feature that we build so that the total value completed each month can be calculated. Keep in mind that the goal is written to be measured from the perspective of the customer, so we have to ensure that the value that we're measuring is from the perspective of the customer as well (that is, we can't measure internal value). What this means, of course, is that technical items that have little or no direct benefit for our customers (like adding support for a new database manager, adding OS service packs to our base product) will provide little in the way of increased value. Also, since we want to derive a baseline value, we will probably need to:

1. Calculate the value produced by previous months' work
2. Use the first month of production as the baseline
3. Guess

In addition, we will need to establish very precise definitions for what is completed, or "done." While there is the concept of earned value, we need to clearly differentiate earned value (which calculates value in terms of how much of the feature is completed) and customer value (which calculates value in terms of completed features). The bottom line is that customers rarely see value in incomplete features. It's either done or it's not. We will talk more about "DONEness" and how it is achieved during agile development in a later chapter.

And, since value is value, we probably won't even have a reason to break the value down into different types, so the resulting graph is fairly simple. As Figure 8.4 clearly shows, value increased from 40 points to 49 points by the end of the two-year period. This represents a 22.5% increase in value, which is, unfortunately, short of the 30% goal. In this case, one of the two goals has been achieved. The organization will have to review the transition plan and decide if they want to continue with the transition as designed, modify the transition plan, or scrap the plan and try something else.

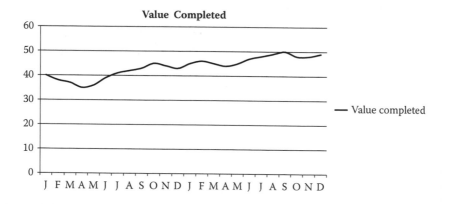

Figure 8.4 Value completed by development.

Setting Control Limits to Manage Corrective Actions

In addition to monitoring and managing the direction of the transition project, you can also use measurements to help manage when to take corrective action. This can be quite useful to help ensure that the organization does not engage in tampering (that is, interfering in the normal course of the development process because it is perceived that something unexpected has occurred) or isolation (that is, not interfering in abnormal course of the development process because it is perceived that nothing unexpected has occurred). We do this by setting upper and lower control limits on our measurements. These control limits are much like the red zone on a gauge or meter. When the needle moves into the portion of the gauge that is red, some user intervention is required; until then, however, no intervention is needed.

In the manufacturing world, control limits are set by observing the manufacturing process and then basing the upper and lower control limits on the data (it is common practice in the United States to use three standard deviations, or 3σ; other statisticians use probability limits). As long as the process remains within the limits, the process is considered to be under statistical control. You can accomplish the same in the software development world. I'll use the defect information from the previous example to show you what I mean. To keep it simple, we'll use only the defects found during the development iteration. You can see the original information in Figure 8.2; Figure 8.5 shows the "During Iteration" data, but with an upper and lower control limit established at three standard deviations above and below the average of the data.

In Figure 8.5 you see the original "During Iteration" data (that is, the number of defects found during the development iterations) and two new lines: the "Upper Control Limit" and the "Lower Control Limit." In this case, both limits have been created based on the organization's ongoing performance and by agreement with

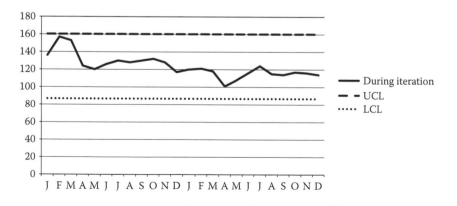

Figure 8.5   Managing defects with upper and lower control limits.

the developers and management. While 3σ has been used in this example, the upper and lower control limits can also be established simply by selecting reasonable upper and lower values. In either case, the concept is simple: if the number of defects crosses above the upper control limit or below the lower control limit, the organization begins an investigation to determine which of the following is true:

1. *Something has happened during development that needs to be corrected.* In this case, further investigation is needed to understand why the defect measurement crossed the control limit. Are more peer reviews or code reviews required? Have some of the developers become lax in their creation and execution of unit tests? Has there been an ongoing problem that has caused continuous integration and testing to not run to completion on a regular basis? Did a number of developers take vacation? Was whatever changed temporary? Is it going to self-correct? You may need to diagnose why the measurement exceeded the control limit and then determine a proper solution.
2. *Something has changed that requires a change to one or more development processes.* This instance occurs when the developers are following the defined processes properly despite the out-of-control measurement. As a result, you will have to determine why the defined process is failing, determine what process or processes need to be changed, make the proper changes, and roll out those changes to the development teams.
3. *Something has happened that requires a change in the control limit.* You may find that your developers are doing everything right and your processes are working fine, but the measurement is crossing the control limit anyway. It is very possible for measurements to cross the control limit because the organization has changed in some fundamental manner. On a positive note, the reported defects measure might cross the lower control limit simply because the organization has gotten much better at finding and eliminating defects before calling a feature done. Likewise, if your organization suddenly sold your product to a number of new customers, you may find yourself dealing with more defects as a result of more users of your product. Value, too, may cross the upper control limit (indicating that the organization is now generating more value than it was before). Did you add more teams? Did your teams simply improve a little each month until the value produced simply crossed the control limit? Did your product owner suddenly add a number of very high-value features to the backlog that your Scrum teams just finished? There are many possibilities. As before, you will need to determine what changed and, if the change is long term (more than three or four months), adjust the control limit appropriately.

As you can see, there are so many reasons for a measurement to cross a control limit that it is foolhardy to rush into a situation with grand notions of quick fixes until a reasonable diagnosis can be made and a solution, if any is required, can be determined and enacted.

Avoiding Organizational Dysfunction Caused by Measurements

Unfortunately, there isn't a single measurement that cannot be easily "cooked" in order to create the desired outcome. For example, if you measure reported defects (as in the example in this chapter), you may discover instances of defects that are found by developers and are simply fixed without being reported. Likewise, measuring reported defects may cause a testing manager to encourage the testers to open more defects. One frequent instance of this is when testers, who previously had opened one defect report to encompass multiple similar defects in the same object or component (for example, a simple problem common to all of the fields on a single dialog box or screen), begin opening defects for each and every field. Suddenly your defect reports unexpectedly increase by a factor of ten or worse. In another case, a product owner began increasing story value estimation by ten to fifteen percent in order to achieve quarterly or annual goals. Examples of this type of dysfunction caused by measurement collection are endless, and many instances are actually damaging to the organization. For example, imagine the overhead that was generated by the testers that began opening ten times as many defect reports as before, not to mention the overhead experienced by the developers trying to work their way through ten times as many defects in their queues.

There are a few ways to avoid these situations, or at least make it harder for these dysfunctions to develop. First, communicate what you're doing and why. When employees become aware of measurements being gathered and reviewed without any kind of explanation, all sorts of unexpected and unwanted behavior occurs.

Communicate what you're collecting, how you are collecting it (this is very important, as you may discover that what you thought was the right value really isn't—or isn't in all cases), and what you're doing with the information.

Second, *do not* use organizational performance measurements in an employee's individual performance plan or performance evaluation. Measurements collected regarding the performance of the organization's agile transition are intended to demonstrate progress toward organization-level goals. They measure the interaction of many people and groups in your organization and can rarely be significantly affected by a single employee. Keep your employee's performance evaluations (if you must have them at all) focused on their soft skills (ability to work with teams, etc.) and the hard skills (technical skills). Organizational measurements measure organizational goals. Personal measurements measure personal goals. Keep these definitions clear and never confuse the two.

Third, consider creating pairs or trios of related measurements that support proper conclusions and help rule out measurement cooking. By creating multiple measurements for each goal, you create checks and balances so that changes in one measurement caused by unwanted organizational dysfunctions can be validated by one or more other measurements. If one measurement of a trio shows a significant change, it may be the result of an unwanted behavioral change. If, however, two or three of the related measurements change, you can be much more certain that something real has changed in the organization.

For example, we've discussed the following goal:

■ Improve software development productivity by reducing software defects by 20% from the point of view of the corporation.

And we've established a measurement:

■ Total defects

In order to ensure that unwanted changes in practices do not unusually inflate the total defects measurement, we need to create one or two other measurements that support the total defects measurement. For example, we could put in place any of the following supporting measurements to help validate the total defects measurement:

1. *Number of test scripts executed*: Counting the number of test scripts being executed during development iterations can help check against sudden increases in defects found.
2. Number of files (or classes or modules) changed: Understanding how much code, in terms of files, classes, or modules, can help validate the number of defects found.
3. Number of new noncritical defects to the number of new critical defects: In general, the proportion of new noncritical to new critical defects should remain relatively constant (within control limits, of course). Should there be a sudden increase in total defects that is coupled with a significant change in this ratio, there might be reasonable cause for investigation into unwanted behavior.

Summary

At the beginning of any transition to agile development, it is vitally important that clear goals for the transition be determined. How long should the transition take? Why are we investing time and money into the transition? Is it about improving quality? What about improving productivity? In all cases, how much? By clarifying your transition goals, many questions about how to deploy your Scrum teams and how to plan your transition can be answered.

Having established your goals, it is also a good idea to determine how to appropriately measure your progress in order to help the organization make the right decisions at the right time. In support of those decisions, your measurements can be combined with upper and lower control limits that can be determined by the organization. These control limits help the organization understand how much process deviation is to be expected and when process changes may be needed when the measurements cross the control limits.

Since measuring any aspect of the organization can produce unwanted behaviors, it is also frequently a good idea to create measurements in pairs or trios that can help validate the primary measurement. If the primary measurement changes significantly without appropriate changes in the supporting measurements, the organization should look for unwanted behavior changes. If, however, the supporting measurements support changes in the primary measurement, the organization should look for evidence that points to needed changes in practices or process.

Endnotes

1. Basili, Victor, Caldiera, Gianluigi, and Rombach, H. Dieter. *The Goal Question Metric Approach*. ftp://ftp.cs.umd.edu/pub/sel/papers/gqm.pdf (accessed on November 12, 2008).
2. This is not to imply that the customer's perspective is unimportant, but merely that, in an agile transition, we are focusing on software built during the transition, not before. If we focus on software defects that the customer finds, we are more than likely going to include a lot of defects created prior to the beginning of the agile transition.

Chapter 9

Create the Transition Backlog

Taken from the Scrum definition of a product backlog, a transition backlog is a list of everything that needs to be done during the transition to agile development. As with the product backlog, the transition backlog is emergent. It changes and is reprioritized constantly in order to ensure that the items that bring the most benefit to the organization are addressed as early and as quickly as possible. Also, like the product backlog, while anyone on the project team can contribute to it, the transition backlog is owned and prioritized by the *transition owner*.

The genesis of the transition backlog is fairly straightforward. We do the initial population of the list by starting with a couple standard planning items. These items, once the transition begins, are then groomed by the transition team(s) into more and more detailed items that will guide the transition project from that point forward. Our transition backlog[1] begins as follows in Figure 9.1.

While this backlog is not nearly complete in order to actually do a transition to agile development, it does have the necessary items on it that will allow the transition teams to continue to groom the backlog once the transition actually begins.

Bringing the Transition Team Together

Once the initial transition backlog is in place, the transition team is kicked off with the following suggested agenda:

Backlog Items

- Create the communication plan.
- Create the transition budget.
- Create the training plan.
- Create the facilities plan.
- Complete the pilot development project.
  - Select the pilot project.
  - Establish the pilot project sprint schedule.
  - Staff and train the initial development teams.
  - Staff and train the remaining development teams.
  - Create the product deployment plan.
  - Create the pilot project product backlog.

Figure 9.1 The initial transition backlog.

1. General introduction
   a. Project introduction: What is the project and what are the goals? If the executive sponsor is available, let him or her deliver this portion of the message, or at least repeat to the team his or her commitment to the project.
   b. Team introduction: Who is everyone and why are they there? If they were selected for the project, why? What strengths do they bring to the table? Who is the transition owner? Explain their responsibilities.
2. Logistics
   a. Project schedule (sprints)
   b. Meeting schedule (locations and times)
   c. Meeting minutes (rotation or assignment)
3. Transition backlog: What's on it? What does every item mean?
4. Structure of transition team
   a. Will there be subordinate teams?
   b. How and when will they be staffed?
   c. Who on the core team will take leadership roles over the subordinate teams? Those who volunteer for this duty should be aware that they are taking on product ownership of that portion of the transition backlog. In other words, within their subordinate team's responsibilities, they become the product owner.
5. Next steps

With the creation of the initial transition backlog completed, the transition project is ready to begin.

Endnote

1. You can find more information about transition backlogs at http://www.bigagiledevelopment.com/transitionbacklog.

STARTING THE TRANSITION

Exciting and Really Challenging

With the initial transition backlog ready and the transition team set up, it's time to actually begin the transition project itself. While this will be a very exciting time, you should also be prepared for it to be a very difficult time. The reason for this is in the nature of how agile development works. In traditional product development methods (including both waterfall and spiral models), there is considerable focus on phases of development. First we analyze, then we design, then we code, then we test. We do this once in waterfall (theoretically, that is), and we do this once an iteration in spiral or iterative models. This approach to development tends to easily absorb the impact of organizational dysfunctions because the transitions from one phase to another happen infrequently and, for the most part, across the entirety of the project (that is, all activities in the project shift from analyze to design, code to test simultaneously).

Given that model, think of an agile development project as extremely high-speed development. Teams move between analysis, design, code, and test as frequently as several times a day, and the only time there is a planned break in the action is at the end of a sprint. In this approach to development, an organization's processes and structures will be tested to the extreme and, in the early days of the transition, will frequently break. Common examples of these "breakages" include:

- Product build times in excess of one hour
- No automated build or the automated build process requires human intervention to complete

- Source code control tools that do not support frequent check-in and check-out
- Source code control practices that do not support code versioning and thus the easy removal of code containing defects
- Scarce skill sets that become in demand across several teams at the same time
- Coding standards are not clear or not defined
- Organizational "DONEness" is not defined
- No automated testing
- Performance requirements are not clearly specified until after development is finished
- Procurement processes that are focused on most significant savings instead of keeping the development teams functioning

As these obstacles occur, one or more development teams will be either partially or completely blocked from making progress until the problem is solved. The nature of Scrum in its daily approach to examining the current reality and making decisions also means that the problems that these obstacles cause will be reported on a day-to-day basis until they are solved. In this book, we'll approach the transition by trying to deal with some of these potential obstacles before they start causing problems.

Basic Approach

The basic approach to the transition project used in this book is to use agile development concepts not only to develop software, but to drive the transition as well. This means that the transition project will be an agile project, using Scrum to manage the schedule and backlog. As each sprint begins, we'll examine the backlog and take the highest-priority items to the transition team(s) for work. During the course of the sprint, we'll look ahead to future sprints by grooming the backlog (i.e., analyzing, estimating, and slicing backlog items into smaller and smaller pieces of work). At the end of each sprint, we'll look at what we accomplished to make sure we did it right, and then discuss how we accomplished it, looking for ways to improve our process. The overall process comes in two parts: (1) beginning the transition and (2) executing pilot agile development projects.

Beginning the transition is all about building the transition backlog, forming the transition teams, setting up the pilot development projects, monitoring the pilot projects, and executing the transition plans. This effort begins first and continues throughout the entire transition. The first month will usually be taken up entirely by:

- Grooming the transition backlog
- Establishing (staffing) the transition subordinate teams (if any)
- Starting to build the training plan

- Starting to build the communication plan
- Starting to build the budget
- Starting to build the facilities plan
- Selecting the pilot projects

Planning for the transition project may take more than a month (depending on the size of the overall organization and the size of the transition team). When it does, the next month or two will be time for:

- Grooming the transition backlog
- Finishing any critical plans that are not finished
- All transition subordinate teams working their backlogs
- Staffing and training one or two Scrum teams for the pilot projects
- Building the product backlog for the pilot projects
- Grooming the product backlog for the pilot projects
- Establishing DONEness criteria for the pilot projects

Executing the pilot agile development projects begins within a month or two of beginning the transition and continues throughout the remainder of the transition project. Once the transition project ends, of course, it is assumed that new development projects will be agile, but they will no longer be pilot projects. When we begin pilot agile development projects, each month will be a repetition of the same development events:

- Groom the product backlog
- Complete the sprint (create some product functionality)
- Do a retrospective that includes a discussion around the effectiveness of:
  - The training
  - Any facilities changes
  - Any new tools
- Anything else that went well or went poorly and needs to be addressed

This last sprint description simply repeats itself over and over again. New projects can be added to this cycle at any time, as long as there are resources available for training. This section of the book will review the work that occurs during the initial month or two of the transition project. We'll discuss communication plans, training plans, facilities plans, and so on.

Chapter 10

Beginning Transition Sprint 1

We begin the transition project with our very first sprint. This chapter will provide an example of much of what will likely happen (good and bad) as you plan that first sprint. We'll also talk about some of the practices that will begin here and continue throughout the rest of the transition project, and some even for as long as you continue to do agile development. We'll start by setting up the sprint schedule, reviewing the transition backlog (as established in a previous chapter), and talking about the grooming process. Then, we'll look at sprint planning and some of the tasks that the transition team will want to focus on during this first sprint. The chapters that follow will discuss, in detail, much of the planning and decisions that you'll have to make during your first couple transition sprints. Finally, we'll look at the sprint review and the sprint retrospective. During the sprint review, our focus will be on what was accomplished and whether or not we'll be able to begin training development teams in the next sprint. We'll also look at what was accomplished, modify the transition backlog appropriately, and then start thinking about sprint 2.

During the sprint retrospective, we'll focus on the process we followed during sprint 1—what worked and what didn't. There are also a number of items we'll take a look at during the sprint retrospective, including:

- Training that the team received. Was it effective? How could it be improved?
- New practices created (or old ones modified) during the sprint. Are there any that need to be properly documented for regulatory reasons?[1]
- The subordinate transition teams. Were they effective? Do any need better direction?

The Sprint Schedule

My preference, over several years of using the Scrum process with software development projects, is to use sprints that are either three or four weeks in length. For the purposes of the transition, I'm going to suggest four-week sprints. Once you begin the pilot project sprints, you should go with either three- or four-week sprints. In the end, the difference between the transition sprints and the development project sprints will not adversely affect the transition. One other suggestion, when there are subordinate transition teams, is to put those teams on a staggered schedule consisting of two-week sprints. What I mean by a staggered schedule is to offset the subordinate team sprints by one week from the beginning of the core team sprint (see Table 10.1).

What this accomplishes is:

1. When there are subordinate teams in place, the core team is generally covering topics that there are no subordinate teams to cover or is simply managing the project and maintaining the transition backlog. Under these conditions, there is no particular reason to run a short sprint.

2. Subordinate teams are generally very productive, moving through items rather quickly if the right resources are in place (and if the right resources aren't in place, you'll want to know about this quickly anyway). By shortening the sprint length of the subordinate teams, you gain the flexibility of receiving and being able to use output from the subordinate teams much more frequently than with longer sprints. Also, the shorter sprint length allows the core transition team to constantly review the backlog and give the subordinate teams new instructions through the reprioritization of each team's portion of the transition backlog. Since many of the subordinate teams have to work together, being able to rapidly and repeatedly realign their priorities comes in quite handy.

3. To a lesser extent, a small degree of mixing the sprint length based on the focus of the individual teams helps to highlight some of the often unrealized flexibility of the Scrum method.

Table 10.1 Suggested Sprint Schedule

Week	1	2	3	4	5	6	7	8	9	10	11	12	13	14	15	16
Core Team		Sprint 1				Sprint 2				Sprint 3				Sprint 4		
Subordinate Teams		S1		S2		S3		S4		S5		S6		S7		

Of course, if there are no subordinate teams and the core team is handling the transition, I would still recommend three- or four-week sprints for the core team, as they would have much to do under these circumstances and may not be able to get much done in the shorter two-week sprints. In the end, the decision is up to the transition team. If there is a high degree of uncertainty in the transition, go with shorter sprints. If, however, the transition backlog grooming is going well and the information you need to get those stories done is available when you need it, the longer sprint lengths (three to four weeks) will work just fine.

The Transition Backlog

As you begin the first transition sprint, the transition backlog[2] will look something like the one presented in Table 10.2.

This backlog doesn't represent everything that you will need to do during the transition at a detailed level, but it does cover the high-level requirements. During your transition sprints, the core team will continuously work on the backlog items, splitting them into smaller and smaller pieces that the core team or a subordinate team can commit to completing during a sprint. As it is right now, the transition backlog has few items that would be considered small enough for a Scrum development team to commit to. Creating items of that size will be one of your goals for the first transition sprint. We'll talk more about the process for getting the items down to the right size in the "Grooming: Reducing Backlog Items to Sprint Size" section. In the meantime, let's discuss the difference between core team backlog items and subordinate team backlog items.

Table 10.2   The Initial Transition Backlog (Unsliced)

Create the communication plan.
Create the transition budget.
Create the training plan.
Create the facilities plan.
Complete the pilot development project: • Select the pilot project. • Establish the pilot project sprint schedule. • Staff and train the initial development teams. • Staff and train the remaining development teams. • Create the product deployment plan.

The Structure of the Transition Backlog

The transition backlog is a prioritized list of items that represents the entirety of everything that needs to be done in order for the transition to agile development to be successful. When there is one core transition team and one transition owner, that list is represented as a single list of items. However, if you charter subordinate teams to handle various aspects of the transition (e.g., a communications team, a facilities team, etc.) *and* those teams are staffed by mostly different people, you will have to make a few changes to how you handle the transition backlog.

To describe it simply, when you create multiple teams, it becomes easier for each team and the team's product owner to manage their own transition backlog. Items on the core transition backlog that are assigned to a subordinate team are moved to that team's backlog, where additional grooming continues until each item is reduced to a sprint size.

Let's look Table 10.3 to see both transition backlog management processes side-by-side.

Once the ownership of a backlog item is transferred to a subordinate team, that team begins grooming the backlog item preparatory to committing to it during sprint planning. One rule, however, must be followed by the subordinate transition teams: the priority of each item on the subordinate team backlog must remain consistent with the relative priority of the parent item on the core team's backlog. In other words, if the core team transfers two backlog items, say item 1 and item 2, to the communications team, where item 1 is a higher priority than item 2, no matter how many times the communication team grooms those items into smaller and smaller items, the items belonging to the original item 1 should continue to be a

Table 10.3 Comparing Transition Backlog Management Processes

When There's Only a Single Core Transition Team, the Core Team Should:	When There Are One or More Subordinate Transition Teams, the Core Team Should:
1. Prioritize the backlog.	1. Prioritize the backlog.
2. Groom the backlog.	2. If an item clearly belongs to a subordinate team, assign the item to the subordinate team and mark it as "owned" by the subordinate team.
3. During sprint planning, select items from the top of the backlog first.	3. If an item may be owned by several teams, groom it (slice it into smaller pieces).
	4. During sprint planning, select items from the top of the backlog that are owned by the core team.

higher priority than the items belonging to the original item 2. Of course, for every rule there is an exception. The exception to this rule is thus: it is not unusual for the team to determine that one item of a lower priority should be done before an item of a higher priority for technical reasons. In such cases, the team should consult with the product owner for his or her consent to reorder the items.

Grooming: Reducing Backlog Items to Sprint Size

Grooming backlog items is an activity that you will spend a lot of time doing throughout any agile project, whether we're talking about the transition project or any typical product development project. Items that are placed on the backlog are usually not placed there ready to be committed to and completed during a sprint. They are often too big, and we usually know too little about them to go ahead and start working on them. Backlog items are often called stories; large stories (stories that contain smaller stories) are called epics. Conversely, a story or item that is small enough to be committed to and completed during a sprint is called sprint-sized or right-sized. There is a general agreement in the Scrum community that a right-sized story is something that can be finished by a development team in less than two weeks. Personally, my preference (and the one used throughout this book) is that a right-sized or sprint-sized story is one that can be completed by two or three people in less than a week. If you aren't sure which standard to use, consider going to the smaller sizing for new teams and let them work up to the larger sizes as they gain experience. This approach will allow you to balance the effort of slicing a story down to a small size with the risk of missing something important because the story wasn't sliced small enough.

To reduce stories to the proper sprint size or right size, we have to groom backlog items. Grooming involves three steps:

1. Learning about the item and saving that information for later
2. Slicing the item down to smaller items
3. Creating estimations about the new items created in step 2

We'll discuss all of these steps in the following paragraphs.

The Scrum master for the team should schedule a series of grooming workshops to be held during the sprint. Ideally, these workshops should take between four and eight hours per week,[3] should be scheduled for the same times each week during the sprint, and no single session should be longer than two hours in length. During the workshops, the team asks questions of the product owner to further clarify the item. This information is often collected in item-specific documentation for later reference. When the team feels they understand the items well enough (usually just a few minutes of questions can do the job), they slice the item down into smaller pieces.

The new items that the team comes up with are placed on the backlog (the parent item they were sliced from is removed from the backlog) and estimated. Estimation is usually done in *story points,* which are values that provide a comparative idea of size and complexity across multiple items or stories. After the items have been estimated, the process repeats on the next item in the backlog. We'll talk much more about grooming, story points, and estimation techniques later in this book. For now, we'll confine our discussion to the first sprint of the transition project.

Sprint Planning

When you enter sprint planning for the first transition sprint, you'll find you have a problem—there aren't any items on the transition backlog that are broken down to a sprint size, and none of the items are estimated. Basically, everything that we try to avoid in a product backlog at sprint planning will be true here. The transition backlog is not ready for the sprint. In a development sprint, this means that the team will spend a lot of time trying to build a sprint backlog—determining all of the required tasks will be difficult, and much of the work cannot be done without the product owner helping to complete the understanding of the team members during the entire planning effort. Even after the sprint begins, there's a high likelihood of overcommitment due to new tasks being added continuously during the first several days of the sprint. Truthfully, the same thing is going to happen to the transition sprint. But we're in the earliest phase of the transition project and you need to expect that the initial sprint or two will not be perfect. They will, however, be quite productive.

Step 1 in sprint planning is to find out what kind of availability you have from your team members during the course of the next sprint (four weeks, if you're going with my recommendations). Find out if anyone is less than 100% committed to the team—you'll want to look into this later anyway. How about vacations? Scheduled training? Department meetings longer than two hours? Let's get all this out on the table from the very beginning so that we can keep an eye on what the team can realistically commit to during the first transition sprint.

With that completed, let's start reviewing the transition backlog from the top down:

1. *Create the communication plan:*[4] If you have a communications team, you can assign this item to them and be done with it for now. Make sure you have someone on the core transition team that will act as the product owner for the communications team. If you've followed the sprint schedule I recommended in Table 10.2, the communications team product owner has a week before the first sprint—he or she can use that week to get part or all of the communications team together and start grooming this item into sprint-sized pieces.
2. *Create the transition budget:*[5] This item is usually managed by the core transition team, even if there are subordinate teams.

3. *Create the training plan*:[6] If you have a training or education team, you can assign this item to them and be done with it for now. Make sure you have someone on the core transition team that will act as the product owner for the education team. If you've followed the sprint schedule I recommended in Table 10.1, the education team product owner has a week before his or her first sprint; he or she can use that week to get part or all of the education team together and start grooming this item into sprint-sized pieces.

4. *Create the facilities plan*: If you have a facilities team, you can assign this item to them and be done with it for now. Make sure you have someone on the core transition team that will act as the product owner for the facilities team. If you've followed the sprint schedule I recommended in Table 10.1, the facilities team product owner has a week before his or her first sprint—he or she can use that week to get part or all of the facilities team together and start grooming this item into sprint-sized pieces.

5. *Complete the pilot development project*: This will be the responsibility of the core transition team, even if we have other subordinate teams. Since we've already sliced this a little, let's look at the pieces:

   a. *Select the pilot project*: This can be a project already in progress or a project that is about to begin. The question, for the purposes of estimation, is this: Can the selection of a pilot project be done by two to three people in less than a week? If the answer is yes, we don't need to do anything. However, the answer could well be no. If so, we need to discuss this item more. For example, perhaps we have no idea what project we could use. Or maybe there are lots of possibilities, but we don't know if the project and resource management are on board. Of the possibilities we know of, perhaps several are simply too critical to be potentially delayed by the transition. So, we might slice this item into several smaller items:

      i. Identify the top five projects that would work well with the transition (small, short, noncritical efforts that will begin shortly).

      ii. Select the best project for the transition (talk with the management in charge of the projects to get a short list of projects where management is willing to be part of the agile transition).

      iii. Identify the remaining projects to be included in the transition during the course of the project (we'll need this for later).

   b. *Establish the pilot project sprint schedule*: This item usually doesn't take too long and can certainly be done in a few days (or less).

   c. *Staff and train the initial development teams*: This one will take a little work, and you should plan on slicing it down to something a little smaller. The end result might look a little like this:

      i. Get a list of developers, analysts, testers, QAers, etc., involved in the target project.

      ii. Work with management to identify potential development teams that are no larger than seven people each.

      iii. Order the teams by starting sprint (which are the first two teams, which two go next, and then after that?) Overload the teams in sprint 1 with two people each from the sprint 2 teams.

      iv. Schedule and execute the training.

  d. *Staff and train the remaining development teams*: This one is similar to the previous. We already know which people are on which teams, so if the plan is to launch two or three more teams in the next month, then:

      i. Overload the teams for sprint 2 with two people each from the sprint 3 teams.

      ii. Schedule and execute the training.

  e. *Create the product deployment plan*: This item is going to be product specific (that is, every product can have a different deployment plan). Is the product an internal application? Is it shrink-wrapped software, or do you deliver to a finite list of customers? How often do you deliver? All of these questions will lead you to a much more specific discussion about how completed software goes from your development factory to your customers. Consider adding some of the following items to your backlog:

      i. Determine what releases occur during the course of the pilot project.

      ii. Determine what extra steps are needed for releases during the course of the pilot project.

So, as you complete the first step of your sprint planning effort, you find yourself with a growing transition backlog before much work has even gotten under way. In fact, with each new transition sprint, you'll see more and more items getting added to the transition backlog even as you and your teams work to take other items off the list by completing them. This is normal and reflects the emergent characteristic of the transition backlog (and the product backlog). You may find that, during the transition project, the transition backlog continues to simply get longer and longer (in estimated size, not just number of items). Don't be discouraged by this. What is happening is that you and your transition teams are essentially evaluating the development capabilities of your organization from top to bottom and creating a very extensive list of items that need to be addressed. As long as you keep the transition backlog prioritized, you can ensure yourself and the organization that you are spending your time working on the most important items first.

Now, we have one more problem to fix. Because the transition backlog is new (and, in fact, we've been pretty much building it through the sprint planning process), it still isn't estimated. In the short term, that doesn't pose a significant problem. However, it won't be long before executive management is going to start asking questions about how much progress you are making and how much longer you need to complete a significant portion of the transition. To do that, you'll need reasonable estimates on your transition backlog items, and the sooner we start estimating transition items, the better off we're going to be.[7] Thankfully, we should be able to do this quite easily, as our backlog is neither lengthy nor terribly complex.

During sprint planning, take an hour and write your entire backlog out on a white board or flipchart. Create two columns: one for the item and one for the estimate. You can also create the clear relationship between a smaller child story and the original parent by adding a theme to the front of the item. I've done so in the following table by adding themes to the front of some backlog items in parentheses and italics. For example, if I had an item about creating the wheels for a car, I might have a child item split off from building a car that would look like this:

(*Build a car*) Create the wheels

This notation indicates that the "Create the wheels" item came ultimately from a "Build a car" parent story.

If you've stuck pretty close to the example we've discussed so far, your backlog will look like Table 10.4. Now, if you don't have a communications team, a facilities team, or a training team, you're going to need to spend a lot more time on those initial items at the top of the list. You will likely find that the entire first two or three transition project sprints will be dedicated to slicing these items down into smaller and smaller child items, building the budget, communication plan, training plan, and facilities plan. For now, however, we can size these items as being too large to be sprint-sized—we call this extra large, or XL.[8]

As for the rest of the backlog, work with your team to review the effort that is entailed within each item. Set a time limit for each item; some teams use a simple egg timer, and others set the limit at five or ten minutes and someone becomes responsible for keeping track of the time. If the time limit expires, the team can very quickly decide to extend the time limit another five or ten minutes or to move on to the next item and come back to the current item later. This method of time boxing the discussion can be quite useful in any analysis effort—it recognizes that, sometimes, our conversations get stalled (ever been in a conversation where people simply repeat themselves over and over again?) and we need some kind of time limit that forces us to stop, check, and decide. At some point, either in the first round of talking or at the end of a couple five- or ten-minute time boxes, the team will decide that they know enough about the item to go ahead and put an effort estimation on it. For now, we'll use t-shirt sizing as a means to shortcut the estimation effort into basic categories of effort.

And here's one of those *big warnings*! When you do any form of agile estimation, there's going to be a real desire to just fall back to hours as we always have in the past. We're used to using hours in our estimates, and when confronted with uncomfortable change, people will naturally migrate back to more comfortable, if less efficient, practices. The question will be asked: What's the big deal between estimating something as eight or sixteen hours or using XS or S? Believe me—it'll happen. The answer to this question will be heard over and over again when you discuss agile analysis, so let's get it nailed down right now.

Table 10.4 The Transition Backlog: Somewhat Expanded/Sliced

Backlog Items	Estimate
Create the communication plan (handed off to communication subteam).	
Create the transition budget.	
Create the training plan (handed off to training subteam).	
Create the facilities plan (handed off to facilities subteam).	
Identify top five projects for the agile transition.	
Select the best pilot project from the candidate list.	
Rank the remaining projects to follow the first.	
Establish the pilot project sprint schedule.	
(*Staff/train*) Get a list of developers involved in the target project.	
(*Staff/train*) Work with management to identify potential Scrum teams.	
(*Staff/train*) Order the teams by starting sprint.	
(*Staff/train*) Overload sprint 1 teams with people allocated to sprint 2 teams.	
(*Staff/train*) Schedule and execute the training (handed off to training subteam).	
(*Staff/train*) Determine the staffing for all remaining teams and overload with two people each from the next sprint's teams.	
(*Staff/train*) Schedule and execute the follow-up training (handed off to training subteam).	
(*Deployment*) Determine what releases occur during the course of the pilot project.	
(*Deployment*) Determine what extra steps are needed for releases during the course of the pilot project.	

What's the Big Difference between Hours and Points?

We've started the process of agile analysis, and no sooner do we get ten minutes into the conversation than someone asks that question: "What's the big deal? This isn't any different than doing estimates in hours the way we always have." After thanking the individual for asking the question and giving you the opportunity to answer it once and for all, you provide the following answer.

1. *Estimation is estimation*: Whether we estimate in hours, days, points, t-shirt sizes, it doesn't matter. When we estimate the size, effort, or risk involved in something, we analyze it for detail and then create an estimate. So, to a certain extent, the questioner is quite right: it isn't any different—on the surface. But then again, a cannon and a small gun both fall under the category of "artillery" too, don't they? However, we don't use them interchangeably. My father, a fantastic auto mechanic, used to say this over and over again: "the right tool for the right job." On to point 2.

2. *Precision costs money*: In this particular meeting (during sprint planning, that is), we aren't looking for significant precision yet. A rough estimation is all I need right now. Certainly, I could get a much more detailed and much more precise estimate *if* I gave an analyst or two many hours to review the item in detail, model out a solution and some tasks, estimate the smaller tasks, and then add them up to come up with a considerably more precise estimate.

3. *Precision increases risk of waste*: In agile development, much of what we do is done "just in time," as opposed to waterfall projects, where we attempt to produce our most detailed estimates at a time in the project (analysis phase) when we know the least about them. When we estimate backlog items, we attempt to do so while spending the least amount of effort on the items. When we've learned enough about an item to estimate it, we probably also know enough about the item to slice it into smaller pieces, learn more, and estimate again. Since we do estimation frequently on items that are getting smaller and more detailed, we don't want to spend a considerable amount of time estimating and reestimating. In addition, should we learn something about a story that forces us to change the entire approach, we would have to rework and reestimate anyway. With simple, nonprecise estimates, we wouldn't lose a lot of time in wasted estimates. Similarly, if we spend a lot of time on a story that is suddenly removed from the project, we would lose a considerable investment in estimation if we had done a detailed analysis up front. Our most detailed estimation effort (creating tasks from the items and estimating them in hours) comes right at the beginning of the sprint, when we're the most certain that we're definitely going to build the items we've committed to.

Estimation in an agile environment, then, is about being prudent about the effort and the precision that we're putting into each item. Waterfall methods require us to learn everything there is to know about an item from the beginning of the project. This one-size-fits-all approach to estimation ignores the possibility that an item may be removed from the project at a later date or that another item may change the design or architectural approach so much that one or more other items will need to be completely rethought and reestimated. Estimation in an agile environment, therefore, applies the proper precision at the proper time in the project and reduces waste rather than applying the maximum precision to every item in the project without regard to its priority or complexity.

Building the Sprint Backlog

Once you finish estimating all of the items on the transition backlog, you're ready to start moving the items to the sprint backlog and deciding how much you'll actually get done during this sprint. How much you can do, however, is going to have to be determined by your team. There are two methods for populating a sprint backlog. The first is called *velocity-based planning*. This method allows you to load the sprint based on how much work the team has been getting done during the past one, two, three, or more sprints. The problem with velocity-based planning, however, is that since this is our first sprint, we don't have an established velocity. So, we have to use the second method: *commitment-based planning*.

Commitment-based planning is a form of sprint planning that adds backlog items to the sprint backlog one at a time, with the team evaluating the total amount of work and then deciding if they can commit to more work. If an item doesn't "overload" the team's ability to commit, the item is kept on the sprint backlog and the team looks at the next item on the backlog. If the team can commit to the second item, they move on to the third, and so on. When the team feels that they've committed to as much as they can, the most recently considered item is not moved to the sprint backlog. Let's take a look at a couple examples:

- A very aggressive transition team with no subordinate transition teams could commit to completing the "Create a transition budget" item (which is quite large), but only feels that they can complete a draft communication plan. So, they slice the "Create the communication plan" item into two items—"Create a draft communication plan" and "Finalize the communication plan"—and then commit only to the former, leaving the latter on the transition backlog for the next sprint.
- A transition team with a full complement of subordinate transition teams could assign the communications plan, training plan, budget, and facilities plan to the subordinate teams and then commit to the rest of the transition backlog.
- A transition team will a full complement of subordinate transition teams could assign the plans and budgeting to the subordinate teams, but hold short of committing to the rest of the transition backlog.

Let's take a brief look at some of the influences that drive over- and undercommitment during sprint planning.

When Teams Attack! (The Backlog, That Is)

Some Scrum teams, for a variety of reasons (both understandable and not so understandable), tend to overcommit to items on the product backlog, learning very quickly during the early part of the sprint that completing what they committed to simply isn't going to happen (or worse, can't be done without cutting corners on product quality). Teams often overcommit because:

1. The items they committed to were actually larger than estimated.
2. The team took an aggressive stance with the expectation that they could get the work done.
3. The team was "asked" (translate as "strongly urged") to complete a certain amount of work.

In a well-managed sprint, teams usually determine their overcommitment within a few days of sprint planning. Whether it's because new tasks are discovered that add to the overall amount of work or because tasks that seemed straightforward seem to take longer and longer to finish, as Figure 10.1 depicts, sprint burn-downs generally show overcommitment within the first week or ten days of the sprint, when the slope of the burn-down line clearly indicates that the team will not finish without heroic, unsustainable, and potentially risky effort.

When teams overcommit, for whatever reason, they need to correct their commitment in order to adjust to the current reality. There should not be a penalty for returning work to the backlog. In fact, the view of the team and the organization needs to be that the work that can't be done by the team *couldn't have been done anyway*.[9] The error made by the team isn't in their inability to follow up on their commitments; the error, in fact, is in the commitment itself. The solution is to simply return the work to the backlog. Unfortunately, the error made by most organizations is to look at sprint planning commitments as written in stone and forcing teams to "stick to their commitments," even at the risk of harming product quality.

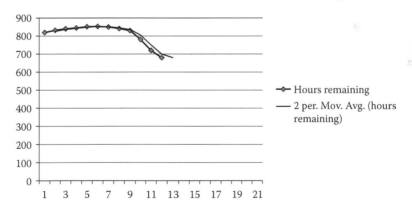

Figure 10.1 Overcommitted sprint burn-down. In this figure, the team started with about 810 hours of work, which grew slightly to 850 before trending downward. However, in the ninth working day of the sprint, the possibility of getting done in time is diminished. By the eleventh or twelfth day of the sprint, it is clear that a correction is needed and some work needs to be returned to the product backlog.

And, of course, bad experiences with overcommitment usually result in an opposite and potentially more harmful reaction: undercommitment.

When Undercommitment Is the Order of the Day

How much your team is willing to commit to during any sprint is going to depend on a lot of things, including how comfortable your team is with not achieving all of the planned results. Many Scrum teams will deliberately undercommit because they work (or are under the impression that they work) in an environment that frowns on not achieving their objectives as stated. This is a pervasive problem in business today; we all work (or have worked) in environments where we make estimates, make objectives based on those estimates, and then are stuck achieving those objectives, even when the estimates were flawed (which they usually are) or the business circumstances change in unpredictable ways, affecting our ability to achieve our objectives. Unfortunately, this type of business promotes individual agendas that often conflict with organizational goals, result in employee overwork (which invites burnout, clinical depression, neglected families, and reduced product quality), and engender creeping mediocrity.

In the agile development environment, undercommitment occurs during sprint planning when teams either deliberately overestimate items or deliberately undercommit to their sprint goals (refer to Figure 10.2). As mentioned before, teams do this because they anticipate unwanted consequences when they don't achieve all of their sprint goals. In one example, a manager decided that an important measurement of his Scrum teams' productivity was the ratio of completed stories over committed stories. Therefore, if his teams completed only half of what

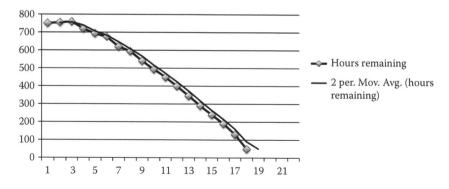

Figure 10.2 Undercommitted sprint burn-down. In this figure, the team started with about 750 hours of work and, after a minor correction during the first couple days, burned down at a fairly even pace, completing all of the team's work with three or four days to spare. In a situation like this, teams should look to the product backlog for more work to do if there's work available that can be done in the remaining time.

they committed to, the measurement would be 50%. Obviously, then, completing everything that was committed to would result in a measurement of 100%. The manager thought that this measure both was useful and would help his teams work toward completing the stories they committed to. What actually happened was that productivity dropped as the Scrum teams deliberately undercommitted sprint after sprint. Even worse, when team members had time at the end of the sprint, they absolutely would not take new work from the product backlog because that would introduce the risk of not completing a story, which of course, would "mess up" their metrics.

Teams either finish their goals during a sprint or they don't. Sprints begin and end on prescheduled dates that have nothing to do with how long stories on the backlog will take to be finished. There will be many reasons for teams to not finish all of their goals, from a lack of experience on the part of the team members to organizational dysfunctions that result in inefficient work patterns to, as mentioned earlier, time simply running out. There's nothing good or bad about not finishing all of the items that a team committed to—it simply happens.

Clearly, we need to take a completely different approach to setting and reacting to Scrum team goals. We need an environment that encourages aggressive, achievable commitments while removing the stigma of failure related to not getting all of the team's commitments completed. Teams need to be encouraged to be reasonably aggressive with their commitments during sprint planning and to continuously take steps to improve team performance. As the sprint progresses, if it seems likely that a team cannot complete all of the stories that they've committed to, they need to be permitted to return the lowest priority items to the backlog and reduce their overall commitment.

Of course, having said all this, there is always that case where a team doesn't finish their sprint goals because they actually did not work in good faith with the organization. They, to be blunt, slacked off. Some would suggest that this is the reason why measurements of Scrum team progress are so important—to quickly identify and deal with situations like this. However, as common sense suggests, if a team is truly not working in good faith with the organization, the signs would be everywhere without having to be specifically measured. Observation of team activities during the sprint, the progress reflected by the sprint burn-down, the results demonstrated during sprint review—all of these will show evidence that the team is not performing to their capabilities. Should this be the case with any Scrum team, some radical changes in the make-up of the team, up to and including disbanding the team entirely, would certainly be called for.

Committing to Work in the First Transition Sprint

Bottom line, then, is that you will need to encourage your transition teams (both the core team and the subordinate teams, if any) to set challenging but achievable goals for their sprints, but not to get too worried if they discover they've committed to too much or too little. That's going to happen. If a team commits to too much, we return the extra work to the backlog. If a team commits to too little, we go back to the backlog for more work. This message also needs to be delivered to the organization's executive management. When the transition project status is reported to management, you'll likely talk about what goals each team has set, and you will almost certainly, from time to time, report goals that have been returned to the transition backlog to be worked on in a later sprint. It's very important to set this expectation early and often with your management and your teams. Unless your teams are slacking off, the assumption must be that they are always doing their best to complete as much work as possible.

Whether or not you have subordinate teams, the first duty of the core transition team is going to be to work on the transition project budget. Without the budget, it's hard to set the organization's expectations for what's going to come next and how to plan financially for the project. The remaining chapters in this part of the book are focused primarily on the types of work that the core transition team and subordinate teams (if any) will have to address. Refer to the proper chapters in this section of the book to help you do your planning.

Sprint Reviews for Transition Sprints

While most of us are used to sprint reviews evaluating the software completed by a Scrum team during a sprint, there's actually nothing in the Scrum method that insists that we build software. So, doing reviews for transition sprints is pretty much the same as doing the typical sprint review. The process is fairly simple and can be summed up as follows:

- Who should be there? The transition team, the transition owner, anyone else who feels like being there. When it's a review for a transition subordinate team, consider having as many members of the core transition team there as possible.
- How long will it take? It really shouldn't take more than an hour. However, if you discover that your transition owner has a lot of questions about what the team produced, you should have a discussion with the owner about being more in touch with what the team is doing during the sprint. A good transition owner or product owner should know beforehand what he or she is going to see during a sprint review.
- What needs to happen? Someone on the team (or different team members at different times) should review each backlog item that the team committed to finish and should show the team's transition owner the evidence that they finished it. For example, if the team committed to finishing a communication plan, the transition owner should expect to see and "touch" a completed

communication plan (yes, it's probably best to print a copy for the transition owner—everyone else can look at an electronic copy perhaps displayed by data projector). The transition owner may ask questions about the plan, may suggest improvements (which are written up and added to the transition backlog to be addressed in a future transition sprint), or may even reject the plan in part or completely. If the team's output is rejected, the backlog item that they thought they completed is moved back to the transition backlog to be readdressed in a future sprint (again, this is why its better for the transition owner to be in constant touch with the transition team—outright rejections like this should be extremely rare).

Depending on the result of the sprint review, the team's transition backlog is updated to remove completed backlog items (if any) and the team moves on to the sprint retrospective.

Sprint Retrospectives for Transition Sprints

As with sprint reviews, sprint retrospectives for transition sprints really aren't all that different. However, there are some important items that should also be discussed during the sprint retrospective. In general, there are many ways to effectively execute a sprint retrospective. Some of the best texts on the subject have been authored by Esther Derby and Diana Larsen. For transition sprints, however, I also recommend that the transition team discuss the following items:

- *Training*: What feedback, if any, has been received from employees who have taken the training provided for the transition? It should be expected that agile development training will undergo some degree of maturation during the course of the transition. Every organization learns in a slightly different way, and no matter how you initially set up the training, you'll find that it needs periodic tuning. Sprint retrospectives for the core transition team are an excellent opportunity to review any feedback and decide what, if any, changes may need to be made to the training. Whatever decisions are made with regard to the training can be added to the transition backlog as new items that can be addressed by the core transition team or the proper subordinate team in the future, depending on the item's prioritization.
- *Process changes*: Since we're doing the transition as an agile effort, we didn't plan to spend a lot of up-front time examining all of our defined practices trying to detect possible impacts with agile development practices. Therefore, once the pilot project(s) begins, Scrum teams will begin encountering problems with previously defined processes. What worked before starting agile development may actually begin blocking (obstructing) Scrum teams. What we'll need is a way to communicate those process issues (and what the team

did about them) to the core transition team so that permanent changes can be made to the defined process. In addition, we will also need a means by which all teams are made aware of process changes so that the same problem isn't encountered in future sprints (this will actually be part of the communication plan).

■ *Effectiveness of subordinate teams*: Lastly, if there are subordinate teams, the transition core team should plan to spend a little discussion time during each retrospective on the progress being made by the subordinate teams. The focus here should be on identifying teams that:

1. Need staffing changes (this will happen as the transition project moves forward, but may also present as a team that is having poor sprint reviews)
2. Are running out of work on the backlog (eventually, the subordinate teams should be disbanded—this is a good thing!)
3. Are not making sufficient progress (watch for reductions in team velocity or signs that the team should be able to accomplish more in the time they have)

Continuing beyond Transition Sprint 1

Once the first transition sprint is completed, you'll have a slightly clearer picture of how much your team can do during a sprint and, therefore, how many sprints it may take before you will be ready to take on the first pilot project. The backlog we've discussed in this chapter, and the details in the chapters that make up the remainder of this part of the book, will help guide you in getting to that point in the transition where you can take on the first pilot project and launch your first teams.

Look carefully at the results of your first transition sprint. Discuss the results in detail during your sprint review and try to decide, based on what you see at that point in time, what's the next most important thing to do (that will help drive possible prioritization changes to the transition backlog before you begin the next transition sprint). Following this, use the sprint retrospective to carefully examine what worked during your first transition sprint and what didn't. Maybe the team had a great time and got a lot of work done. That's good—whatever you did during the first sprint, make sure you repeat it. Even more likely, however, is that the team felt that they didn't have enough "free time" allocated to the project to get the important stuff done. What can you do to change this? How important is the transition to the organization and what is it willing to do to make the transition work? Make sure you clearly communicate any organizational-related difficulties to your executive sponsor (or, better yet, get him or her to attend the retrospective unless you feel the team won't speak up with the executive there) immediately. Leverage the transition backlog to show how much needs to be done and how much didn't get done because of the transition team members' other commitments. If this is going to be a problem in your transition project, you'll want to deal with it early and decisively.

With the sprint review and the sprint retrospective behind you, get sprint planning for the second transition sprint under way. The process is the same as discussed throughout this chapter. For specific information on the budget, communications plan, training plan, facilities plan, and more, see the remaining chapters in this section of the book.

Endnotes

1. This should be done during the sprint (and as your teams get more experience, it will get done during the sprint), but in my experience, it often isn't clear that we need to do this until after the sprint ends. Dealing with it during the sprint retrospective helps ensure that nothing in missed in the early sprints and reminds the team to do this activity during the sprints instead.
2. You can find more information about the transition backlog at http://www.bigagiledevelopment.com/transitionbacklog.
3. In cases where there are subordinate teams, the core team may not need more than four hours per week in the early sprints, and possibly quite a bit less later in the transition project because the core team does not groom items that clearly belong to a subordinate team. Those items are simply transferred to another team, which becomes responsible for the grooming of the item.
4. You can find more information at http://www.bigagiledevelopment.com/communicationplan.
5. You can find more information at http://www.bigagiledevelopment.com/transitionbudget.
6. You can find more information at http://www.bigagiledevelopment.com/trainingplan.
7. In addition, the sooner the transition team starts doing story point estimation on backlog items, the sooner they'll become more familiar with the estimation process.
8. There are, in fact, XXL and XXXL sizes that are often used by some agile teams, but for the purposes of simplification, I recommend going light on the X's.
9. For more information on this point, see http://www.artisansoftwareconsulting.com/file/Blogs/Entries/2009/8/11_Whatever_Happens_Is_The_Only_Thing_That_Could_Have.html.

Chapter 11

Create the Transition Budget

While a successful transition to agile development will result in higher performance, better-quality software, and a stronger working relationship with your customers, there are costs that most organizations will likely occur during the transition. We'll discuss a lot of those possibilities in this section. However, since prices vary and an organization's readiness and size will vary, I cannot provide adequate cost estimates. So, as with much of this book, use this section as a way of helping to ensure that your planning is as detailed and comprehensive as you can make it, but fill in the particular details based on the needs and capabilities of your organization.

The major budgetary items[1] that will likely occur during a transition to agile development will fall into these categories:

- Training and coaching
- Software and hardware
- Facilities
- Travel
- Personnel

We'll discuss each of these categories in the sections that follow.

Training and Coaching

By far the largest portion of your budget will be spent in training and coaching. A degree of understanding of agile development can be acquired through reading books (thus, the tome you are currently perusing). However, much of agile development is behavioral and even cultural in content. So, while you can easily learn the concepts of Scrum by reading a few books (and even the litany of articles currently available for free), you will benefit greatly by hiring or training some Certified Scrum Masters who have some experience in how to take advantage of the roles, artifacts, and meetings that make up Scrum. Similarly, test-driven development (TDD) is easily understood through a number of books and, again, free material available on the web. However, it takes a developer with experience to really understand the various nuances and situations that cannot adequately be described in a book or article.

The list of areas of expertise that are important if not critical to the implementation of agile development is rather extensive, and each comes with a similar cautionary tale that, while book learning is important, direct training and coaching is absolutely invaluable. Some of those areas, many of which are discussed to some extent in this book, include:

- Agile analysis (user stories, estimation, grooming)
- Agile development
  - Automated acceptance testing
  - Configuration management and source code control
  - Continuous integration and testing
  - Test-driven development
- Application build (compile and link)
- Project management, release management, and reporting
- Scrum

In general, you will find coaches that specialize in Scrum (and basic agile concepts), agile programming (primarily Extreme Programming (XP)-based practices), and agile analysis. In fact, even when you can find the rare but exceptional coaches that can address all aspects of agile development quite well, you'll still get more flexibility in how you use your coaches by hiring specifically for the categories previously mentioned. From a cost perspective, you will need to estimate the number of Scrum teams that will be created and active at the same time and then base your coaching requirements on the following approximations:

- One Scrum/agile principles coach for every six to eight Scrum teams
- One agile programming coach for every two to three Scrum teams
- One agile analysis coach for every four or five Scrum teams

Fortunately, there are many good consultants available that can help you in several of these areas of expertise—you won't have to find a different source of information for each area. The Agile Alliance (http://www.agilealliance.org) and the Scrum Alliance (http://www.scrumalliance.org) web sites are good places to start to learn about some of the vendors that may be available to help you through the transition.

Software and Hardware

The secret behind agile development's success in improving software quality has a lot to do with rapid software development cycles. In the typical agile development team, software tests and code are written nearly simultaneously, and as each small piece of software is finished and tested, the code and the tests are added to the rest of the product code and tests. In order to ensure that the aggregated code continues to work properly, the entire product is frequently rebuilt and retested by running some or all of the tests. For two or three developers working together on a small piece of a feature, this cycle of clarifying the requirements, writing the tests and the code, testing the code, and adding the new code and tests to the rest of the application can happen in thirty minutes or less (some very experienced agile developers can complete the cycle in fifteen minutes or less). Within one Scrum team, new or changed tests and code can be added to the rest of the product ten or twenty times a day for each of the typical two or three subteams working on a separate story or feature, meaning that your product code base could be modified thirty to sixty times a day. Multiply this by three, four, or even twenty Scrum teams, and your product code base is generally under constant modification.

Under these conditions, it is not unusual for your product to be rebuilt and tested two, three, or four times an hour, each time incorporating new additions to the code base that require testing. In order to keep this continuous build, integrate, and test cycle running while your developers are working, you'll need some software and some hardware to make it all happen.

In addition to the challenges of continuously building and testing your software, you may also need new tools to support the management of teams, products, and their respective backlogs (lists of things to do—stories, features, defects, etc.). In a smaller organization, some simple tools can be created by using readily available spreadsheet programs and even web-based wiki engines. However, as the size of the organization grows and the need for supporting multiple development sites, reporting, and the consolidation of data increases, a backlog and team management tool will prove to be invaluable. Backlog tools can also help:

- Track the relationship of large stories (epics) when those stories are split into smaller stories (children). This creates traceability, something that is often absolutely critical in organizations that are heavily regulated or have stringent quality management practices.

■ Track the required sequence of stories and tasks. Despite the fact that product owners have ultimate responsibility for the prioritization of the product backlog, many stories and tasks have to be done in a specific order or sequence. It is quite difficult in a spreadsheet to track sequence effectively.

■ Flag when the sequence is broken. It is a fairly common occurrence for an item that is being worked on by one Scrum team and is a predecessor for multiple other items to be scoped out of a sprint. Backlog tools can help flag when this happens and can notify the responsible individuals in case additional action needs to be taken.

■ Manage the team's sprint burn-down, relieving the team from this responsibility.

Here's a list of some of the items you may want to consider when planning your software and hardware budget for your transition:

■ Hardware: To the extent that you can, take full advantage of server virtualization.

  – One application environment for the live (production) version of your backlog and team management tool and database.

  – One integration environment per product: This environment receives updates on a continuous basis and represents the most current integration version of the software at any point in time.

  – One integration environment per Scrum team: This environment is updated with the latest version of the product at least once or twice a day (more often hourly if the software can be easily and automatically installed).

    • For products where each developer can install a separate environment on their laptop or PC:

      1. The developer will test their changes on their laptop or PC

      2. Because the developer's environment will not be the most up-to-date version of the product (it can't be, the up-to-date version is constantly changing), he or she will move anything he or she has tested on his or her laptop or PC to the team's server environment.

      3. If the software works on the team's server environment, it is moved to the main code base, where it is tested again on the product integration server.

    • For products where each developer must use a common environment that cannot be built on his or her laptop or PC (because the personal environment is too small, too underpowered, or the full install of the product takes too long to apply):

      1. The developer will code his or her changes on his or her laptop or PC, but test them on the team's environment.

      2. If the software works on the team's environment, it is moved to the main code base, where it is tested again on the product integration server.

■ One environment per active release: While optional, it is still strongly recommended that you keep one environment available for every active configuration of software that exists in the customer base. Defects will be reported on old releases, and you will not want your potentially delicate development environment ruined by developers retrofitting software releases in order to fix a defect.
   – Other optional hardware
      • Webcams: If your teams are not co-located, you will want to do whatever you can to eliminate as much of the effects of physical separation as possible. One of the easiest ways to do this is to install webcams in team rooms and to provide webcams to any individuals who are telecommuting. Then, when team meetings are held, the webcams can be employed to provide as close to face-to-face contact as possible. Some teams may even leave the webcams active (regardless of whether or not a meeting is in progress) in order to give the remote employees more of a "part of the team" feel.
      • Data projectors: Teams that are trying to display code, story information, backlog information, etc., will benefit from having their own data projector. These devices used to be quite expensive. However, recent innovations have made data projectors quite affordable so that every agile development team should have one as part of their equipment. Included in this, of course, is some kind of free-standing projection screen upon which the team can display their information (unless a good flat area of wall is available to the team).
      • Dry-erase boards and markers: Teams will also need a place upon which to draw, discuss, revise, and (sometimes) argue over their ideas. Dry-erase boards (particularly free-standing boards that can be easily rolled from one location to another) are particularly suited for this purpose.
      • Status lights: I've seen some teams use lava lamps; others use simple red and green lights. Some use an old CRT attached to their server or another old laptop or PC that cannot be used for development any longer. In any event, teams gain some effectiveness when there's a clear and large indication of when their product builds are working (green) and when they've failed (red). An agile development team is required to respond immediately when they've broken the product build, and these clear indicators can become a tremendous part of a team's productivity.
■ Software
   – Automated testing: You will need software that is capable of running not just your unit tests, but your functional acceptance tests as well. Further, you want your software to let you know if there's a problem.
      • Fitnesse: This is a great acceptance test automation tool written by the folks at ObjectMentor. This tool is free and can be downloaded and

installed rather quickly. Fitnesse's strongest feature is its use of a wiki environment, which makes it surprisingly easy to write new tests.

- Selenium: This is another fantastic tool for testing web-based pages through scripting. Selenium and Fitnesse can be combined to allow full UI testing driven by a Fitnesse page. Selenium is also free. However, as with all UI testing tools, be careful. Selenium may not handle everything you want it to.

– Cruise Control or Hudson: Both of these tools (again, free) provide an automated build and test capability. On a specific schedule, each tool checks to see if any product files have been changed since the last build. If any files are found to be different, these tools automatically start a scripted build process (you have to write the script). After the build is completed, the script can also kick off the existing automated tests. In order to work, however, your build process needs to be rewritten to be completely unattended.

– Backlog and team management tool

- Rally and Version One: Both of these tools provide all of the functionality you'll need from a backlog management tool. The only issue I've seen with both products is that the vendors that provide them seem to be trying to leverage interest in agile development to be the everything tool vendor to their customers. While both products have their strong points, be careful to purchase the tool that actually fits your needs, and be wary of modifying your process to fit the tool.

- ScrumWorks Pro: This tool is straightforward and built on the principles of Scrum. It is easy to install and easy to use with most of the features of its competitors. Because the tool is written specifically for Scrum teams, you will usually be able to fit it into your existing practices quite well.

– Optional software tools

- Collaboration tools: Agile software development is driven by a high degree of collaboration. Therefore, you will want to look for tools that support the ability for the teams to communicate with themselves and with other teams in a manner that supports the rapid entry of large amounts of data, can track who is responsible for adding and changing data, support the ability to alert one or more people when specific events occur, and support easy searching capabilities. Wiki tools are quite effective here, as are other collaboration tools, such as Microsoft's SharePoint® and IBM's Lotus® Notes®.

- Code inspection: You might also want to purchase and use code inspection tools during your build process that help to ensure that your developers are following your organization's standards.

- Code formatters: Some organizations like their code to be formatted in a very specific manner in order to improve readability. Code formatters can run after-code inspection tools during the build process.

Facilities

As has been and will be said a few more times before you finish this book, agile development is more than just a different way of developing application software. It has a whole different culture of its own. Teams of developers are managed as teams—not in separate offices, but like a team on a playing field with the supporting personnel and equipment on the sidelines, ready whenever the team needs them.

In order for any agile development team to be successful, it has to be in a single, open location. You need to encourage your team members to talk directly to one another instead of using emails, instant messaging, or hand-written notes dropped on their chairs. Unfortunately, if you leave absolutely any kind of divider between your team members, they will often resort to these tools instead of talking face-to-face.

I often tell the story of the members of one team who sat in single-person cubicles before I could set up their first team room. It was very frequent that a team member in one cubicle would send an email to the team member in the very next cubicle. Between the delay in the second person receiving the email and actually reading and responding to the email, a few hours could easily pass before an answer (if indeed the response email contained an answer) was sent back. When I discussed this phenomenon with the team, they agreed that email took too long and immediately installed and began using an instant messaging program instead. They then found that the IMs were very distracting and started to set their system status to "offline" or "busy." In the end, the turnaround of answers to questions, even if the team members were next door to one another, was simply too long. The only answer that actually worked was to remove the walls altogether. By doing this, not only could one team member easily see if another was too busy to answer a question, but they could just as easily see when that team member (or any other team member) was available, and they could get a very rapid answer to their query.

As odd as it might seem that one person would not stand up and walk ten steps to ask the person next to them a question, it is, in fact, quite common. Studies have clearly shown that any kind of separation between workers—whether it's a wall, a room, a floor, a building, a city, or an ocean—has the same effect. Interactions are delayed and group-driven innovation can never get off the ground.

All this means one thing: if you're going to have a successful transition to agile development, you need to plan to rebuild your facilities to provide team rooms rather than "cube jungles" or offices. That's going to mean moving a lot of employees, changing the office space, and rewiring. It also means that you'll need to consider two very interesting problems:

1. How will you re-create your corporate directory so that the location of an employee is updated even if they move from team to team when projects end?
2. How will you manage your internal telephone system if employees move from team to team (and location to location) in between projects?

Both of these problems are critical to solve and will also test your commitment to the success of the transition. If you believe that your employees can have a home location that never changes and they go from there to their teams each morning when they come to work, well, you might not have completely bought into the team concept yet.

Some organizations manage their corporate directory with a simple database and modify their procedures to update the directory anytime an employee moves from one team to another. A different process, however, kicks in when an entire project ends and lots of people move simultaneously. Some organizations solve the telephone problem by giving their employees a wireless "house" phone that they keep with them no matter where they are working. The wireless phones work over an internal voice-over-Internet-protocol (VOIP).

On the sidelines of the agile development team's playing field you will find the servers and other tools that the team uses to do their jobs. In some instances, you may find that you'll also have to plan for additional space to house the servers needed by your teams, and security concerns or environmental concerns (cooling, for example) may also play a part in your facilities planning.

Travel

Travel as part of a transition to agile development will be widely varied depending on the specific organizational circumstances, but will likely include travel for the following reasons:

1. *Travel to/from agile development conferences*: There are a couple conferences each year that offer organizations an opportunity to learn from the experiences of others with case studies and reports that address topics central to agile development. By sending one or two individuals from your organization to these conferences each year, you can create a continuous flow of useful information into the organization.
2. *Travel for coaches and trainers*: You may decide to include coach/trainer travel in your training/education budget or travel. But however you decide to do it, be sure to remember the travel and living expenses for your trainers in your planning. Ask your prospective trainers how they book their transportation and lodging, how long they expect to need to be on site, and how often they go home during longer engagements. Also, consider multiple development

sites in your budgeting. Will the trainers work only at one site, or will they need to repeat the same training in multiple locations.

3. *Travel for multiple development sites*: If your developers work in multiple locations or from home, you will need to consider how often you will bring remote or offshore employees to the home location in order to work directly with their teams or to get centrally scheduled training. In cases where teams cannot be co-located, there is still considerable gain to be had by ensuring that everyone on the team has worked directly, face-to-face with everyone else at least once.

4. *Travel for customers*: Agile development teams work best when they have direct contact with their customers. While this can sometimes be difficult to arrange, when you do have a customer willing to work directly with one or more development teams (perhaps on critical or market differentiating features), you should be willing to subsidize if not completely pay for the customer's expenses.

People

While most transitions to agile development can be done without altering your total employee count, you should carefully consider some of the following possibilities:

- The installation and setup of a large number of new server environments may require a temporary increase in server administrators.
- The possible one-time need to convert your product installation to an unattended script could potentially be done by consultant developers.
- The organization may wish to seed their Scrum master ranks with experienced, certified Scrum masters on a short-term or long-term basis.
- While coaching and training are effective tools in integrating new concepts and behaviors, your organization may see a real benefit in hiring contract programmers that are already experienced agile developers to join some or all of your teams and provide daily examples of how agile developers work.

Summary

Creating a budget for your agile transition is a necessary step that will help your organization plan for the many types of changes you may have to make during the course of the transition. From new hardware and software to facilities changes, personnel changes, and setting aside money for travel, there is much to consider. However, being completely clear about the costs that will be incurred in a transition is extremely important. Ensuring that the transition has the funding it needs to be successful avoids unwanted delays caused by getting separate approvals for everything you'll need, while also clearly outlining the types of expenses and the extent of those expenses for the organization's management to make carefully considered decisions.

Endnote

1. You can find more information about transition backlogs at http://www. bigagiledevelopment.com/transitionbacklog.

Chapter 12

Develop the Transition Communication Plan

As you begin to prepare to launch your transition to agile development, communication[1] to *all* stakeholders should be a significant part of your planning. Everything you do in the course of the transition is going to impact people that you will depend on in order to make the transition successful. Changing development processes will have an impact on your developers and managers, your customer support departments, and your training/education groups (for starters).

How you plan releases in an agile project will affect all of the aforementioned people as well as your sales and marketing groups, your customers, and various levels of management. Changing to a very team-oriented environment will have a significant impact on your developers and managers as well as the human resources, staffing, and legal departments. In other words, you're going to need to evaluate every step of the transition to agile development with all of your stakeholders.

Some of the most common stakeholders include:

1. *Developers and development managers* (including analysts, testers, technical writers, product management, project management, etc.)
2. *Training personnel*: Those who offer classes to customers as well as those who are responsible for internal training of employees.
3. *Legal, human resources*: These groups are most affected by changes to contracting policy, communication with external stakeholders, changes to staffing policies, changes to compensatory policies (raises, promotions, incentives).

4. *Customer support/service*: These groups are most affected by changes in how the product is developed, changes in tools used to develop the product, and (to some degree) how the development teams are organized.

5. *Sales and marketing*: These groups are most affected by changes in how product releases are scheduled, how customers are involved in the planning of release content or with development teams directly, how release content may or may not change during the course of the development project, how the product is priced/contracted.

6. *Corporate/executive management*: In a corporation, executive management usually doesn't get involved in the day-to-day development activities; however, they usually are uncomfortable unless they get periodic reports of development progress and how the product is received and perceived by their customers.

7. *Facilities management*: Regardless of the size of the organization, someone is responsible for the physical arrangement of the employees within the organization's offices. The creation of team rooms will have a tremendous impact on the facilities.

8. *Procurement/legal/internal information technology (IT)*: While implementing new practices in Scrum and Extreme Programming (XP), it's not at all unusual for large purchases of new tools (software), new hardware, and new physical equipment (e.g., whiteboards and tables, etc.). Getting your procurement, legal, and IT departments involved in the transition early and keeping them involved will help clear the way for the materials you need at a price that the organization can live with.

In order to keep everyone aligned initially on what the transition is and why you are doing it, and then later, the progress of the transition and changes being made as part of the transition, you will need a communication plan (see Figure 12.1). This plan should determine the channels of communication you plan to use for each type of stakeholder and the type of information that will be communicated along each channel and how often communication will occur. Typical communication channels that you can use include:

1. Internal and external web sites
2. Email
3. Posters
4. Newsletters
5. Internal closed-circuit TV
6. Tip sheets
7. Internal meetings (group/team, department)
8. Customer meetings (with one or more customers)
9. Trade conferences

Backlog Items

Create the communication plan:

- Define a central location for all project and practice documentation.
- Define a means/schedule that determines what information is communicated to whom and by which means.
- Create a means by which information can be quickly communicated to all Scrum teams.
- Create a means for employees to understand who is on which team.
- Create a means for everyone to understand which team is working on what
- Create a means for communication of standards, design principles, and coding practices across Scrum teams.

Figure 12.1 Slicing the "Create a Communication Plan" transition backlog item.

For example, you can easily communicate with your developers and managers via email for important, time-sensitive information, but you probably don't want to overload this already overused channel for routine information like transition updates, training announcements, etc. Another channel, posters or time during already scheduled department meetings, could be used for this information. On the other hand, your customers don't have a need for a lot of information about the specifics of the transition, nor are you likely to want to discuss this information via email, where information can be easily stolen and even more easily misinterpreted; face-to-face communication via account managers might be better.

A completed communication plan for your transition might look something like the one presented in Table 12.1.

Project Information Storage

Once the agile transition begins, you will need a common location in which to store all of the transition's artifacts, including items like:

- The communication plan
- The facilities plan
- The training plan
- The training materials
- Project communications
- Project reports

Table 12.1 A Sample Communications Plan

Stakeholder(s)	Information	Channel	Frequency
Developers, managers	Detailed transition status	Email	First of month
Executive management	Summary transition status, project status	Email, presentation	Monthly (or more often, as required)
All other internal departments, customer service/support, procurement	Summary transition status, planning information	Email	Monthly
	Transition information and progress (with legal and sales and marketing approvals)	Press releases, customer letters	Quarterly or semiannually
External customers	More detailed transition information with regard to product improvements	Face-to-face via account manager	Monthly or quarterly
	Customer role training, working with Scrum teams	Face-to-face or web-based training	As needed
	Development process changes	Email	As needed
Developers (including analysis, testers, technical writers, etc.)	Development process training, tool training	Classroom or web-based training	As needed
	Development process training	Classroom, web-based, large group presentation	Monthly or as needed
Human resources, legal, staffing	Any changes to roles, job descriptions, staffing requirements, job titles, compensation	Face-to-face	As needed

You may also find it useful to create an artifact-naming standard that helps employees to find documents faster when your project information storage becomes heavily populated. The naming standard need not be difficult or elaborate—it only needs to help employees easily and quickly find the document that they are looking for.

Here's a couple sample naming standards:

1. In a simple directory structure, with one product and no change control:

    yymmdd-documentname.document-type

    ex. 090101-communication-plan.doc
    ex. 090108-training-plan.doc
    ex. 081112-Team-Diamond-Scrum-Backlog-Sprint-0811.doc

2. In a simple directory structure, with two products and no change control:

    productname-yymmdd-documentname.document-type

    ex. productA-081101-product-backlog-snapshot.doc
    ex. productA-081201-scrum-team-membership.doc
    ex. productB-081202-training-plan.doc

3. In a change control directory with one product:

    documentname.document-type

    ex. product-backlog-snapshot.doc
    ex. training-plan.doc

4. In a change control directory with two products:

    productname-documentname.document-type

    ex. productA-training-plan.doc
    ex. productA-communication-plan.doc

Endnote

1. You can find more information at http://www.bigagiledevelopment.com/communicationplan.

Chapter 13

Create the Training Plan

A key element of a successful transition to agile development includes careful planning of effective training and coaching[1] that addresses the various roles involved in the transition and is sensitive to providing the right education in the right manner at the right time. This chapter will discuss the four elements of the training plan (role, topic, manner, and timing) in detail, with the goal of providing you with a basic structure for a training plan that can be incorporated with the overarching transition plan (see Figure 13.1).

Basic Concepts

The training plan follows some tried but true concepts that help to maximize the benefit of training while, at the same time, attempting to reduce the risk to your product development efforts by ensuring that employees working on an agile development team have had the proper requisite training.

The first concept used throughout the training plan is also widely used in medical practice. Put simply, the concept is summed up as "learn, watch, do." In other words, prior to actually writing code in an agile development team, every developer will learn how to develop code in an agile manner, will then work with other more experienced developers, and only then will actually work on an agile development team, producing code in the manner in which they've been taught. Similar approaches are taken with agile analysis, story point estimation, scrum mastering, etc.

The second concept used throughout the training plan recognizes the importance of the development team in an agile environment. All non-role-specific training is planned for intact development teams; in other words, as much as possible, teams will be trained as intact units to ensure that they all hear the same message

---

Backlog Items

Create the training plan:

- Identify the roles that your projects will use (product owners, Scrum masters, project manager, etc.).
- Identify the skills needed by each role.
- For each skill area, create a training module.
- Combine the training modules to create a curriculum.
- Create a team of coaches to support Scrum teams.
- Create a schedule of courses.
- Determine external coaching needs (how can teams request help?)
- Create a means to capture retrospective feedback and improve the training.

Figure 13.1 Slicing the "Create a Training Plan" transition backlog item.

and that they all acquire the same shared experiences during the transition period. When the two concepts are combined, you see that the foundations of the training plan are based on teams learning, watching, and doing and, by this approach, learning how to create their own agile development identities.

The third concept used in the training program has to do with how we create it. This chapter will describe an open approach that will allow you to customize the training program as needed simply by following the same steps as laid out in this chapter. Those steps are:

1. Identify the roles that your agile projects will use. I'll list many of those roles in the following section.
2. Identify the skills needed for each role. I'll provide much of this later in the chapter.
3. For each skill area, create a training module that teaches the skill (could be classroom work, independent work, team instruction, coaching, or any combination).
4. Combine the modules together to create the curriculum. Your curriculum will have five distinct tracks from which most of your employees will select or be selected for training: external stakeholders, project management, resource management, and two team membership tracks—one for technical personnel and the other for analytical personnel.

Having discussed the basic concepts of the training plan, we now need to explore the basic structure of a large-scale agile project as well as the roles that make up the large-scale agile environment.

Agile Project Structure

The agile project structure, while similar in many ways to more conventional projects, has a very distinctive organization that focuses on self-organizing teams "swarming" around a project or *release* backlog, continuously pushing new software updates into a single code base that also contains a self-correcting mechanism should faulty software be introduced into the code base.

As you can see from Figure 13.2, in addition to the release backlog and the product itself (which includes the software and any documentation), there are four types of teams in an agile project:

- *Quality assurance team*: This team continuously monitors and tests the condition of the product above and beyond what the development teams do. This team develops new tests in addition to what the development teams create as part of the product development effort. Defects found in the product are diagnosed to determine responsibility for the source of the defect; once determined, the defect is sent to the proper development team with critical priority.
- *Development teams*: These teams (including customers that may be involved in the development effort from time to time) develop all of the new features and feature changes in the product. They accept their work from the release backlog and send the results to the product. Defects found by teams are fixed immediately. Defects found in the product are identified by the quality

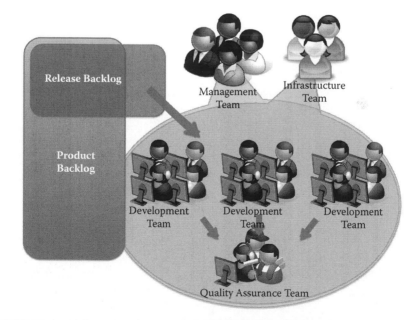

Figure 13.2   Overview of an agile project.

assurance (QA) team and returned directly to the responsible development team for immediate correction.

■ *Infrastructure teams*: These teams keep the entire "factory" working by managing server environments and source code configurations.

■ *Management team*: This team usually consists of a release manager, a project manager, and an executive sponsor. They, together and separately, make the decisions that keep the project on track.

The teams are made up of a variety of roles that employees either will hold for the duration of the project or will switch between a few times during the project or even several times a day during the project. Understanding these roles is very important, as a clear knowledge of which roles an individual will play during the project will provide you with a clear idea of the training that he or she will need to have in order to do his or her jobs well. For example, while a project manager is likely to only play the role of project management during the project, it is entirely possible that an application analyst may also play the role of a documentation writer or that your coders may also take on the roles of analyst, designer, and tester. Agile development requires that employees be willing to take on whatever roles they can to meet the team's objectives, so it is particularly important that those who participate on an agile team have a well-rounded education in agile development methods.

Roles in an Agile Project

In this section, we'll talk about the roles that you will likely find in an agile project with particular emphasis on the aspects of the roles that are distinct to agile development.

■ *Management roles*: Management roles on a project manage the project budget, handle the decision making, provide resources, and keep the project on track.
  - *Development (R&D) manager*: Supports the agile transition plan by ensuring that his or her teams have the resources and support that they need to get the job done. Handles conflicts and impediments that cannot be handled by the Scrum teams.
  - *Product manager*: Supports the project by setting the goals and providing direction for a product. Usually, the product owners report to the product manager who is, in essence, an uber product owner.
  - *Program manager*: Supports multiple projects by setting the goals and providing direction for a product family (or otherwise related products). The product owners may report directly to the program manager or to uber product owners that, in turn, report to the program manager.
  - *Project manager*: Supports the project by managing the project schedule and handling all external issues that may have a direct impact on the project; communicates project status on a regular basis.

- *Quality manager*: Supports the quality of the finished product by managing the quality assurance team, providing testing resources directly to the development teams, sometimes maintaining separate QA teams that verify product quality independent of the development Scrum teams, and providing and continuously improving organizational testing skills.
- *Quality process manager*: Supports the organization through the proper documentation of all practices used by the organization. Helps to ensure that the organization abides by defined quality practices, prepares the organization for internal and external quality system audits of the organization, and drives resolution of corrective actions that may result from internal or external audits.
- *Resource manager*: Supports the project by providing resources to the development teams. Responsible for supporting the continuous improvement of employee performance and skills.

■ External roles
- *Sales and marketing*: Supports the project by generating customer interest in the product in time for the eventual release of the product to the customer population.
- *Executive sponsor*: Supports the project by strongly supporting the transition plan.

■ Supporting roles
- *Configuration manager*: Supports the project by maintaining the artifact version control configuration, software, access/security, and practices.
- *Environment manager*: Supports the project by helping to maintain the various hardware and software environments necessary for software development. This may include the Scrum team-specific development environments, product integration environments, demonstration environments for sales, and support environments for customer service.

■ Team roles
- *Analyst*: Writes and clarifies stories, supports coders and designers to build the product properly, and often provides interim acceptance of stories during sprints as a step prior to QA review.
- *Coder*: Writes code, responsible for writing unit tests and acceptance tests while also writing the product code.
- *Designer*: Creates conceptual approaches to building the application based on the information contained in the backlog items.
- *Product owner*: Responsible for the product, its business plan, vision, and return on investment. The product owner determines the prioritization of the release backlog and is the final arbiter with regard to questions about release backlog items.
- *Quality assurance analyst*: Supports product quality by testing the application beyond the unit and acceptance tests designed and built by the developers.

- *Scrum master*: Enforces the Scrum process within the project teams, and helps to keep everyone focused on their commitments.
- *Tester*: Creates conceptual approaches to testing the application based on the information contained in the backlog items. Helps write or clarify the acceptance criteria.
■ *Writer, technical writer*: Writes most customers and some internal documentation.

Before continuing, consider your organization. What additional roles might you have in your projects? For the purposes of training, I have deliberately not included roles like database designer, UI analyst, and architect, as these roles are generally covered under the designer, analyst, coder, and Scrum team member descriptions. As much as possible, try to relate your new roles to the roles defined in this section: On what teams do your new roles work? What do they do? In the next section, we'll take a role-by-role look at what skills are needed and what training can be provided.

Matching Skills to Roles

The advantage of breaking the responsibilities into roles is that each role can then be matched with a mostly distinct set of skills. Then, by understanding what roles an individual will take on during a project, you can plan his or her training accordingly. In this section, we'll take each role and list the necessary skills. For each skill, take the additional step of identifying if the person in the role needs a basic knowledge of the topic or an advanced knowledge. Associate basic knowledge with an understanding that allows individuals to be familiar with the terms and concepts of a skill; they can perform the skill reasonably well with supervision. Advanced knowledge is when an employee understands both the concepts and the applications of the skill, and helps others perform the skill effectively. For our current purposes, the ability to teach others a skill will be considered beyond even the advanced level of knowledge.

Tables 13.1 and 13.2 provide a list of all of the roles listed earlier in the chapter and show the basic skills that each role will need in order to be successful in an agile environment. For your organization, you may wish to change this table by adding, modifying, or deleting roles; adding, modifying, or deleting skills; or changing the entire table. Regardless of what you choose to do, when making your training plan, start with this table to decide what roles you will have and how each role should be skilled.

One note: Unless really necessary, don't combine two or more of the listed roles into one (there may be a real temptation to do so with designer and coder). Unless there's a real strong reason to combine roles together, continue to think

Table 13.1 Necessary Skills for Management, External, and Supporting Roles

Roles	*Skills Required* *(Level = Talking Points, Basic, or Advanced)*
• All	• Introduction to Agile Development (Basic)
• Development manager	• Scrum (Basic) • Test-Driven Development (Basic) • Continuous Integration and Testing (Basic) • Agile Analysis (Basic)
• Resource manager	• Scrum (Basic)
• Product manager, program manager, project manager, quality process manager	• Scrum (Basic) • Agile Analysis (Basic)
• Quality manager	• Scrum (Basic) • Agile Analysis (Basic) • Software Deployment
• Sales and marketing, executive sponsor	• Scrum (Talking Points) • Software Deployment (Talking Points)
• Configuration manager, environment manager	• Scrum (Advanced) • Continuous Integration and Testing (Advanced) • Software Deployment (Advanced)
• Customer	• Scrum (Basic) • A Customer's Responsibilities

of them as independent things that people do, sometimes in a sequence and sometimes all at the same time. Keeping roles separate helps to modularize the training and thus keep you from teaching the same thing in two or more inconsistent ways.

Skills Become Training Modules

Once you complete the table in the previous section, you essentially have an inventory of skills that you need across your organization and for which you need training materials created. If we review the table of roles and skills and list only the skills (removing the duplications), we come up with the following list:

Table 13.2 Necessary Skills for Scrum Team Member Roles

Roles	Skills Required (Level = Talking Points, Basic, or Advanced)
• Analyst, designer, writer/technical writer	• Scrum (Advanced) • Agile Analysis (Advanced)
• Coder	• Scrum (Advanced) • Agile Analysis (Advanced) • Test-Driven Development (Advanced) • Continuous Integration and Testing (Advanced)
• Product owner	• Certified Scrum Product Owner (CSPO) • Agile Analysis (Advanced)
• Scrum master	• Certified Scrum Master (CSM) • Certified Scrum Master—Practicing (CSP) • Agile Analysis (Advanced)
• Quality assurance analyst, tester	• Scrum (Advanced) • Agile Analysis (Advanced) • Continuous Integration and Testing (Advanced)

- Introduction to Agile Development
- Software Deployment in an Agile Environment (Basic, Advanced, and Talking Points)
- Certified Scrum Master
- Certified Scrum Product Owner
- Scrum (Basic, Advanced, and Talking Points)
- Test-Driven Development (Basic and Advanced)
- Continuous Integration and Testing (Basic and Advanced)
- Agile Analysis (Basic and Advanced)
- A Customer's Responsibilities

This list of skills is essentially a list of the training modules that we will need to create. These modules, in turn, can be combined (or not) in multiple ways to create the training sessions that will enable us to complete the training plan. A few of the modules (those without the "basic" or "advanced" designations) either include the skill level in their title (e.g., Introduction to Agile Development is clearly an introductory module and therefore can be considered basic) or are complete, defined courses (e.g., Certified Scrum Master and Certified Scrum Product Owner).

Two of the skills list "talking points" as a skill level. In these cases, we're looking for a simple page or two that can be used by senior employees that do not have the availability for even a half-day work session, but need to be able to discuss the topics at a high level. These materials are generally easily created from the basic materials of the same skill.

The Training Modules

With the list of skills and the level (basic or advanced) defined, you're ready to detail out the content of the modules that you will need to build to complete your training plan. This book includes the training module definition for the skills identified in the previous section. For any roles you may have added and new skills you may have identified, you will also need to create the new training modules.

Training modules are "pieces" of a class or workshop. They can be as short as fifteen minutes or as long as a day. If you find yourself building a module larger in length than one day (approximately six hours), consider the possibility that you're actually creating multiple modules. Look for clear delineations of topic material in the class outline; if you see a clear change in direction, try splitting the module there.

The remainder of this section describes the training modules. The course numbers are added to help facilitate an understanding of prerequisite courses. In other words, 100-level modules should occur in the training before 200-level modules, which should occur in the training before the 300-level modules, and so on (see Table 13.3).

Defining the Tracks

With the modules clearly defined, we can now define our curriculum paths and assign roles to them. If you recall from earlier in the chapter, we will define four tracks in our agile training curriculum: external stakeholders, project management, resource management, and team membership technical and team membership analytical. In this section, we'll define each track, the roles that are in the track, and the arrangement of the training modules as presented in Table 13.4.

Executing the Tracks

If you follow the basic transition plan described later in this book, you will begin the transition to agile development by staffing your transition team, building the transition backlog, identifying a project that will be the pilot project, staffing that project, and building that project's initial backlog all in the first transition sprint. Your second sprint will therefore consist of a transition team and one or two project teams during which both transitional and project work is completed. The third sprint consists of the transition team and even more project teams, and so on. Your

Table 13.3 Descriptions of Courses in the Agile Training Plan

Course Title	Course Length/Format	Course Description
100—Introduction to Agile Development (Basic)	2.5 hours, classroom	Introduces the student to the basic concepts of agile development. This course can be used as a primer for those who are new to agile development. The course contents include: the Agile Manifesto, agile principles, brief history of agile development, types of agile methods (Scrum, XP, FDD, DSDM, etc.), quality infusion through DONEness, description of the transition plan and the current state
101—Scrum (Basic)	4 hours, classroom	Introduces the student to Scrum through a combination of lecture and team-oriented exercises that explore the basics of Scrum, roles (product owner, team, Scrum master), artifacts (release backlog, sprint backlog), meetings (sprint planning, sprint review, daily Scrum, sprint retrospective)
102—A Customer's Responsibilities (Basic)	2 hours, web-based training	Introduces customers to their responsibilities on a Scrum team
105—Introduction to Test-Driven Development (Basic)	2 hours, classroom	Introduces the student to TDD through a combination of lecture and group-oriented exercises that explore concepts and procedure
106—Introduction to Continuous Integration and Testing (CIT; Basic)	2 hours, classroom	Introduces the student to CIT through a combination of lecture and group-oriented exercises that explore the concepts and methods
107—Introduction to Agile Analysis (Basic)	4 hours, classroom	Introduces the student to agile analysis through a combination of lecture and group-oriented exercises that explore concepts, user stories, story point estimation, managing story backgrounds

Course	Duration/Format	Description
110—Introduction to Software Deployment in an Agile Environment (Basic)	1 hour, classroom	Introduces the student to the basic concepts of software deployment in an agile environment; the course contents include discussion of concepts and challenges
201—Scrum (Advanced)	1 day, classroom	Continues the student's education in Scrum through a combination of lecture and team-oriented exercises that explore backlog grooming, writing story agreements, story point estimation, quality infusion (DONEness), retrospective techniques
202—Certified Scrum Master (CSM) (Advanced)	2 days, classroom; must be provided by a Certified Scrum Trainer (CST)	Introduces the student to being a Scrum master through a combination of lecture and team-oriented exercises that explore Scrum basics, roles (product owner, team, Scrum master), artifacts (product backlog, sprint backlog), meetings (sprint planning, sprint review, sprint retrospective, daily Scrum, user stories, backlog grooming, story point estimation, team leadership)
203—Certified Scrum Product Owner (CSPO) (Advanced)	2 days, classroom; must be provided by a Certified Scrum Trainer (CST)	Introduces the student to being a Scrum product owner through a combination of lecture and team-oriented exercises that explore Scrum basics, roles (product owner, team, Scrum master), artifacts (product backlog, sprint backlog), meetings (sprint planning, sprint review, sprint retrospective, daily Scrum), building/prioritizing/grooming a backlog, understanding business value
205—Test-Driven Development for Developers (Advanced)	4 hours, classroom; must be followed by on-the-job coaching	Continues the student's training on TDD through a combination of lecture and individually oriented exercises that explore handling exception conditions, writing complex unit tests, staying away from the database, refactoring

(continued on next page)

Table 13.3 (continued) Descriptions of Courses in the Agile Training Plan

Course Title	Course Length/Format	Course Description
206—Continuous Integration and Testing for Developers (Advanced)	2 days, classroom; must be followed by on-the-job coaching	Continues the student's training on CIT through a combination of lecture and individually oriented exercises that explore smoke testing, regression testing, and using tools (Fitnesse, Cruise Control, Hudson)
207—Agile Analysis (Advanced)	4 hours, classroom; must be followed by on-the-job coaching	Continues the student's training in agile analysis through a combination of lecture and individually oriented exercises that explore story slicing and writing effective agreements
210—Software Deployment in an Agile Environment (Advanced)	4 hours, classroom; must be followed by on-the-job coaching	Continues the student's training in software deployment through a combination of lecture and individually oriented exercises that explore branching strategies and story back-out strategies

Table 13.4 Training Tracks

External Stakeholders Track	
Notes: These modules can be given as a one-day class or two half-day sessions or as independent training. There are no specific timing issues with this track.	
Roles	*Modules*
• Sales and marketing	• Introduction to Agile (100) —*except customer and sales and marketing*
• Executive sponsor	• Scrum (101)
• Resource manager	• Scrum (Talking Points) —*only executive sponsor and sales and marketing*
• Customer	• A Customer's Responsibilities —*only customer*

Project Management Track	
Notes: Recommended arrangement is to offer as three classes (100/101, 107, and 110). Classes should be provided just in time for the beginning of an agile project.	
Roles	*Modules*
• Project manager	• Introduction to Agile (100)
• Product manager	• Scrum (101)
• Program manager	• Agile Analysis (107)
• Quality manager	• Software Deployment (110) —*only quality manager*
• Quality process manager	

Team Membership Technical Track	
Notes: Recommended arrangement is to offer as five classes (100, 101/201, 105/205, 106/206, and 107). Consider offering the 100, 101/201, and 107 classes prior to the beginning of the project, then offer the 105/205 and 106/206 training during the first sprint. Coaching for 205 and 206 courses should be done on a follow-up basis within one or two weeks and then again for a couple days during the next two or three sprints.	
Roles	*Modules*
• Coder	• Introduction to Agile (100)
• Configuration manager	• Scrum (101 and 201)

(continued on next page)

Table 13.4 (continued)   Training Tracks

Roles	Modules
• Designer	• Test-Driven Development (105 and 205)—*only coders*
• Environment manager	• Continuous Integration (106 and 206)—*except designers*
• Quality assurance analyst	• Agile Analysis (107)
• Tester	

Team Membership Analytical Track

Notes: Recommended arrangement is to offer as four classes (100, 101/201, 105/205, and 107/207). Consider offering the 100, 101/201, and 107 classes prior to the beginning of the project, then offer the 207 training during the first sprint. Coaching for 207 courses should be done on a follow-up basis within one or two weeks and then again for a couple days during the next two or three Sprints.

Roles	Modules
• Analyst	• Introduction to Agile (100)
• Product owner	• Scrum (101 and 201)
• Scrum master	• Agile Analysis (107 and 207)
• Writer/technical writer	• Certified Scrum Master—*only Scrum master* • Certified Scrum Product Owner—*only product owner*

training will therefore follow similar cycles. A reasonable schedule for your training is given in Table 13.5.

This pattern will help to ensure that (1) new Scrum team members will get the proper training right before they will use it and (2) constant retrospection on the training materials will guarantee that gaps in the training are quickly corrected.

The Role of Coaches in the Agile Transition

Teaching Scrum, Extreme Programming (XP), and other agile concepts isn't terribly difficult. Much of agile development is about common sense. However, while the concepts may be easy to explain and easy to grasp, putting the concepts to work in your daily job can prove to be a major challenge. I have seen many instances

Table 13.5 A Sample Training Schedule

Sprint	Week	Training Tracks
1	1	Project management **Note:** Transition team also attends Introduction to Agile and Basic Scrum courses (100 and 101)
	2	External stakeholder
	3	Team membership analytical
	4	Team membership technical
	Retro	Sprint retrospective, including review of training
2	1	Make training improvements and corrections based on feedback
	2–3	Team membership analytical (all team members to attend basic agile analysis)
	4	Team membership technical
	Retro	Retrospective on all training materials

where developers were trained in intensive immersion courses, only to return to their desks to continue to do things the way they did it before. This isn't a sign of resistance, however. It's simply that learning a skill like, for example, test-driven development (TDD), doesn't prepare you to know exactly where to start when you return to your desk. The only way to make skills like this effective is to follow the same methods that American surgeons do in their training: learn, watch, do. First they learn something, then they watch someone do it, then they do it themselves.

We've covered the *learn* part pretty thoroughly in this chapter. Coaches handle the *watch* part by giving newly trained employees someone to watch who is actually doing the work. They *exemplify* the proper behaviors. After watching, the *doing* part becomes much easier to internalize. In exemplifying proper behaviors and skills, good coaches also provide another form of assistance: "*remind.*" Good agile skills are as often associated with good habits as anything else. In other words, using TDD as an example again, most coders in today's world have been taught to write code, then write their tests (if they write any tests at all, that is). When you learn how to do TDD, your perspective as a coder undergoes a significant paradigm shift when you learn to write your tests and code at the same time (with the tests going first, though not by much). This is a radical shift in thinking that, when the pressure is on or when they simply get a little lazy, many coders forget and go back to how they used to write code. Coaches provide an ongoing reminder to their teams to keep building their code the right way by example and by discussion.

Planning for coaching is part of the training plan (though we also discussed it, at a high level, as part of the transition budgeting, because coaching can be a major portion of the overall transition costs). Each team that you create will have additional coaching requirements, and some of the roles in your organization will also need coaching. Let's look at both instances here.

Team Coaching Requirements

Scrum teams require coaching in general concepts (like Scrum, customer involvement on a team, and DONEness), coding practices (like test-driven development, continuous integration and testing, paired programming, refactoring), and analysis practices (writing user stories, estimating user stories, etc.). Newer teams need more coaching; more experienced teams need less. There are some coaches that are very good at coaching in all of these skills; however, you may find greater flexibility by hiring coaches that specialize. Table 13.6 provides approximate coaching needs per team during the critical first six months of any development project.

Table 13.6 demonstrates that you should consider providing a total of almost five hundred hours of coaching to each Scrum team during the first six months of their existence. You'll need an expert in Scrum and basic agile principles to spend about seventy hours with the team during this time. They'll help ensure that the Scrum method is being properly enforced, will support your new Scrum masters, and will also help the team stay focused on delivering done software at the end of every sprint. During this same time, you should plan on about 280 hours of time from a coach that can help the team understand test-driven development, how to write unit and functional tests, and how to keep from breaking build when they check code while, at the same time, checking code on a frequent basis.

Also, you'll need a coach who has, and can teach, a clear understanding of how to write, use, slice, and estimate user stories. Maintaining the product backlog

Table 13.6 Approximate Coaching Time by Type of Coaching and Sprint in Hours

Skill	Sprint 1	Sprint 2	Sprint 3	Sprint 4	Sprint 5	Sprint 6	Total Hours
Scrum and agile principles	30	20	10	10			70
Coding practices	100	80	40	20	20	20	280
Agile analysis	40	20	20	20	20	20	140
Totals	170	120	70	50	40	40	490

can be a very difficult task, and good agile analysis coaches will be able to provide many different exercises for learning the most about user stories as quickly and as efficiently as possible.

The big questions, of course, when planning for how many coaches you will need are:

1. How many Scrum teams will you create each month of each development project?
2. How long before you feel you will be able to provide coaches from within the organization?

Based on the approximate times shown in Table 13.2, you will need one Scrum/ agile concepts coach for every six to eight Scrum teams. For the coaches that provide support with agile coding practices, you will need one coding practices coach for every two or three Scrum teams. For the coaches that provide support with agile analysis, you will probably need one agile analysis coach for every four or five Scrum teams.

Coaching should always be done with an eye toward training internal employees to provide the coaching in the future. As coaching is one of the most crucial pieces of the agile transition and one of the most expensive, your long-term planning needs to consider how soon teams can coach themselves rather than having an external coach assigned. At the same time, be very careful not to try to save expenses by hiring fewer coaches than recommended. Coaching is as crucial an aspect of the agile transition as training classes and, indeed, will have a much longer-term impact in terms of teams that have truly internalized what they've been taught. Reducing the coaching availability for your teams will have a lasting impact on your Scrum teams' velocity, effectiveness, and on the quality of the software they produce.

Overload the Scrum Teams

As the new Scrum teams are being formed during the transition, consider overloading the Scrum teams with one or two extra members that will become the experienced team members on new teams in the next sprint. For example, during transition sprint 1, the first one or two scrum teams are formed and trained. Staff the first two teams with up to nine team members, seven of which are permanent team members and two of which will move on to be permanent members of the next two teams. These temporary team members are placed with an initial team for a sprint in order to internalize what they have learned and then benefit from any follow-up coaching. At the beginning of the next sprint, they join their new permanent teams (who received their initial training during the previous sprint) and, along with the coaches, pass on what they have learned in the previous sprint.

Normally, it isn't considered good practice to change the team makeup, but in this case, the membership is known to be temporary in the first place and, more importantly, the benefit of setting good behaviors in the first Scrum teams will be realized in all of the following teams as long as the training and coaching remain reasonably consistent.

Scrum Masters and Scrum Product Owners

Because proper training of Scrum masters and product owners usually involves someone certified to train these roles (Certified Scrum Trainers), you will find that the availability of the courses is not in line with your sprints. Your best move here is to train two or three Scrum masters and Scrum product owners and use them to mentor newer Scrum masters and product owners until such time as the training is available again. Even if you can select and train all of your Scrum masters and product owners all at once, I do not recommend it unless they will have teams to work with immediately upon completing the course. Like the rest of agile development, Scrum is very much a behavioral experience. If you cannot immediately apply what is learned, you will find yourself with a large number of Certified Scrum Masters and Certified Scrum Product Owners that do not remember how to do what they were taught.

Prove Your Skill First

New scrum teams should be considered probationary teams during the first three sprints. This means that the teams have not yet proven their skills at agile development and the results of their work are to be carefully scrutinized. The most effective way to do this is to examine the team's overall behavior and two elements of the team's product output:

1. Sprint review results
2. Continuous integration impact

We can look at the team's sprint review results to see if the team finished any stories during the sprint. It's important not to worry too much about *how much work* got done in the first couple sprints; instead, focus on the *quality of the work*. If the team is completing work and their story acceptance criteria are sufficiently detailed and rigorous, the team's sprint review results should be considered to be positive.

Regardless, however, of the quality of the completed work, we also have to be very concerned about the quality of the slices of work being added to the product code base during the sprint. Even new scrum teams should be putting code and tests in the product code base at least once a day (this number should increase to several times a day as the team matures, but initially the number will be relatively small). More importantly, you will need to be sure that when code is pushed to the product code base, the team's contributions do not cause repeated failures in the continuous build and test process that the product code base should be going through on a constant basis. If a team repeatedly stops the continuous build and test process, they may not fully understand the concepts of test-driven development or quality infusion through story agreements.

In terms of the team's overall behavior, just because you put them together on a team doesn't mean that the members will work well together. If you see significant conflicts within the team, consider taking it apart and starting over, or identifying the problem team members and trying them on a new team in the near future.

In any case, should a team prove to be a problem during the probationary period, the following must occur to ensure that their problems do not spread to other, successful teams:

1. A coach must be assigned to the team for the next sprint to help with every step of the sprint.
2. A retrospective, facilitated by someone outside the team, must be held to review the exact details of the team's issues and determine both root causes and a course of action to correct.
3. If the team is overloaded in order to provide experienced team members to another new team, those temporary team members usually should not be allowed to move to their new teams until the team successfully completes at least one successful sprint.

Summary

The training plan is a pivotal aspect of the overall transition plan. It is linked closely with the transition schedule and, when well executed, creates the foundation of a successful transition. We start with the roles that we need in our projects, determine the skills that each role requires, and then build our training modules around the roles. The training plan is also tied closely to how teams are created, such that training is offered to all who are going to participate on the agile project and the training cycle is repeated continuously as long as there are more teams to create. During each cycle, the training is assessed and improved for the next round.

In addition to the classes and coaching, teams should also be overloaded with one or two temporary members that spend one sprint with their initial team to learn and be coached; those members can then move to their permanent teams when those teams are created and act as semiexperienced members for the rest of the team.

Newly created Scrum teams, even with the coaching and training provided, are still considered to be probationary until they are able to complete two or three sprints where their sprint review results show a solid trend of work being complete in a manner consistent with each feature's acceptance criteria and the team's interim deliveries to the product code base do not cause repeated failures in the product's continuous build and test process.

By following the training plan and ensuring that Scrum teams are understanding and using the concepts they are taught during the training, you can ensure that you install not only the proper concepts and skills, but also the right behaviors needed in order for your transition to agile development to be successful.

Endnote

1. Find more information at http://www.bigagiledevelopment.com/trainingplan.

Chapter 14

Facilities Planning

To some extent, it almost seems extreme to be talking about modifying your facilities in order to introduce a software development method. However, as has been and will be stated several times in this book, agile development focuses on people producing software that satisfy customer needs. In order to create the best environment we can to support effective software development, we have to change much of the thinking of the past that puts software developers alone or in pairs into offices and cubicles (refer to Figure 14.1).

Software development teams work best when they are co-located. They need to be able to work together, ask each other questions, bounce ideas off of one another, and to be able to do all of these things without necessarily having a scheduled time to do so. In many organizations, we stifle the creative possibilities of our development teams by separating them. Then when they need to get together to meet, they are confronted with scheduling hassles that create unnecessary delays in our projects and do even more damage to our developers' creativity. By creating team rooms for our Scrum teams, we encourage creativeness, teamwork, innovation, and imagination, and we remove delays caused by unavailable rooms and trying to work important conversations into everyone's schedule.

This chapter reviews the many aspects of how the adoption of agile development in an organization may affect your facilities and the types of changes you may want to consider planning for. At a high level, we will be discussing the following:

- Team rooms: Where our Scrum teams will work.
- Server rooms: Where the servers needed to provide Scrum teams with independent development and testing environments will be set up.
- Private rooms: Where employees can be temporarily seated when necessary and where employees, typically in team rooms, can go for short periods of time to hold private meetings or handle private phone conversations.

Backlog Items

Create the facilities plan:

- Determine how many team rooms are needed.
- Determine whether or not server rooms are needed and, if so, how many.
- Locate space within which teams can be located.
- Locate space for server rooms to be created.
- Build initial server room.
- Create team room plan.
- Build initial team room.
- Create remaining team rooms and determine how to move personnel.
- Determine how the employee directory will be maintained.
- Determine how employee phones will be maintained.
- Determine plans for dealing with noise (if needed).

Figure 14.1 Slicing the "Create a Facilities Plan" transition backlog item.

Team Rooms

Team rooms are a key element in the successful implementation of agile development. Team rooms support the need for developers to work very closely together by removing any remaining walls or other obstructions that interfere with development progress. When creating a team room, one has to carefully consider several properties that help to make team rooms more and more effective for the developers that use them. We'll discuss many of those properties through the rest of this section.

Size

When planning the creation of team rooms, you will have to consider the number of people on your Scrum teams. Assuming that the organization will abide by the generally accepted practices that Scrum teams should be between five and nine people in size, you will be best served by creating team rooms that can easily support six people (for teams of five and six) and ten people (for teams between seven and nine). Team rooms of this size leave a little extra room for each team and also facilitate planning in large organizations by giving your floor space planning only two room types to deal with.

Location

When locating and organizing your team rooms, there are some additional factors that you will want to consider to improve your teams' experience. These include:

- *Traffic*: There are few things more distracting to a Scrum team than having their team room used as a shortcut to get from "here to there." Many Scrum teams adapt to team rooms by quickly interrupting themselves when someone walks in; there's an assumption that, if someone walks in the team room, he or she needs something from the team. When people simply "pass through," it becomes a major distraction. When planning for team rooms:
  - Consider whether team rooms can be limited to single entrances (unless, of course, not having the second or third entrance might create an unsafe situation).
  - Don't put team rooms near public entrances.
  - Create "hallways" between team rooms to encourage walking through them instead of through team rooms.
  - Label the entrances to team rooms with some kind of sign that says, "Hey! This is a team room." In organizations using a lot of modular walls to build team rooms, it is often difficult to tell the difference between an entrance to a team room and a passageway between team rooms until it's too late and you've already interrupted someone.
  - Establish a rule in your organization that team rooms are to be treated like offices. You don't just walk in unless you work there or need someone.
- *Natural lighting*: The International Labor Organization, an agency of the United Nations, advises that "the quality of lighting in a workplace can have a significant effect on productivity"[1] and "using daylight improves morale and is free."[2] Proper lighting reduces errors; helps to improve productivity; decreases eyestrain, headaches, nausea, and neck pain; and allows employees to concentrate better on their work. A rather interesting study of school children in Alberta, Canada, used four different kinds of lighting and tracked the benefits of classroom day-lighting.[3] They found:
  - Exposure to daylight resulted in better attendance (3.5 fewer days absent each year).
  - Day-lit libraries had significantly reduced noise levels, due to increased concentration levels among the children.
  - Day-lighting induced more positive moods, resulting in better scholastic performance.
- *Proximity to related teams*: While teams work better when they are co-located, it is also important to make sure that teams working on closely related software are placed in close proximity to one another. As these teams frequently have to work together to make design changes and improvements to their

application, you need to ensure that you reduce the walking time in between these teams. In addition to reducing unwanted movement (identified as waste in Lean software development), putting too much distance[4] between teams that frequently work together results in less efficient behaviors, like sending emails or using the phone to get answers.

Noise

There are two kinds of noise prevalent around team rooms: noise that comes from within the team room as a by-product of the team working, and noise that comes from outside the team room. Both can be quite disruptive to the team if there's too much noise or noise at the wrong time. Some of the noise can be reduced with noise-reducing modular wall panels and ceiling panels. White noise generators can reduce more noise. However, rather than implementing costly solutions up front (and white noise generators often cause more problems than they're worth), consider making the noise problem something that the teams have to solve on their own. In general, it is the teams that create noise as a by-product of working closely together. Part of the self-management that teams are supposed to exhibit is the ability to solve these types of problems.

Setting Up a Team Room

With your floor plans in place to build your team rooms, you'll then want to move on to thinking about how each team room will be configured and what kinds of supplies and materials you'll need. We'll talk about some of that in this section.

- *Configuration*: How will you set up the interior of the team room? Generally this is something you will want to leave to your teams. They will know best what they want their workplace to look like. However, you can give them some basic configurations upon which they can expand.
  - *Central table*: Sometimes, teams work around a central table, sitting along the sides of a table much like a family sitting down for dinner. This leaves a lot of wall space around the sides of the team and also puts everyone face-to-face, making conversation and working together that much easier. The disadvantages to this approach include the problem that some team members may have with a lack of privacy or a lack of working space. Also, the number of cables and wires that collect under a table in this situation can be quite a problem.
  - *Around the walls*: Some teams prefer to work at personal stations while having a table in the center of the room for meetings and work sessions. This works well for most teams, but can sometimes permit team members to disengage from the rest of the team.

In general, you can support both configurations by creating team rooms that support individual workstations, but with a large central table. If the team chooses to work around the table, provide the additional assistance to help them clean up the cables and keep them safe.

Keep in mind, of course, all pertinent regulations regarding occupational and fire safety to ensure that your team rooms are both safe and legal. Some great examples of team rooms can be found at http://www.xp123.com/xplor/room-gallery/index.shtml and http://www.scissor.com/resources/teamroom.

■ *What to put in the team room*: For a team room to be truly effective, there are a number of items you may want to consider ensuring are in it when the team moves in:

- *Wall space*: Teams are usually taught to use walls to keep track of their work. Teams will often use wall space for task boards (boards that show what the team is currently working on), storyboards (boards that show what work is due to be worked on in the near future), and burn-down or burn-up charts (graphs that illustrate the progress and trends of the team). Teams need a lot of clean, smooth space on which Post-it® notes will stick, or corkboard space on which index cards can be pinned.

- *Meeting table*: Discussed in previous paragraphs, this table should be long enough to support everyone on the team plus two or three more "guests" sitting at it at the same time.

- *White board*: White boards (or dry-erase boards) are invaluable tools for Scrum teams to do brainstorming, group design, etc. In addition, you should also consider having a number of digital cameras available to employees to take pictures of white boards in order to take the board content and preserve it.

- *Data projector*: Team members often have the need to show segments of code, text, or working software to the entire team at the same time. Sprint reviews are excellent examples of when this is needed. Some teams will also use data projectors to support code reviews, document reviews, and special presentations done by team members for the rest of the team. Data projectors often drastically reduce the amount of paper used by Scrum teams, reducing paper supply costs, copier costs, and time wasted by employees making and organizing copies preparatory to a team meeting.

- *Projection screen*: If your team will be using a data projector, they will also likely need a projection screen. In some cases, these can be hung from the ceiling, reducing the footprint of the screen when not in use.

- *Speakerphone*: Your team will likely need a speakerphone during the course of normal development to support meetings with remote customers or remote employees.

- *For remote employees*: If a team also has one or more members working remotely, you may wish to also provide one or more web cams in order to improve

communication and remote desktop sharing software to allow employees to access each other's desktops as needed (i.e., for pair programming).
- *Miscellaneous supplies*:
  - Post-it notes
  - Index cards and push pins
  - Dry-erase markers
- *Other options*: While not every option is good for every team, here are some additional features that many teams find add to their productivity:
  - Plants: A study[5] done with computer operators showed a twelve percent improvement in productivity when plants were present compared to when plants were not present.
  - Game tables: A small table in the room on which the team can build a puzzle, play chess or checkers, or board games.
  - Permanently projected electronic task board: A real disadvantage of backlog management tools that support online task boards is the fact that they are only visible when displayed. Some teams solve this problem with an old workstation with a keyboard, mouse, and a very large monitor (twenty-one inches or better). The workstation is always left displaying the task board. Team members take tasks, update statuses, and update hours remaining using the workstation.
  - Large monitors for developers' workstations: Some Scrum teams engage in an Extreme Programming (XP) practice known as pair programming. This requires two developers to sit side-by-side to write code. In order for this to be done without causing eye or neck strain, you may want to consider purchasing larger monitors than the typical fifteen- or seventeen-inch screens.

Employee Directories

When an organization gets large enough that it becomes impossible to know who everyone is and where everyone sits, the organization's first employee directory is created. When team rooms are implemented, you'll be faced with one or two new challenges. First, when the team rooms are initially built, your entire directory will have to be reworked. Instead of everyone having office numbers or cubicle numbers, many employees will now be located in team rooms. You'll have to find a way to number or name your team rooms, making the names easy to read by posting them outside the team room walls, and you'll need to find a way to make your team rooms easy to find.

The difficulty gets a little worse, however, if your organization begins to change team membership from time to time (as it should). When that begins, tracking employee location gets more and more problematic. Your organization will likely have to create a procedure that allows for the easy setting and resetting of employee location.

Employee Telephones

Similar to the problems with employees moving from team to team are the problems with the employee telephones. Moving employee telephones every time an employee moves from one location to another can be very expensive. Your organization may wish to look into voice-over-Internet-protocol (VOIP) systems or other options that allow employees to easily move their phone with them as they change teams.

Private Spaces

Part of your facilities planning should also result in the creation of several regular offices that can be used as quiet spaces when needed or for small meetings. These offices should have doors that when open, mean that the space is available, and when closed, mean that the space is in use. The office can be set up with basic furniture: a desk or table, two or three chairs, a white board, and a telephone or speakerphone.

Server Rooms

The final item to discuss in this chapter is the server room. While this is by no means a guaranteed portion of your facilities plan, agile development teams generally require development environments in which to test the application and at least one additional environment to support continuous application building and testing. When there are enough teams, it becomes more effective to build one or more secure rooms in which to place the servers. Even when there aren't many Scrum teams, each server that is not properly protected, from both a hardware and a software perspective, becomes a potential liability should the server be damaged or become unavailable. Each organization has to make this decision based on its willingness to manage the risk.

The Facilities Plan

This chapter is intended to give you an idea of what to expect when trying to decide what kinds of facility changes will be necessary during your transition to agile development. We've discussed team rooms, including how to configure, locate, and supply them. We've discussed private spaces and server rooms. We've discussed some of the problems you will have to deal with regarding employee directories and employee telephones. My hope is that the content of this chapter will help you create a more complete and comprehensive facilities plan.

Endnotes

1. "Lighting in the Workplace." http://www.ilo.org/public/english/protection/safework/hazardwk/ergono/lighting.pdf, p. 1.
2. Ibid., p. 2.
3. Hathaway, W. E., Hargreaves, J. A., Thompson, G. W., and Novitsky, D. *A Study Into the Effects of Light on Children of Elementary School Age: A Case of Daylight Robbery.* Edmonton, Alberta, Canada: Alberta Education, 1992.
4. Some have suggested that this distance can be as short as one hundred feet.
5. Pearson-Mims, C. H., and Lohr, V. I. Reported Impacts of Interior Plantscaping in Office Environments in the United States. *HortTechnology* 10 (2000): 82–86.

Chapter 15

Selecting the Pilot Projects for the Agile Transition

The first quality for a commander-in-chief is a cool head to receive a correct impression of things. He should not allow himself to be confused by either good or bad news.

Napoleon Bonaparte

Americans live in an interesting culture. We are a wary bunch, perhaps because the earliest pages of our history are written by individuals run out of their homelands due to their beliefs. Perhaps our reluctance to trust comes through our British roots: "First impressions are often the truest, as we find (not infrequently) to our cost, when we have been wheedled out of them by plausible professions or studied actions."[1] Wherever our wariness comes from, it is most succinctly stated in the more well-known phrase: "You never get a second chance to make a first impression." Blow your first chance and it's over.

Agile development, on the other hand, is about learning enough to take your first steps, learning from your successes and mistakes, and using that information to take your next step. In fact, a purely agile development saying goes like this: "Fail fast, fail often." This saying reflects a basic belief that agile developers hold that there is much more to be learned in failure (or, perhaps, mistakes) than in continuous success. Mistakes provide the raw materials for new ideas and new ways of doing things. Repeated success, over time, tends to limit the innovativeness of the product developers: "If it ain't broke, don't fix it."

This outlines the biggest problem that we have in the most crucial aspect of a successful transition to agile development. Agile projects aren't expected to be perfect from the start; they are expected to get better from sprint to sprint. However, if the organization's first impression of an agile project is that it failed, your organization's transition to agile development may come to a rapid conclusion for reasons that may have had little to nothing to do with agile development. You will hear phrases like "Agile won't work for us" and "Our environment is too complex for agile development."

The selection of a pilot project for a transition to agile is one of the most critical decisions that can be made early in the transition itself. I have, therefore, dedicated an entire chapter to this single topic.

In the selection of a pilot project, you will need to accomplish several tasks, each of which will be discussed in this chapter.

1. *Define your goals*: What is it you want to achieve with the pilot project? Is it simply how you plan to create your initial teams, or do you hope to learn something specific in a short period of time. By understanding your goals, you can make better pilot project selections.
2. *Set expectations*: What should the organization expect of this project? Will it produce code faster or is the focus elsewhere? Will the organization be abandoning any portion of the organization's quality processes in order to achieve real agility?
3. *Choose the best project to meet your goals*: How long of a project should be selected? What about staff size? What about the criticality of the project or the project's cost? How do these factors weigh in the final decision?
4. *Set your project up for success*: In order to make the best first impression that we can, we will want to not only select the best project, but also take steps that give that project the best chance of success that we can provide.

The rest of this chapter will review each of previously mentioned topics with the goal of giving you the information you will need to help your organization make the best decision possible when selecting a pilot project.

Define Your Goals

The first step in selecting a pilot project for the agile transition is to determine what, exactly, are the goals of the pilot in the first place. Pilot projects can be undertaken for a number of reasons. We might want to simply see if our training is effective by training the right people in the proper manner and then letting them start a project. We might want to uncover some of the organizational dysfunction that we're going to find during the transition, but in a more controlled manner and at a slower pace. Many pilot projects are nothing more than the beginning of a ramping-up process whereby more and more Scrum teams are added each month. The initial project, in this case, is unimportant, though it is still important to understand what you want out of your pilot project, even in this instance. In addition, understanding your goals helps you to understand something very important to agile developers: When are you done? In other words, when has the pilot project served its purpose and is considered complete?

When setting the goals for a pilot project, you must ask yourself a few questions:

1. *Why do we want to do this?* By asking this question, we hope to understand better what it is we want to prove by doing a pilot. Perhaps the organization is not satisfied with the rate at which projects are being completed and the pilot project is about measuring improvements in productivity. In difficult economic times, agile development is often positioned as a means by which more features can be produced with higher quality without changing current staffing levels. The organization may be uncomfortable with agile development for a variety of different reasons and management wants to see it in a smaller, controlled setting. Or, the organization may not be satisfied with the product quality and is looking to agile development to help improve it.

2. *What do we hope to learn?* In asking this question, we clarify the scope of potential pilot projects as we seek to determine whether or not the organization is even up to the challenge of performing a transition to agile development. Organizations want to know what kinds of challenges will be surfaced during the initial months of the transition. And of course, though most coaches will tell you that agile development will work with your organization, there are always the nagging doubts that agile development will be too vague or random or touchy-feely for the real world.

3. *How long will we wait for results?* As mentioned earlier, agile projects are geared toward continuous improvement. We learn enough to get started, take our first steps, and then use the information (good and bad) resulting from our first steps to take the next steps. Looking for productivity improvements from a Scrum team may take four to six months, at least (in fact, there's often a drop-off in productivity for a new Scrum team as they all learn how to embrace new roles). If you are looking for improvements in quality, it is not unusual for new defects to be found on new or changed code several months after the code was completed (even with a formal source code control system). How long is the organization willing to wait for results? Three months? Nine months? Longer? How long will the organization be patient before it begins tampering or fixing processes, or giving up entirely? By defining this length of time early, you can either pick a project that will be amenable to changes during the latter half of the project or short enough that it can finish before management begins to start changing agile practices.

4. *How much are we willing to spend?* If your pilot project is supposed to test the real environment, you will find it necessary to spend money on training your project personnel. This will possibly include training for your Scrum masters, product owner, team personnel, and some management. In addition, you may wish to add some coaching hours from an outside consultancy to help your teams understand what is expected of them and to give them ways to complete their work.

Next comes the issue of how much agile development will be done during the sprint. If your Scrum teams are doing nothing more than Scrum, you will want to ensure that there's enough money in the project budget to support rework in these areas and that you can afford to create one or two Scrum team rooms for the purposes of the pilot project.

Should you, however, find yourself in a situation where your Scrum teams will be instituting Extreme Programming (XP) practices, such as continuous integration and testing, and test-driven development (TDD), you may have to invest in new tools and new hardware to implement these practices. For example, continuous integration requires an environment in which your application software can be repeatedly built and tested automatically, twenty-four hours a day, seven days a week. While there's plenty of good, reliable, and free software to handle the building and testing,[2] you may need to find a clean machine (perhaps server quality) in which to actually run these CPU-intensive activities. Likewise, test-driven development may initially appear to make everything take longer (though you'll find that, if it's done right, the positive impact on quality and reduction in support time later in the development process makes it all worth it) and paired programming may require you to pick up some larger monitors for your developers' desktops or laptops in order for more than one person to easily see what is on the screen at the same time.

Set Organizational Expectations

Even with your goals set, it will still be very important to prepare your organization for what will happen while the pilot project is under way. Remember, the goals that you are trying to achieve will not magically occur during the first sprint of the project. More than likely, some bad things will occur before good things start to happen. By setting the organization's expectations up front, you can avoid some of the panic that might otherwise set in.

So, what are some of the expectations you'll want to set up front? Well, they will vary considerably based on the organization, the people, and the software being developed, but here are some of the common things you'll want to discuss within the organization:

- *Short-term decreases in productivity*: Any time you introduce new people, new practices, new tools, or new methods to an existing development situation, you can expect that there will be some loss in productivity as the team adapts to the new situation. New people on the team will require training and coaching from an experienced team member, and the time spent results in a loss of productivity. Learning how to use new tools, and cleaning up the messes made from using them wrong, can result in significant losses of productivity.
- *Lots of questions and "retakes"*: As the pilot progresses, the team may discover reasons that would lead them to wanting to modify the Scrum process to fix (or rather, hide) an organizational problem. This may lead to frustration and arguments within the team and from the product owner. It will have many of the characteristics of Bruce Tuckman's team storming phase,[3] where the team has difficulty working together and reaching consensus on a variety of ideas, including how to design software and how to use Scrum and other agile methods.
- *Some deviations from established quality practices or company standards*: As the Scrum team strives to improve their use of Scrum and agile development, there will be "collisions" with established quality practices or company standards. Agile development encourages challenging the status quo and, often, will cause teams to question the existence of company standards or quality practices when they do not perceive the value in the standard or practice. Discussion between team members and your organization's management regarding these disagreements should be encouraged. There are many stories of company and quality policies existing for so long that the reasons for their original creation were no longer valid. Policies and standards that seem like they are obsolete should be closely examined*; they should be changed or dropped as needed. For the purposes of the pilot project, try to err on the side of the pilot project and, at minimum, temporarily change or suspend practices or standards if the pilot project might benefit. You can always decide

---

* The best example of obsolete standards that I know of comes from the reasons for the distance between the rails of U.S. railroad tracks. It is a precise 4 feet 8½ inches. The reason for this unusual measurement comes from the fact that English railroads were built the same way, and it was English expatriates that built the first U.S. railroads. Of course, the English built their railroads that way because that's how they built the prerailroad tramways (used in mining and logging operations), which were built that way because the jigs and tools used by those who built the tramway cars were also used to build wagons and that's how far apart the wagon wheels were. The wagon wheels had that unusual spacing because if they were farther apart or closer together, they would break on old, long-distance roads because of the spacing of the wheel ruts in the old roads. The old roads were built by Imperial Rome—it was their chariots that formed the initial ruts in the roads. The spacing between the wheels of the chariot was a standard set by Imperial Rome because it was the rough total distance of two Roman warhorses standing side-by-side. So, the 4-foot-8½-inch width of today's railroads is based on the width of the rear ends of two Roman warhorses standing side-by-side. It is easy to set a standard and then get stuck with it.

later to reinstate the changed or suspended policies or standards later in the pilot project or at its conclusion.

The pilot project may also produce results that leave room to interpret good outcomes in a negative light. For example, what will your organization think when:

- The pilot project team discovers major errors in design early in the project? The good news is that the team discovered the error before it could be built into the product. The bad news is that the design changes will result in significant delays bringing the project to completion. From a software engineering perspective, finding the design flaws early in the project is considerably less expensive than finding it in the product at a customer site. This is the type of thing that we would want to encourage. However, from the business standpoint, the appearance may be that the design was fine until the pilot project began.
- The pilot project team produces fewer lines of code each sprint, but it becomes clear during independent testing that the quality of the application is significantly improved? The good news, clearly, is that the quality of the software has been improved. The bad news is that perceived/interpreted productivity dropped as soon as the pilot project began. How will this be by your organization?
- The pilot project team, charged with finding the obstacles to the agile transition, succeeds quite well, finding problem after problem? At what point does the organization blame the problems on the pilot project and not on the likely fact that the pilot project is simply surfacing obstacles that had been in existence all along? Organizations, even those willing to change how they develop software, have a limited tolerance to being exposed to all of the obstacles that exist within themselves. At some point, there is a natural tendency to want to blame some external force (in this case, agile development and the pilot project) for the problems.
- The pilot project team, dealing with unrealistic timeframes and software that tends to be quite buggy, is unsuccessful in completing anything close to what is hoped during the course of a sprint? The bad news, of course, is that the team isn't making any progress getting the product features built. On the other hand, neither were teams prior to trying to use agile development. There is clearly no good news here. But what does the organization see? That the pilot project team was unsuccessful, or that they had a Herculean task set for them in the first place?

The answer here is to set expectations with everyone even remotely involved with the pilot project and to continue to communicate (and interpret) ongoing results. One way of doing this is to clearly define what it means to hold a successful pilot. What kinds of outcomes are you expecting to see, and how will you interpret those outcomes during and after each sprint in the project? Here are some of the questions you should ask yourself when defining success for the pilot project:

- Which do you value more: quality or quantity?
  - In other words, which is more valuable: less functionality with higher quality or more functionality with the same or less quality? This will help you understand which—quality or quantity—is more important.
- Are you hoping to find obstacles, or hoping that none will be found?
  - Some pilot projects are started to see how well the organization performs (in a small space) within the existing organization. This helps the transition team understand what will need to be addressed before any large projects get started. If you are hoping that no obstacles are found during the project, your assumption is probably that your organization is already pretty lean and agile is begin implemented in order to achieve additional gains.
- Are you hoping to perfect the process during the project, or just get a handle on what works?
  - If you're hoping to perfect the process, there's going to be a lot more focus during the sprints on identifying and correcting broken practices and standards and a bit less focus on getting software done. You might also be more willing to extend the project until the organization agrees that significant gains in removing waste have been achieved.
- If the project falls behind schedule will you cancel the pilot or keep going until it is finished?
  - This is almost a trick question; agile projects don't have a predefined schedule. Progress is made based on the established velocity of the teams. If your expectation is that a predetermined project schedule should drive the teams' activities, try to redefine the pilot to simply run for a predefined period of time, regardless of what gets finished. Evaluate the project success on how development occurred, not how fast.
- Which do you value more: the project timeframes or the completed functionality?
  - This is a follow-up to the previous question. Which do you want more: that the teams stick to a specific schedule or that they produce working functionality? If any portion of the organization is insisting on keeping to a predefined schedule, try to reset expectations before beginning the pilot.
- Under what conditions would you consider the pilot to be a failure?
  - Is there a point at which you or the organization would cancel the pilot altogether, considering it a failure and moving away from agile development? What are those conditions? Can you mitigate them in some way? Are they appropriate?

Now, define success. Your definition will usually include some discussion of the use of Scrum and agile methods, the creation of the product backlog, the definition of roles and responsibilities, how the overall process is improved, and of course, making progress in the completion of new or updated features. At first glance, it may appear that your goals and your definition of success are the same thing. However, while they are related in that your definition of success should support and clarify the goals that you set for the project, the definition of success also gives you an opportunity to address expectations. For example, one project's definition of success might look like this:

> The pilot project will include four sprints, each sprint set to one calendar month in length. The team will be co-located in a conference room for the duration of the project. By the end of the project, we will have completed the following:
>
> 1. All team members will have been properly trained to fulfill the requirements of their role.
> 2. The Scrum method will be initially applied in terms of roles, meetings, and artifacts as defined in "Agile Software Development with Scrum."
> 3. Obstacles will be recorded on an impediments list by the teams' Scrum master and will be worked during the project and reviewed during sprint retrospectives.
> 4. The Scrum teams may make standards and process changes during the sprint, but the nature and reasons for such changes must be reviewed and approved by appropriate personnel during sprint retrospectives.
> 5. The Scrum teams will make as much progress as possible in completing items on the project's product backlog. The project length will not be enough to determine velocity, and therefore, teams are to complete as much as they effectively can.

This definition of success, while driven by the project goals, also clarifies the expectation that the team is to focus on putting agile development in motion and identifying and solving impediments while also getting as much of the product backlog done as possible. There is less of a focus on developing features and more of a focus on implementing agile development. You could, of course, create a pilot project with a completely different definition of success, as follows:

> The pilot project will include six sprints, each sprint set to one calendar month in length. The team will be co-located in a conference room for the duration of the project. By the end of the project, we will have completed the following:
>
> 1. All of the content identified for inclusion in release 2.2 will be completed. Progress will be reviewed and discussed at each sprint review to determine if the team's velocity is sufficient and, if not, how to improve it.

2. The Scrum method will be initially applied in terms of roles, meetings, and artifacts as defined in "Agile Software Development with Scrum."
3. The teams' Scrum master will record obstacles on an impediments list, but only critical impediments will be addressed. All others will be reviewed at the end of the pilot.
4. Key team members will have been properly trained to fulfill the requirements of their roles and will coach others to ensure that all team members have been educated.
5. The Scrum teams may not deviate from company standards and quality policies. These standards and policies exist for reasons that are verified annually. Scrum teams should incorporate tasks made necessary by company standards and quality policies during sprint planning.

In this version of the project's definition of success, there is a clear focus on getting a software release completed and ready for customer use by the end of the project. An organization with a definition of success such as this is evidently focused on ensuring itself that agile development does not jeopardize the company's ability to produce a product release. In addition, this definition defers the reviewing of all noncritical defects until after the project and restricts the Scrum teams from making any changes to existing standards or quality policies (since those standards and policies are being reviewed on an annual basis, it makes sense that the organization would expect that they would not change because of agile development).

Both definitions are equally valid and both represent the legitimate concerns of two different organizations—one that is focused on the process and willing (to some degree) to sacrifice delivery dates, and one that is willing to adapt to agile development but not willing to change software delivery dates that may have already been announced to their customers. Your organization may be like one of these, or may be somewhere in between. While most organizations will be more than willing to set the pilot project goal to something like "Test out Scrum and XP practices to prove that they will work in our organization," when you start defining what that really looks like in terms of what the organization is willing to negotiate, you will get a much clearer picture of what kind of a project you want to select in order to begin your piloting effort.

Selecting Your Pilot Project

Determining your goals and definition of success will help you make a good selection for a pilot project. However, let's discuss some common elements of projects that make them good pilot choices first. Good candidates for pilot projects are:

■ Small staff sizes: Because the pilot project is all about learning and applying new skills, dealing with unexpected impediments, and trying to create good working environments for Scrum teams, you will find that a project that has no more than twenty development personnel assigned to it is easier to manage. The additional administrative and logistical overhead introduced by larger staff sizes does not contribute much value to the outcome of a pilot project.

■ Short duration: Pilot projects are intended to be tests of new methods or new tools (sometimes both). The idea is to put the new methods in action, observe, and then decide what to do. Projects that last between three and six months provide ample opportunity to experiment and work out most of the major problems. Projects that run longer than six months tend to delay the decision to move forward with the agile transition and provide very little new information after the first few months. Remember, the purpose of a pilot project is to see how agile development will work and what types of changes you may have to make in your organization. Pilot projects are not intended to resolve all of the problems of your transition.

■ Spotlighted: Pilot projects need to be noticed. They should have an impact on your organization. Creating a pilot project around a little used, little known internal utility will not garner the lasting attention and appreciation of senior and executive management. A successful pilot project should both satisfy the definition of success and have an impact on your organization's bottom line. Will customers be happy when the project is successfully completed? Will anybody care?

Now that we've identified some good candidate projects, let's trim the list by reviewing our goals and definition of success. Here are some guidelines that you can use to help select a good pilot project:

If your organization values working software over evaluating agile development, you should strongly consider projects that:

■ Develop mature products that are already stable and of good quality. This will help ensure that the team is not bogged down in fixing defects and working with brittle code.

■ Have a lot of product expertise available in the organization to help answer questions and make decisions. Mature products often result in a number of individuals in the organization that understand the products and their users quite well. Having these people available, in addition to the product owner, can help ensure that the team does not get stuck in drawn-out discussions to make critical decisions.

■ Are focused on major releases of functionality. Small updates of mature products do not tend to get a lot of attention from senior and executive management. Go with a project that will produce something new and exciting in the mature product; a successful pilot will succeed both by beginning the agile transition and by putting out a new key feature—not a bad start for your transition.

If your organization values the evaluation of agile development practices over working software, you should strongly consider projects that:

- Develop a new product. New products have a lot of room for negotiation in how features are implemented, and there are no preconceived ideas about what the product is supposed to look like (except, maybe, in the head of your product owner). This maximizes the potential of Scrum and agile development practices to truly explore the possibilities of the product while developing the product iteratively. This allows the product owner (and senior/executive management) to see pieces of the new product early and improve the design as you go. There's no better advertisement for the advantages of agile development than this.

- Have a strong proponent in the organization. The trouble with new products is that we sometimes lack proper guidance and a clear vision of the product's direction. The development of a new product will be nearly impossible to do with any efficiency without a good, strong product owner that can guide the Scrum teams' efforts.

If you have projects to choose from for your pilot, consider what we've covered in this section. While some projects make good candidates for piloting, others certainly do not.

Before we continue, one final note on selecting a good candidate project for your pilot: Talk with the managers and developers that will be part of your first or second choice for the pilot. Are they excited about the opportunity? Are they critical but willing to keep an open mind? Or, are they critical, convinced that agile development "won't work here." People are your project's biggest asset or your greatest liability. Make sure you make the choice that improves your chances for success. Other than people, there are a number of obstacles that can reduce any project's chances for success. If you are prepared for these obstacles, you can take steps to remove them before they cause a serious problem. We'll discuss the obstacles to a successful pilot in the next section.

Obstacles to a Successful Pilot Project

No matter how good a choice you make in your project selection, all you've really done is mitigated some of the major risks inherent in the success or failure of any project. There are many more potential obstacles for which you need to be prepared. We'll discuss a number of them in this section.

Dysfunctions Come with the Territory

As any Scrum trainer or coach will tell you, understanding Scrum is easy, but implementing it is hard. When you implement Scrum and agile methods in a pilot project, there is often an expectation that Scrum is a sort of silver bullet that will solve a number of organizational problems and speed your project along to a successful delivery. However, the truth is that all successful Scrum projects start with a period of time during which many of an organization's dysfunctional processes are raised and fixed. Part of the success of Scrum, in fact, is the removal of waste from the development process. Implementing Scrum will not remove the dysfunctions that come with the organization. Whether it's a security process that results in a two-week delay during which your teammates cannot access a particular database, or a procurement process that results in a three-month delay before a new server can be delivered, Scrum will ensure that these impediments are brought to the attention of the Scrum master, the team, and probably management as well. Your job will be managing the expectations of the organization so that everyone realizes that the identification and removal of these dysfunctions is part of how Scrum works.

Team Co-location

Even if you choose the perfect pilot project, if rooms, floors, buildings, cities, or even oceans separate the team members, communication between them will be impeded to some degree. This will negatively impact all team activities. You will need to take additional steps to improve communication as much as possible. Installation of web cams, speakerphones, and team collaboration tools are a good start. Bringing the team members together for the duration of the project would be ideal.

Lack of Expertise or Necessary Skills

If the project you choose comes with a staff that lacks the proper skills or any experts on the product, you may want to spend some initial time, prior to actual development, getting the developers the requisite training they need to be effective with the product. Asking your developers to learn new methods, new tools, *and* a new product at the same time will create a very frustrating experience and will likely have a substantial negative impact on the success of your project.

Improper Development Metrics

Many organizations measure progress and productivity based on the number of lines of code produced or other metrics based on the amount of code produced.

Agile development, on the other hand, focuses on completed and working functionality rather than how many lines of code were written to complete the function. By measuring our developers improperly, we unwittingly invite unwanted behaviors into the Scrum team that will negatively affect the performance of the team. In general, all development metrics, save those included in the project's definition of success, should be suspended for the duration of the pilot project in order to ensure that they do not affect the outcome of the project.

In this section, we've covered some of the obstacles that can have a detrimental effect on the success of your pilot project. In the next section, we'll discuss some things you can do to help ensure success.

Setting Your Project Up for Success

Given how critical the pilot project is to the success of your Agile transition, it only makes sense that you would want to do whatever was reasonable to ensure success. In this section, we'll discuss some of the things you can do to improve the odds of success.

People First

First, and most importantly, remember that Scrum is not a development method! Scrum is a method for organizing work and making teams of people more efficient. *Always focus on the people and let the process emerge.* From how quickly they learn and adapt to the new practices and new tools to the respect and commitment they give to one another in putting the team first and the individual second, people will drive the success or failure of your pilot project. People that are convinced that agile development will not work will make sure, consciously or subconsciously, that the pilot project does not succeed. Conversely, dedicated team members that have bought into what Scrum and agile development are all about will internalize the concepts quickly and, instead of complaining about things that go wrong, will always be on the lookout for solutions to new problems.

In addition, I also mentioned "let the process emerge." In too many instances, I have seen organizations try to solve problems with processes and standards that really only resulted from misunderstandings and poor training. Processes need to be defined around the developers and the products, not vice versa. Start with the most basic process you need to get the job done (of course, if you are building a heavily regulated product, like a medical device or air traffic control software, you will have a lot of regulatory requirements that you will have to translate into a minimal set of process steps) and try it out. You will have ample opportunities during sprint retrospectives to review the existing process and revise it accordingly.

Everyone Needs to Know Their Job

Training is critical when introducing Scrum and agile development to an organization. In particular, Scrum relies on a clear separation of responsibilities and accountability that is defined in the roles that it includes (e.g., Scrum master, product owner, team member). When everyone knows his or her job, there is less likelihood of confusion and unnecessary adaption of practices. Make sure that everyone that participates in the pilot project receives the proper training. In fact, you may even want to restrict participation in the project to only those who have completed the training.

Include management in as much training as you can get them to attend. At minimum, managers must understand that the critical role they play in an agile project is making sure that the Scrum teams within their sphere of influence have everything they need to get the job done, that no obstacles are left unsolved, and that any conflicts that escalate outside the team are resolve quickly and effectively.

Introduce XP Practices Carefully

While Scrum is an effective tool for making teams of people efficient, most organizations combine Scrum with XP in order to improve software quality and help improve productivity beyond what Scrum alone accomplishes. This means that your pilot project might also include test-driven development (TDD), pair programming, and continuous integration and testing, among other possibilities. You may find that introducing all of Scrum and all of the XP practices all at once is too much for your teams to focus on and use effectively. All of these concepts are more than skills, they are new behaviors; new behaviors take time to be appreciated and internalized by your developers. Try starting your pilot project and introducing Scrum and, perhaps, pair programming.[4] In the second Sprint, you can begin introducing continuous integration by setting up the continuous integration server, doing builds, and running whatever automated tests exist at the current time. Then, introduce test-driven development to augment the tests running in the continuous integration server. However you do it, introduce these skills one or two at a time. Let your team learn, practice, and begin to master the skill before you introduce another.

Get a Good Product Owner

In an organization with established agile skills and Scrum-based projects, with experienced developers and strong Scrum masters, a bad product owner can turn an effective team into a frustrated and ineffective mess. Obviously, this is not something you want to happen to your pilot project. So, even if there are individuals in your organization that know your product better, your product owner must also be able to clearly communicate the product vision, resolve conflicts among team members, and be available to your Scrum teams.

Whether or not your product owner derives the product vision from discussion with several experts and managers or does it on his or her own, the key is that the product owner needs to be able to effectively communicate this vision to the Scrum team. When the team has a clear idea of the product vision, they become much more effective at estimating and completing product backlog items.

When team members disagree over how to resolve issues with backlog items, the product owner needs to be able to step in and resolve the problem with a clear and consistent answer and in a way that preserves everyone's self-respect.

Scrum teams need constant access to their product owner to clarify questions about backlog items. They need input during backlog grooming workshops, during sprint planning, during sprint reviews, and during most days of the sprint. If the product owner is available, the team can complete backlog items at a rapid pace and be quite successful. If the product owner is difficult to get in touch with or does a poor job answering questions, your team could find itself frustrated, angry, and worse, completely unable to complete backlog items. For a successful pilot project, a good product owner makes all the difference in the world.

Keep It Visible

No matter what, you don't want your pilot project to be perceived as hiding anything. Agile development is intended to be open and visible to all in the organization. At the beginning of the pilot project, determine how (and how often) you will communicate pilot project progress to management and stick to it. The expectation should be that there will be problems, obstacles, and false starts during the pilot project. Therefore, be clear, and leave little room for doubt that you've communicated the entire and complete status—the good and the not so good.

Never Skip the Retrospective

There is an underlying assumption when you begin the pilot project that things won't go perfectly. There will be organizational obstacles, problems with how the Scrum method is applied, difficulties with how the backlog is managed, and so on. Problems and inefficiencies can appear at any time and as a result of any action that the team or the organization takes. This is to be expected and is why you should never skip the sprint retrospective.

The sprint retrospective is an opportunity for the team to look at what they accomplished during the previous sprint and discuss ways to identify and proliferate the good things and improve the things that could have gone better. If the team doesn't like the way the daily Scrums went, they can suggest better ways. If they don't like how the task board was updated, they can change it. If they thought the backlog grooming workshops could have been better, they can improve them. But, more than that, the sprint retrospective is also a good opportunity to examine the pilot project itself and decide what kinds of changes to make. Was the training that everyone took sufficient, or was there anything that caught employees by surprise? Was the product owner available enough, or does the team need more help? Are there company standards or quality practices that interfered with meeting the goals of the sprint? Are there too many new practices being introduced at the same time (i.e., does the team need more time to get better at Scrum before introducing, for instance, test-driven development)?

When the team identifies things that went well, there should be a general awareness that they want to keep doing those things. On the other hand, retrospective meeting attendees analyze activities that could have gone better to determine why they were deficient and how they will be improved. The findings of a sprint retrospective during the pilot project should be organized as:

1. A list of three or four items that the Scrum teams will carry into the next sprint in order to improve performance
2. A list of items about the pilot project that will be reviewed by the transition team in order to improve how the organization adapts to agile development.

The Scrum teams are responsible for taking their part of the retrospective findings and making those actions a part of their next sprint. The team responsible for the agile transition is responsible for taking the remaining findings and making the appropriate changes to organizational process and practices. For example, if the team determines that the test-driven development training missed some major points, the agile transition team should take that input and modify the test-driven development training.

As with everything else in agile development, you take your best shot. Evaluate the results, make the proper changes, and make sure that everyone knows what changes were made—and then try again. That's the true power of the sprint!

Summary

The pilot project is a tool for seeing how agile development works in your organization, for seeing what kinds of changes you may have to make, and to prove to those in your organization who might not yet be totally convinced that agile development is the right move. In order to improve your odds of being successful, try the following steps:

Set your goals: Understand why you are doing the pilot project and what it is you hope to learn.
Set the organization's expectations: Pilot projects are not always about getting software written. Frequently they are about the training, the organization, and the people. Make sure that the organization understands the goals and priorities of the project so that there's no misunderstandings or miscommunications with regard to the status and success of the project.

Pick the right project for the pilot: You wouldn't use a hammer to swat a fly, right? It is equally important to pick the right project for the pilot. Pilot projects should not take more than six months and generally shouldn't have more than twenty people on staff. Projects that take too long simply delay the transition without good cause. Projects that have more than twenty people on staff tend to create overcomplicated situations that dilute the focus from the important goals of the pilot.

Set your project up for success: Even if you pick the best project in your organization to be your pilot project, you still will want to do everything you can to improve the odds of success. First, focus on people and let the process emerge from the pilot. People are the difference between success and failure. Process should never be the priority in the pilot—start with a basic approach to agile development and Scrum, and let process changes and improvements emerge from the sprint retrospective efforts. Second, communicate constantly to all stakeholders in the organization. Be clear, consistent, and comprehensive. Don't hide the failures (they're good—we learn from them), and shout loudly about your successes (they're pretty good too)!

Use retrospection to review what's worked and what hasn't. Take the good things and remind people repeatedly to do that again. Take the things that need improvement, figure out how to improve them, and do it. Your pilot's first sprint will not be its best, but doing retrospectives on a regular basis will help ensure that it gets better quickly.

Endnotes

1. William Hazlitt (1778–1830) was an English writer who is remembered for his humanistic essays and literary criticism. Hazlitt was a prominent English literary critic, grammarian, and philosopher.
2. I recommend Fitnesse (http://www.fitnesse.org/) for automated functional testing, Selenium (http://selenium.seleniumhq.org/) for automated user interface (UI) testing, and either CruiseControl (http://cruisecontrol.sourceforge.net/) or Hudson (https://hudson.dev.java.net/) for automated scheduling of builds and for kicking off your tests.
3. Bruce Tuckman (1938–) is a psychologist specializing in the study of group dynamics. He formalized a model of team development in "Developmental Sequence in Small Groups" in 1965. The model has been very accurate in its depiction of team dynamics and has been only slightly modified since its creation.
4. Pair programming is a good choice for early introduction because it doesn't require that everyone on the team do it all the time. The more you do it, the better you get, but unlike continuous integration, it doesn't affect everyone as soon as you introduce it.

Chapter 16

Tools in the Agile Enterprise

Give us the tools and we will finish the job.

Winston Churchill

Agile development recognizes the reality that we often do not have a clear idea of what we need to build until after we start building it. For agile developers, this means that we will frequently be building software based on the best information we have at the time. As we complete pieces of functionality, we show our customers and users in the hopes that, on seeing what's been created, that they will be able to further elaborate a direction for us to continue. The natural result of building software in this manner is that we will not always have a clear picture of what the completed software application will look like until late in its construction. This means that we will often refactor our software to remove unnecessary logic and to improve efficiencies between the new code and the rest of the existing system.

The continuous integration of new code with preexisting code means that our code base will be under constant modification, which places both our developers and our software in a somewhat stressed situation. Software in an agile environment requires constant monitoring while it is under development in order to ensure that it continues to work as expected. Developers in an agile environment require a continuous stream of information, helping them keep track of the latest intelligence from their customers and users to ensure that they continue to build software that meets the customers' current requirements and guidelines. Software development tools help us to fulfill the needs of both the monitoring of software and the providing of a continuous stream of information to our developers.

Software development tools improve agile development by automatically handling mundane tasks. For example, some tools help coders refactor lines of software by providing functions that automatically modify code based on coders' instructions. Most modern integrated development environments (e.g., Eclipse™, NetBeans, Microsoft® Visual Studio®) provide refactoring tools that can remove iterated code from a larger routine, place it in a new function, and then modify the original routine to call the new function. Other tools automate the continuous building and rebuilding of a product and automatically kick off unit and functional tests when the build is successful. Still others support Scrum teams by providing backlog management, sprint management, and automated reporting.

Software development tools also assist agile developers by speeding up complex tasks and, through automation, making those tasks far less apt to fail due to human error. A perfect example of this is scripting tools like Ant, which provide a means by which Java™ applications can be automatically and repeatedly built. By automating these processes, we not only remove the possibility of unexpected human error forcing us to redo the work later, but also reduce the cost of many tasks by removing the human developer from the equation.

Tools improve progress and status reporting by creating consistency across all teams in a project. Teams update task and item status on a daily basis, and reporting tools remove much of the work required to turn that information into useful and up-to-date statuses for project and organizational management.

Tools also go a long way toward removing some of the barriers introduced when all team members are not in the same location. For example, online story and task boards (displays that help team members understand what stories and tasks are being worked on in the current sprint, provide the means for team members to assign themselves to tasks, and allow team members to update task status) are a must for teams that are not co-located. These electronic boards provide a way for teams to stay up-to-date with one another and give everyone something to reference during daily Scrum meetings so that everyone understands what everyone else is talking about during a conference call.

With all the good that tools can do to help agile developers, there are good reasons (beyond just the cost of the tool and the support that comes with it) to be concerned when planning to add a tool to your development system. Some of those reasons are:

- Tools need to add value to what your teams do.
- Tools should complement process, not override it.
- Tools usually introduce a standard of usage; you will need to take time to get everyone on board. Improper usage can lead to incorrect reporting and additional time spent fixing what was done wrong.

First, and most importantly, put your people first when considering a tool. There are a lot of good tools out there, but you shouldn't be considering them unless you can determine that having the tool will add more value than the cost of implementing it (your best bet in finding this out is by polling your teams and finding out if they see value in the tool you are proposing). When you implement a tool, there are a lot of hidden and not so hidden costs. After the tool is purchased and installed, you will need to determine the best way to use the tool for your environment. This may be quite easy to do, or it may be a trial-and-error process with a couple of teams piloting the tool to see what happens (which also adds to the cost of the tool). Once the decisions have been made regarding the tool and how to use it, you will then need to put together the materials and training needed to roll out how the tool is to be used by all of the Scrum teams. Lastly, you'll also need to monitor usage of the tool (both statistically and by talking with team members that use the tool) to ensure that it is being used properly and is, in fact, providing value to your Scrum teams.

Second, tools need to complement your existing processes, not override them. In an agile environment, processes are built as needed from a fundamental process skeleton, changing and maturing from sprint to sprint as your organization and your Scrum teams determine they need to be changed. When evaluating tools, you must take into account the existing process. Bringing in the wrong tool could completely invalidate the current process, forcing your teams to somehow reconcile a process that they've built with a process introduced by an outside party (i.e., the tool vendor). Aside from the fact that this may have a demoralizing effect on your Scrum teams, it may also result in your teams being unable or unwilling to use the tool properly. Ideally, you should seek out tools that are flexible in their usage and can be made to easily adapt to your processes rather than forcing your processes and your teams to adapt to the tool.

The rest of this chapter will review some of the common types of tools that you might decide to use. Some of the common requirements of these tools are provided as well. Where possible, examples of effective tools are listed for you to consider.

Continuous Integration/Build

Because of the way software is undergoing continuous changes in agile development, it is important that we ensure that the software continues to successfully build. Building the software once a day is fine, but the sooner your developers know that the software doesn't build, the faster the problem can be isolated and corrected. But of course, having someone manually run these builds opens the possibility for no one running the builds.

Requirements

Before implementing continuous builds, the product build must be completely automated; no human intervention can be required.

The minimum requirements for a continuous integration tool are as follows:

1. The tool must be able to initiate the product build automatically.
2. The tool must be able to automatically save build results for a period of four weeks and allow reports to be retrieved and reviewed.
3. The tool must be able to alert someone immediately if the build fails.

Sample Products

Good tools for continuous integration include:

- Ant (http://ant.apache.org): This build tool is a much more flexible approach to building Java application. It supports the creation of repeatable processes that support complete automation of the build process.
- CruiseControl (http://cruisecontrol.sourceforge.net): This tool supports continuous integration and works very well with Ant.
- Hudson (https://hudson.dev.java.net/): This tool supports continuous integration.

Automated Testing

As mentioned earlier in the chapter, agile development creates a certain degree of stress on software because the software is continuously being updated. Because of this situation, it is necessary to continuously test the software, both when new features are added and on an ongoing basis, to ensure that some other unexpected change doesn't cause the existing code base to break down. Clearly, it is too expensive and too ineffective to have someone manually testing your product twenty-four hours a day, seven days a week. Automated testing tools are among the most common tools used by agile and nonagile developers alike.

Requirements

The minimum requirements for an automated testing tool are as follows (and just for the exercise, I've written them as user stories with Rachel Davies'[1] template):

1. As an agile developer, I want all of the functional and unit tests to be run whenever the code base changes automatically and continuously against my product so that I know that my product still works.
2. As an agile developer, I want to be able to look at two weeks of test run results so that I can see a history of test successes and failures.
3. As an agile developer, I want to be informed by email whenever a test run fails so that I can quickly fix what broke and run the tests again.

Sample Products

Good tools for automated testing include:

- Fitnesse (http://www.fitnesse.org): This wiki-based product allows you to very easily build functional tests in a format that is clearly self-documenting. Fitnesse can be combined with tools like CruiseControl or Hudson to run functional tests on a schedule or continuously.
- Selenium (http://selenium.seleniumhq.org): This product does a pretty good job of user-interface (UI) testing and can be combined with Fitnesse to identify test cases and CruiseControl or Hudson to run functional tests on a schedule or continuously.

Sprint and Backlog Management

As projects get larger and larger and there are more Scrum teams working and more product backlogs to work with, it becomes more and more difficult to keep track of progress. Similarly, as product backlogs become more complicated, backlog items are sliced into smaller pieces, and interdependencies are found between items, it becomes more and more difficult to manage the product backlog and detect issues with backlog item interdependencies. For these reasons, and many more, backlog management tools are becoming a common fixture in agile development environments.

Requirements

The minimum requirements for a backlog management tool are as follows:

1. The tool should help Scrum teams build and maintain their sprint backlogs. This includes the creation of tasks and an electronic task board upon which team members can see task status, take ownership of a task, change the task's remaining hours, and change the task status (up to and including "complete").
2. All project personnel, no matter where they are located, can easily access the tool's electronic task board.
3. The tool must be able to automatically generate sprint burn-downs from the information maintained in the sprint backlog.
4. The tool must be able to help product owners create, display, revise, and delete product backlog items.
5. The tool must be able to allow product owners to group product backlog items into releases.
6. The tool must be able to help product owners easily prioritize backlog items.

7. The tool should be flexible in the units used to support estimation of risk, value, and cost.
8. The tool should be able to alert the proper personnel when backlog items are not properly prepared for sprint planning.
9. The tool should be able to record and maintain interdependency information about backlog items and, when items are in danger of being done out of sequence, alert the proper personnel.
10. The tool should be able to provide project status reporting using the combination of product backlog and sprint backlog data.
11. The tool should be able to provide multiple views of the product backlog to support:
    a. A release view of backlog to define a release
    b. A team view of the backlog to support backlog grooming and sprint planning
    c. A themed view (or otherwise tagged view) of the backlog to support a variety of different viewing needs
12. The tool should be able to identify the stakeholder(s) for a backlog item.

Sample Products

■ ScrumWorks Pro (http://www.scrumworks.com)
■ Rally (http://www.rallydev.com)
■ VersionOne (http://www.versionone.com)

Team Communication

The power of Scrum lies in collaboration between team members. When those team members are separated by walls, floors, buildings, cities, or oceans, the degree of collaboration and the effectiveness of the teams decrease. Co-locating the teams until they have created a team identity and have internalized the team processes and practices can circumvent much of the difficulty in non-co-located teams. However, even when teams have spent a lot of time together, it is very common for a variety of solutions to be employed to help improve communication between teams.

Common solutions for bringing teams together include:

■ Wiki servers: These allow teams to easily post and share information in a manner that is easy to update and easy to access.
■ Instant messaging: IM clients provide a means for non-co-located team members to easily, quickly, and quietly communicate with one another. Some IM clients also support the ability to know if someone is "in the office" or

"in a meeting" or "away," thus ensuring that people don't wait around for a response from someone who might not even be available.

■ Document repositories: While wiki servers provide a lot of support for text and pictures, the team still needs a way to electronically share and collaborate on documents.

■ Web cams: Depending on the circumstances, web cams can be useful in eliminating the feeling of separation between teams. By installing web cams and large monitors, team members can "see the other side of the room" and know who is available and who is not.

Summary

Tools are a common staple in agile development. They can help ensure that the application continues to work as designed (continuous integration and automated testing tools), they can help ensure that everyone in the project knows what they are doing and can manage their work to the best of their abilities (backlog management tools), and they can bring pieces of teams together that are separated by minutes or by many miles (team collaboration tools and web cams). Tools are also intended to take repetitive and mundane chores away from Scrum team members to allow them to focus on developing features.

Tools are supposed to enforce and enhance development practices. When tools are implemented without regard to the value (or lack of value) that they provide or without regard to the effect they have on the existing practices, they generally have a negative effect on the productivity of Scrum teams and never quite provide the value that was originally intended.

In order to ensure that tools create the value that they are expected to create, make sure you consider your people first. Will they use the tool? Do they feel that the tool addresses an important need in the right way? Then, also consider the impacted processes. How will they need to change? Are there any unwanted consequences to those changes? Will you be able to train all of the developers quickly?

Endnote

1. Rachel Davies, an agile coach based in the UK, has suggested the following template for user stories: "As a <role>, I want to <action>, so that <justification or value>" This template does an excellent job of ensuring that we capture the real purpose of a user story. I suggest this template to all of my Product Owners for their user stories.

Chapter 17

Managing Customer Involvement

In software development projects, customer involvement is second only to executive management support in factors that support project success. This is recognized in Extreme Programming (XP) practices and the Scrum method, where we invite the customer to become a member of the development team. For companies operating in highly competitive environments, good customer involvement can be a clear differentiator between your product and everyone else's. When I discuss customer involvement with my Scrum masters, I tell them that customer involvement can be the difference between a product that works and a product that works the way your customers work.

Getting your customers involved in your Scrum teams does more than improve your product. A customer that works successfully on a Scrum team forms a bond with your developers. Because they have worked closely together with analysts, testers, coders, and product owners, customers understand what works and what doesn't; they understand why certain decisions were made the way they were; they understand how much work and dedication go into creating an application. They learn to trust the team.

Your customers might also, speaking figuratively, form a bond with your product. By being involved in the prioritization efforts and the design decisions, and the UI decisions, they become more aware of why the product works the way it does. They understand why certain features were added and why others were removed. Because they put their time and effort into the product and, in many cases, they can see pieces of the software on which they had an influence, they can defend your product with their peers.

Competitive advantages aside, there's no marketing you can buy that is worth as much as one of your customers speaking to other customers or potential customers about the advantages of your product over the competition's.

There are a lot of advantages to having your customers involved in your development efforts: you get a better product and you get an ardent supporter of your product that can be much more effective than any marketing campaigns that you can field. However, none of this comes without some real work to understand how to effectively involve your customers, how to select the right customer for your teams, and what to do with customers when you make the wrong decision.

Selecting the Right Customer

Finding the right customer is the key to successful customer involvement in your development projects. A good customer can galvanize a team, suggest the right changes at the right time, and improve your product, your team's morale, and his or her own satisfaction with the product. On the other hand, the wrong choice can cause the team's morale to sink, have no positive impact on your product (or even a negative impact), and even become a security risk when you are trying to keep the announcement of critical features secret until a key meeting in the near future.

Selection of a customer to be involved with a Scrum team is generally the responsibility of the product owner. The product owner, of course, would be well advised to discuss possible candidates with any account representative that the organization may have assigned to that customer. There are good reasons, from contract negotiation to general politics, that a good candidate may need to be passed over, due to reasons that an account manager could discuss with the product owner. Similarly, having identified a good candidate, the product owner might also want to review the candidate's skills with the Scrum team to see if the candidate is a good fit for the team.

In addition to ensuring that the political landscape is conducive to a good relationship, the product owner should also consider the following:

- Is the candidate qualified to assist the Scrum team?
- Does the candidate pose a potential threat to the organization?
- Will the candidate cooperate with the Scrum team?

Is the Candidate Qualified?

Customer involvement with a Scrum team is only effective when the customer that works with the Scrum team has something significant to contribute. Customers that have not worked with the product for long or have not worked in the specific field of expertise for long would not be able to offer much useful information to the Scrum team. Qualified candidates are experts in their field and are often looked to within their organizations as such. They are often considered visionaries, finding better ways to do things and coming up with ideas, approaches, or techniques that have not yet been explored or even identified. Qualified candidates are willing to share this information with the Scrum team in order to make some of their expertise and vision part of the product in question.

Qualified candidates must also be able to represent the market segments critical to the product development. Solutions built with a customer's involvement should address all of the customers that are in this product's target market and should not be customized solutions that only a few customers could possibly benefit from. In many cases, the product owner will have to help some qualified candidates better understand their role as market representatives rather than simply as a customer representative.

Is the Candidate a Potential Threat?

People come in infinite varieties and can even change from one day to the next. When product owners are attempting to select a customer to work with their Scrum teams, they also have to consider each candidate's potential to be a threat to the organization. When I use *threat* in this context, I'm not talking about physical threats (also, certainly, if there's a danger there, you might want to advise your product owner to move on). What I'm talking about is the likelihood of your customer candidate to:

1. *Leak confidential information despite a nondisclosure agreement*: Even if you have your candidate sign a nondisclosure agreement (more on this later), he or she can break confidence and cost your organization more in the way of lost revenue potential than anything that you might be able to recover by enforcing the agreement. The wrong information given to the wrong person at the wrong time could ruin your organization or, at the very least, trim your profit margins considerably.
2. *Force their own agenda with your Scrum team*: When you get a customer involved with a Scrum team, the idea is to use his or her knowledge and experience to create a better product. However, should your customer decide to force his or her own ideas into the product backlog or change the existing stories in ways that suits his or her own needs, he or she can cause considerable damage to your development efforts and, in particular, your Scrum teams.
3. *"The customer is always right"*: Customer involvement is about using knowledge and expertise to build a better product by making the customer an integral part of the Scrum team. It should be expected that customers on Scrum teams will take part in discussions, express their ideas, listen to other team members, and collaborate to find the best solution from all of the ideas and options discussed. When the customer short-circuits discussions by saying "I'm the one using the product, not you" or "I'm the customer and I'm right" or "Who's the expert here anyway?" he or she constrains the team's ability to

innovate to only what the customer suggests; all other opinions and options are suppressed.

4. *Poor team player*: Some people simply don't work well on teams. They lack the ability to communicate tactfully, to show respect for others, or to constructively negotiate to create the best possible solution. Anyone on a Scrum team must exemplify values such as openness, respect, and courage. Being a customer is not an excuse to disrespect Scrum team members.

5. *Prefers to place blame*: Scrum teams succeed together and, of course, sometimes fail together. But whatever they do, they do it as a team, not as individuals. Individuals on teams that prefer to place blame ("Last week, you said this" or "If you had done it my way, none of this would have happened") cause teamwork and collaboration to disappear as each team member scrambles to reduce his or her risk of being blamed for anything. Worse, a lot of time is lost in identifying who is responsible, what he or she should have done, and arguing about all of it rather than simply accepting where the team is and resolving the situation as a team.

Will the Candidate Cooperate?

Cooperation is the key to whether or not a candidate contributes to a Scrum team. Candidates have to be willing to share their ideas and work with the Scrum team to succeed. Here are some of the things that your product owner will want to look for in a good customer candidate:

1. *Willing to participate in discussions*: Good candidates will be willing to work with a Scrum team and discuss their ideas and the ideas of the team freely and without prejudice. They can handle critical feedback on their ideas and, when necessary, constructively assert the advantages of their position without being overbearing. Good candidates will work with the Scrum team to devise the best solution from everyone's knowledge and experience.

2. *Open-minded*: Good candidates will keep an open mind about the product, their own ideas, the members of the Scrum team, and your organization in general. They should be as willing to learn as to teach, and as willing to change their minds as to challenge the rest of the team with their ideas.

3. *Willing to work on backlog tasks*: When possible, excellent customer candidates will be willing to take tasks off the team's backlog that they are qualified to perform and work on those tasks with the team. If the customer candidates are not able to work on team tasks, it should be because they are not qualified, not because they see themselves as somehow special or different from the rest of the team. Because most tasks in a sprint are done by multiple people (and not by individuals), even the "not qualified" excuse should be short-lived. Customers can be easily guided in writing test cases, creating test

data, adding information to internal and external documentation, and even running tests and evaluating the results.

4. *Good team player*: At no time should someone who is unable or unwilling to work on a team be made a member of a Scrum team. This is as true for customer candidates as it is for the organization's own employees.

5. *Respected by other customers*: Excellent customer candidates have earned the respect of their peers, both inside their own organization and across their specific industry. Individuals that have earned respect have done so, usually, by consistently demonstrating their abilities to their peers and providing useful and accurate information. These are the types of individuals that frequently provide invaluable insight to the product. When these customers can contribute to a product through participation on a Scrum team, they bring respect to the product itself and can sometimes provide priceless marketing in discussions with other customers and presentations or seminars at industry conferences.

Managing the Involved Customer

Once a customer candidate has been selected for a Scrum team, you will want to ensure that he or she is properly trained for the role. In fact, most of the dysfunctions caused by customer involvement in a Scrum team are related to either or both the customer and the Scrum team not properly understanding the role of the customer in the sprint. Therefore, when you are ready to get a customer involved with a Scrum team, make sure that the team is properly trained in the customer's role on the team. Deal with any questions of how the customer will be involved with the team, where he or she will sit (if embedded with the team), and how he or she is to interact with the team clearly and completely. Similarly, your customer candidate should be familiar with Scrum, the customer's role on a Scrum team, and in some cases the customer's role in agile analysis. You may also need to protect your intellectual property rights.

When customers are involved with Scrum teams, they can be part of conversations that can reveal information that provides a competitive advantage over a competitor's product. Your organization probably already has agreements with your employees that protect against the release of confidential information. However, you might not be protected against the involved customer should he or she decide to speak publicly about confidential information. Similarly, the involved customer might be part of discussions that could reveal new concepts or techniques that the organization might consider to be intellectual property that could be confidential or might even be under consideration as a patentable idea. In either case, revealing the information publicly could cause the organization serious damage. To protect the organization from the accidental (or purposeful) release of information against the organization's wishes, you may want to consider asking any involved customer to sign a nondisclosure agreement in which he or she is made aware that

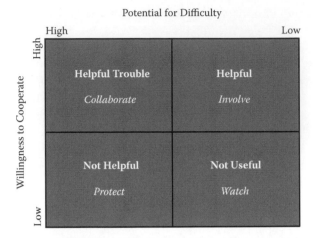

Figure 17.1 Assessing a customer.

he or she could be involved in sensitive discussions and to avoid revealing the content of any discussion to outside parties. Again, check with your legal council when deciding whether or not to do this—you might also discover that the sales agreement you have with your customers already includes such protection (although that should not stop you from discussing the need for confidentiality with any customer involved with a Scrum team).

As I mentioned in the previous section, it is the product owner's responsibility to identify the best customer candidate that he or she can. Candidates are evaluated in terms of their qualifications, threat potential, and cooperativeness. While a candidate's qualifications can usually be clearly delineated, his or her threat potential and cooperativeness can not only be hidden or masked, but can even change during the course of his or her involvement with the Scrum team. We'll use the rest of this chapter section to discuss strategies for handling customers on a Scrum team based on their threat potential and their willingness to cooperate with the team. To select the proper strategy, the team and the product owner will need to assess the involved customer's potential for difficulty as high or low, as well as the customer's willingness to cooperate, again in terms of high or low (refer to Figure 17.1).

The Helpful Customer Strategy: Involve

In the involve strategy, you can involve the customer completely in all team activities, including sprint planning, sprint reviews, daily Scrums, group design sessions, UI design sessions, etc. The customer should be working with team members to complete tasks from the sprint backlog. The customer should be sitting in the team room with the Scrum team and can be entrusted with knowledge of the product's and the organization's weaknesses as well as their strengths.

The Not Useful Customer Strategy: Watch

The watch strategy assumes that the involved customer has only a small focus of concern with regard to what the Scrum team is doing and does not wish to be involved with the team any more than necessary. In these cases, it is usually best to have the customer with the team only when discussing issues that need the customer's opinions. Defer debate and arguments about the customer's contributions until later, when they can be held without the customer in attendance.

As soon as the team moves on to backlog items that do not interest the involved customer, work with the product owner to gracefully end the relationship.

The Not Helpful Candidate Strategy: Protect

The protect strategy focuses on limiting the involved customer's exposure to the team and to sensitive information regarding both the product and the organization. Have the customer work with only a few representatives of the Scrum team and the product owner, and have the discussions away from the rest of the team and, if possible, away from all other Scrum teams. Hold no confidential conversations with this customer; all team discussions should be held separate from this customer at a later time. This customer should not attend any of the team's regular meetings (sprint planning, sprint review, daily Scrums). Additionally, work with the product owner to find other customer candidates to provide the desired information, as your goal should be to end the relationship with the current involved customer before any serious damage can be done to your organization.

The Helpful Trouble Customer Strategy: Collaborate

The collaborate strategy assumes that the customer wants to help the Scrum as much as possible. Keep the customer involved in discussions as much as possible, but ensure that team members are sensitive to the customer's mood at any given time. Should the customer appear to be getting angry or frustrated, the team should switch to more of an interview type discussion, getting information from the customer, rather than the more interactive discussion that the team prefers. As long as the cooperativeness persists, involve the customer in as much as possible. Allow the customer to sit with the team, but make sure that the team understands that no sensitive or confidential information should be discussed unless it is directly relevant to the backlog items currently being addressed. Confidential matters should be discussed in the customer's absence or privately in a manager's office. Should the relationship appear to become challenged, work one-on-one with the customer to reassess his or her cooperativeness with the Scrum team. Adjust your strategy appropriately.

Remember that a customer's potential for threat as well as his or her cooperativeness with the Scrum team can change at any time. Always be watching for changes in the customer's attitude and react accordingly. As much as we would all prefer openness and transparency, I don't believe anyone would be willing to risk his or her organization's future on the principle that all customer involvement must be completely open and transparent, no matter what. Most of us are not often in a position to dismiss a customer employee from a Scrum team because we didn't like their attitude. As with many good business strategies, we set our sights high, but we plan for the worst.

Managing Customer Involvement in a Large Organization

In a large organization, we face challenges above and beyond those discussed previously in this chapter. As you might imagine, finding the right customer candidate for a Scrum team tends to eliminate many of the possibilities. Even in a large customer base, there are usually only a few customers that are even willing to provide employees to assist your organization's Scrum teams. In a shrinking economy, it becomes even more difficult. When you have a project with up to five or six teams, you can often find the right candidates at the right times for these teams. What happens, however, when we scale up?

Imagine a project with forty Scrum teams. Many of them will benefit from customer involvement, but each wants different skills sets that will possibly change during the course of the project. To make matters even worse, projects that are staffed by a large number of teams are often creating high-end, specialized products with a relatively small number of customers. This means, of course, that though they need more candidates, the pool of potential candidates is much smaller. In turn, we end up with a difficult problem that faces many large projects: How do we maximize the benefit of customer involvement across many Scrum teams without overwhelming customers at the same time?

In this section, we will discuss the creation and responsibilities of a customer involvement team to handle the coordination of team needs and customer willingness and availability. This team could be created in a number of ways; the two most likely options are:

1. Virtual team: Since your product owners bear most of the responsibility for the proper selection of customer candidates, a good option is to create a virtual team from your product owners. Even in this case, however, you should plan on staffing the team with one or two permanent employees to handle the many administrative details (to follow). A disadvantage to this option is that your product owners are usually very busy with customers, business stakeholders, and Scrum teams to take on the activities of a virtual team.
2. New, real team: Staff a completely new team (possibly a function of your organization's project management, product management, or sales support

department). This staff would handle the administrative responsibilities of the customer involvement, possibly working directly with customer account managers to identify potential candidates, and then working with product owners to determine their suitability for the role. A disadvantage to this option is that the creation of a new, separate team could invite the creation of processes or more dysfunctional handoffs during software development.

Regardless of how the team is staffed, its responsibilities are as follows:

1. Working with account management, directly with customers, or both, identify:
   a. Which customers are willing to even provide time to have one of their employees work with your organization's Scrum teams
   b. What kind of participation the customer is willing to provide: on site or remote
   c. What is the extent of the customer's willingness to participate: a few hours a month, a few hours a week, every day?
2. Working with product owners and account managers, identify the potential candidates from the willing customers.
   a. Product owners will need to assess each candidate (qualifications, threat potential, willingness to cooperate).
   b. The customer's management will need to specifically sign off on the selected candidate's participation.
3. Your organization may require that any customer that is working directly with a Scrum team be specifically bound by a nondisclosure agreement. This is meant to protect the organization should the customer candidate chose to publicly reveal information that was considered confidential by your organization. In truth, these agreements do not actually protect your organization from damage. While a nondisclosure agreement does a good job of making sure that the candidate understands his or her responsibilities with regard to confidential information, should he or she choose to ignore it, it is unlikely your organization could correct the damage done by the revelation. Of course, as with all legal matters, discuss the necessity and appropriateness of a nondisclosure agreement with corporate council before deciding how to proceed.
4. Work with Scrum teams to identify their specific needs. What skills do they need? When do they need those skills and for how long? What mode would be preferable: on site or remote? Of course, many Scrum teams will also know exactly whom they want to get involved with their teams. When the Scrum team can indicate a preference, the customer involvement team should attempt to honor it as best they can.
5. Keep track of customers that are or were involved with Scrum teams and how it worked out. If a Scrum team had a poor experience with a customer employee, that experience should be taken into account if the same employee

is ever considered again in the future. Likewise, customer employees that work well with Scrum teams should be considered in the future if the skills match and the customer is still willing. At the same time, try to keep your pool of potential candidates as large as possible. This not only protects you should a candidate's behavior or a customer's decision remove him or her from the pool, but it also has the advantage of bringing in as many new, fresh ideas as possible. Sticking with the same customer candidates over and over again can stifle innovation.

Summary

Customer involvement in Scrum teams is a key factor in project success. Having customers work directly with Scrum teams can create key market differentiation for your product. It can also result in better relationships with customer employees and can even result in customers providing priceless public relations for your organization and your product. In order to gain these advantages, however, you must carefully select the right candidates by considering their technical qualifications, their potential as a threat to your organization, and their willingness to cooperate with your Scrum teams. There are strategies you can choose from, based on the candidate's threat potential and cooperativeness, but regardless, if the customer is not very cooperative, the best move is to discontinue the relationship as quickly as possible.

In a large organization where projects can have a large number of Scrum teams, you may want to create a team to help manage customer involvement. This team, which can be made up of product owners or staffed separately and consulting with product owners, has a number of responsibilities that can help coordinate matching of customer candidates with Scrum teams. In brief, these responsibilities include working directly with customers and account managers to identify customers that are willing to work with your Scrum teams, working directly with product owners to identify good candidates for your Scrum teams, and working directly with your Scrum teams to clearly understand their needs and timeframes.

CREATING THE AGILE ORGANIZATION

Within two or three months of beginning the agile transition project, you will probably find yourself ready to start the first pilot project and ready to begin transforming your organization into an agile one. You may, however, feel quite reticent about starting a pilot project, because you aren't ready (or some such reason). Welcome to agile development! Get used to this feeling. Agile development is about doing just enough to move to the next step. That can be unnerving in an industry that generally feels that you should plan for every contingency before getting started.

Planning for every contingency, theoretically, helps you to prepare for all those obstacles that often present themselves during any project. The problem, unfortunately, is that it costs a lot of money and time to plan for everything that might happen. The return on investment for trying to think of everything ahead of time is frequently poor. For all of the contingencies that don't happen during a project, the time spent planning for them is wasted. As for all of the contingencies that happen but were not planned for, the value of all of the up-front planning similarly diminishes.

Agile development suggests doing high-level planning at the beginning of a project, some medium-level planning on project iteration boundaries, and the real in-the-trenches, low-level planning on a daily basis. So, if you've read the previous sections of this book and taken what I've said into account in your planning, you've done the up-front planning for the organization, for the transition project, and for your pilot project. Whether or not you feel ready, it's time to take the next step.

The transition project now has a working transition backlog and teams that are working the backlog—as long as there are no significant changes in direction, the transition project will run through the transition backlog and then end. However, agile development projects don't flourish unless they take place in an agile organization. That's what this section of the book is all about. In the following chapters, we'll look at:

- *Managing an agile development project*: How do we start an agile development project? Should the sprints all run at the same time, or can each team determine that? How do we produce project status reports, and how will they be different from before?
- *Agile analysis*: The transition backlog started as a fairly straightforward list. Breaking down took a little time, but not real detailed analysis. Analysis in a development project is considerably more complex and, in some cases, is affected by quality regulations. So, how should we plan to do this? What do we need? Who manages it?
- *Launching Scrum teams*: In addition to people and a team room, what else does a Scrum team need? We'll discuss common problems, tools, hardware, etc.
- *Managing Scrum teams*: If Scrum teams are self-managing, what role do resource managers play? How do Scrum teams grow and improve?
- *Agile product management*: How does product management change in an agile environment, and what impacts do agile projects have on product management? How do we monitor and control our projects?

I recommend that you read this section of the book *before* you begin the transition, and then come back as you begin planning and running agile projects. What you will find in this section may help you create your transition backlog, select your pilot projects, and even launch those projects.

My greatest difficulty in writing this section was in the ordering of the chapters. Should I go in time sequence (that is, what would you encounter first, second, third, etc.)? Should I go in order of importance? Maybe I could group them—infrastructure stuff followed by team stuff, then management, and so on. The problem with time sequencing is that all of these disciplines occur all of the time, so there really isn't a first, second, or third. It's all at once, all of the time. Ordering by importance is too relative; what might be really critical for one organization might be only a minor concern for another. My decision, then, was to attempt to group the chapters as best I could. You should, however, plan to jump around after your initial reading in order to find what you need when you need it.

So, read this section once or twice to become familiar with its contents and arrangement. Then, use the chapters for reference material as the situation demands.

Chapter 18

Agile Project Management— Getting Started

As your organization converts to agile development, you will find that many traditional roles will change—some slightly, some considerably. The role of the project manager is one of those that changes considerably when agile development is taken on. With the introduction of Scrum, which eliminates much of the project scheduling effort, and the Scrum master, who handles some of the project manager's former responsibilities, the project manager will have to learn some new skills in order to remain valuable to the organization.

In a traditional project, a schedule is built and maintained by a project manager. This schedule lists nearly all of the tasks that must be performed during a project. Each item on the schedule generally identifies who is responsible for performing the task, when the task can be started, and by when it must be finished in order for the project to be completed on time. The schedule also reflects the necessary sequence of the tasks, frequently based on each task's predecessors and successors or by the availability of certain resources (or both). Because of the detail and precision that goes into the schedule, and the inherently emergent nature of the work, the schedule is almost always obsolete when published. The schedule therefore becomes the object of considerable effort and rework to adapt to the nearly continuous changes in tasks, priorities, resources, and timeframes.

In an agile project that uses Scrum, the product backlog and the sprint backlog replace the project schedule. All work in a Scrum-based project is derived from the prioritization and content of the product backlog. The sprint backlog is built and maintained by each Scrum team throughout the course of each sprint. The ordering of features and tasks emerges as the product backlog is groomed and Scrum teams organize themselves around the work.

Scheduling in an Agile Project

Scheduling work in an agile project is quite different than in most other project management methods. Agile projects execute in a manner similar to how an assembly line takes on work. Just like an assembly line completes work based on how quickly that work moves from the beginning to the end of the line, agile projects work at a rate defined by the velocity of the teams on the project. Agile projects also "stop the line" at the end of every sprint to see what we've produced and decide what needs to happen next. Throughout the rest of this chapter, we'll talk about how to create an agile project schedule and how to deal with the many activities and events that you will need to take into account when building and maintaining your schedule.

Scheduling Challenges

Schedules in an agile project are cut up into time boxes called sprints. A project could be one sprint in length or twenty or more sprints in length. There's no practical limit on the length of an agile project except those imposed by business needs (i.e., how long your customer waits for the product to be finished). When setting up your schedule, you will need to consider the following:

1. How much work is there to do?
2. How many teams/people will be assigned to the project?
3. How long will each sprint be?
4. Will all teams use the same sprint length?

One of the hardest questions to answer deals with how much work there is to do and how much it will cost to do it. Unfortunately, this is also quite frequently the question that needs to be answered first in order for a corporation to properly plan or for a software company to bid for a customer opportunity.

Determining the Project's Estimated Costs

With no clear estimate of the agile project cost, we cannot create a reasonable schedule. To solve this problem, we need to learn enough about our product backlog that we can do some educated guessing about costs. The method for doing this focuses on maintaining a balance between creating a reasonable estimate and the cost of creating the estimate at a point in the project when you know the least about it.

Briefly described, we will use backlog-grooming methods to complete a high-level estimation of our product backlog and then turn to sprint planning methods to determine the rough size of our product backlog in hours. Once we have the hours, we can decide the length of the project and the level of staffing needed. By using an example of building a web site to purchase airline tickets, let's examine how to determine a project's estimated costs. We'll start with a basic list (shortened a bit) of product backlog items (PBIs), shown in Table 18.1, that I frequently use in my classes:

Here's what we need to do:

1. Start a one-week sprint for the estimation work. We do this first to set the tone for the rest of the project. It also time boxes the team's effort so that we can look at our progress at reasonable intervals to ensure that we are still making sufficient progress. Finally, doing your estimation in sprints helps to keep the team focused on the goal of estimating the project's total cost. You should plan on one or more one-week sprints during which the estimation work is performed.

   Usually, however, unless the backlog is extensive and complex or the estimation team's resources aren't dedicated to the effort, the estimation work won't take more than one week to complete.

2. Estimate the backlog. We'll use t-shirt sizing for this work; we only need a rough sizing of effort to make this method work. We're also going to assume that two or three people on a team will work all items on the backlog. For our current purposes, we can use three t-shirt sizes: small, medium, and large. And we'll define them as follows:
   - Small (S)—work that will take less than one week to finish
   - Medium (M)—work that may take up to two weeks to finish
   - Large (L)—work that will take about a month to finish

   The team will more extensively discuss any features larger than "large." It may even be necessary to assign a portion of the team to do more detailed analysis on a "larger than large" story before the team discusses the story again. The end goal, of course, is to learn enough about the story to allow the team to slice the story into smaller pieces that can be categorized as, at most, "large."

3. Add up the number of small, medium, and large stories. Let's go back to the original backlog for our ticket purchasing web site. After estimation, it might look like Table 18.2.

This gives us five small stories, nine medium stories, and five large stories. From here, we can approximate best-case and worst-care estimation by equating

Table 18.1 An Abbreviated Sample Product Backlog

■ Search for tickets
• From origin city to destination city
– By airport code
– By U.S. city
– By international city
• Leaving by a specific time
• Leaving after a specific time
• Arriving by a specific time
• Arriving after a specific time
• One preferred airline
• List of preferred airlines
• One-way only
■ Purchase tickets
• Using VISA
• Using American Express
• Using debit card
• Using credit from returned tickets
■ Deliver tickets
• Deliver electronically
• Deliver by mail
• E-ticket (get at airport)
■ Other stuff
• Return incorrect tickets
• Exchange ticket

Table 18.2   A Sample Product Backlog with T-Shirt Estimates

■ Search for tickets	
• From origin city to destination city	
– By airport code	M
– By U.S. city	M
– By international city	M
• Leaving by a specific time	S
• Leaving after a specific time	S
• Arriving by a specific time	M
• Arriving after a specific time	M
• One preferred airline	M
• List of preferred airlines	L
• One-way only	S
■ Purchase tickets	
• Using VISA	S
• Using American Express	S
• Using debit card	M
• Using credit from returned tickets	L
■ Deliver tickets	
• Deliver electronically	L
• Deliver by mail	M
• E-ticket (get at airport)	M
■ Other stuff	
• Return incorrect tickets	L
• Exchange ticket	L

Table 18.3 Determining Best- and Worst-Case Hours for T-Shirt Sizes

Stories	Best Case	Worst Case	Best Case Total	Worst Case Total
5 small stories	20	40	100	200
9 medium stories	60	80	540	720
5 large stories	120	160	600	800
Totals			1,240	1,720

small, medium, and large with different numbers of hours. An example is given in Table 18.3.

This gives us a total product estimate of 1,240 hours (best case) and 1,720 hours (worst case). From here, you can use one of the two values (best case if you anticipate few surprises, worst case if you anticipate lots of surprises), any value in between, or even a value outside this range, depending on how comfortable you are with the estimations.

Further, if you feel that the estimation process needs a little more rigor (which will result in a potentially more precise estimate, but will most certainly cost more to produce), you can do any or all of the following:

1. Add extra-small and extra-large sizes to your t-shirt sizes. This will give you a bit more precision without adding excessively to your estimation costs. However, try not to create sizes much larger than a month. For example:
   ■ Extra small (XS)—a couple days
   ■ Small (S)—a week
   ■ Medium (M)—two weeks
   ■ Large (L)—less than a month
   ■ Extra large (XL)—approximately one month
2. Consider taking some estimation samples. In this method, you pick a small sampling of stories of each size and test their sizing by doing enough analysis to reduce each selected sample down to specific tasks. In other words, what you would normally do during backlog grooming and would finish during sprint planning, you'll do during this early estimation process instead. So, during the estimation effort, the team would select a number of small stories and continue doing in-depth analysis and design until the story was broken down into clear and concise tasks, none of which should be larger than ten to sixteen hours. For example, let's assume we sampled five small stories and came up with the following totals:
   ■ Small story 1—15 hours
   ■ Small story 2—5 hours

- Small story 3–12 hours
- Small story 4–25 hours
- Small story 5–18 hours

These samples help us to ensure that our assumption of roughly twenty hours is accurate. If our estimates were not in line with "small," we can correct the size of small up or down as appropriate.

Of course, if you require more accuracy, sample more stories. However, the more stories you sample, the more expensive your estimation effort will cost you. You and your organization have to decide how much effort is reasonable and how much precision is necessary in order to complete the project estimate.

Planning and Staffing

With the project effort estimated, you can turn your attention to staffing teams and setting the overall schedule. While staffing and timeframes generally have an inverse relationship (that is, the more staffing you have, the faster you can get done), the reality is that *staffing* is a term that oversimplifies the relationship between the individual developer and the work that he or she can do. In other words, having two hundred coders on a project doesn't really do you much good if you need some detailed analysis during the project. Likewise, two hundred analysts won't get you very far in actually building the product. However, we often tend to refer to two hundred full-time employees (FTEs) without regard to how many of those employees are analysts, coders, designers, architects, testers, writers, database designers, and so on.

In this section, we'll talk about the concerns that will drive your project planning and team staffing. We'll divide this discussion into the following areas:

1. Specialization: Many applications are so complex that they require specialized skills that may have a lengthy learning curve in order to achieve proficiency.
2. Architecture definition: Prior to beginning feature development, it is imperative that your product's architecture is fully defined. How will common functions throughout the product be handled? How will authorization and authentication of users be managed?[1]
3. Unprepared backlog: While we may have completed a high-level evaluation of the backlog for budgeting purposes, we still need backlog items that are of the highest priority and are able to be completed in less than a week by two or three members of a Scrum team.

Specialization and the Unbalanced Backlog

The reality in large project staffing is that Scrum teams frequently have the skills to work on only one major piece of a product. For example, our ticket purchasing web site might be divided into major functions (or modules) like:

- Searching
- Purchasing/refunds
- Advertising
- Third-party relationships (hotels, auto rentals, airport parking)

In such a situation, it is very likely that some number of Scrum teams would be assigned to the searching module, while others would be assigned to the purchasing/refunds module, and so on. Each team would, in a short time, *specialize* in these areas of the product and the movement of personnel across modules would become more difficult. These are called *product specializations*.

Similarly, while we work to encourage all individuals in an agile development situation to take on whatever tasks are needed to help their team achieve their goals, it will always continue to be the case that some employees are analysts, others are designers/coders, and still others are testers or writers or database designers or user interface (UI) analysts. Each individual on a Scrum team will excel in one or two skill areas and will tend to commit to sprint backlog tasks that play to those strengths. These are called *skill specializations*.

While we will often describe our project staffing in terms of the number of people, it is critically important that we also think in terms of product specializations and skill specializations. We attempt to address skill specializations by providing adequate staffing to every Scrum team.

Scrum teams are best when they are between five and nine people in size. These limits keep the teams small enough to have the skills they need and small enough that everyone on the team can easily (through the daily Scrum) understand what everyone else on the team is doing. In the Table 18.4, you'll find a suggested staffing of a Scrum

Table 18.4 Suggested Skills Breakdown Based on Scrum Team Size

Team Size	Analysts	Coders/Designers	Testers/QA	Writers
5	1	2	2	0
6	1	3	2	0
7	2	3	2	0
8	2	3	2	1
9	2	4	2	1

team in terms of skill specializations. You are invited to use this table as a guideline, but make the final decision based on your own experience in your organization.

We have a very different problem to deal with when we address product specialization. Product backlog items tend to stay within single modules, frequently using the communications services provided by the system architecture to provide communication between modules. This means that many stories can simply be assigned to the module teams (the final selection of which team gets a particular story might rely solely on who gets to it first), and this works fine when there are enough module teams to get all of the items done during the project. However, when the number of module teams available is insufficient to complete that module's product backlog items before the anticipated end of the project, you have to consider lengthening the project, increasing the staffing, or removing some of the extra items from the backlog. Likewise, you may discover that you have more teams than you need to complete the scoped product backlog. In this case, you can shorten the project, decrease the staffing, or add more items to the scoped portion of the product backlog. In short, you will frequently be faced with projects that do not have backlogs balanced against the teams that are qualified to do the work, and you will likely need to be able to quantify the imbalance and potentially correct for it.

When considering how much work one or more specialized teams have on the backlog, I calculate something that I call the developer load, a value that gives you a rough idea of how much work a team would have to do to get their entire backlog done instantaneously. I use this value in the beginning of the project. Once the project is started and the Scrum teams are formed, however, I set the expectation that each team is responsible for determining what skills are needed and taking steps to acquire those skills. A team with a higher developer load will take longer to get their portion of the backlog done than a team with a lower development load. This value can be useful if you want to determine (1) how much imbalance there is in the backlog and (2) if it's possible to move people or teams to help level the imbalance.

Using the earlier example of the ticket purchasing web site, let's look at three different modules in the web site: searching for flights, purchasing tickets, and the delivery of tickets to the purchaser. Having completed the project budget, we've also determined how much work there is to do for each of the aforementioned modules. For a breakdown of work, see Table 18.5.

Table 18.5 Adding Up the T-Shirt Sizes

Module	Best Case	Worst Case
Searching (1L, 6M, 3S)	540	760
Purchasing (1L, 1M, 2S)	300	320
Delivery (1L, 2M, 0S)	240	320
Total estimate in hours	1,080	1,400

Table 18.6 Sample Distribution of Team Skills

Module	Analysts	Coders/Designers	Testers/QA	Writers
Searching	1	2	2	0
Purchasing	1	3	2	0
Delivery	1	3	2	0

Let's assume worst-case estimation. That would mean that there was 760 hours of work in the searching module and 320 hours of work each in the purchasing and delivery modules. Now, let's look at the Scrum teams that we have for this project. To keep it simple, we'll have one team for each module, broken down as in Table 18.6.

With this information, we can calculate developer load for each module. The formula is simple: divide the total number of hours for each module by the total number of coders available for each module. For example, if I had three coders and three hundred hours of work to do, my developer load would be one hundred hours per developer. Even if the team had two analysts, two testers, and a database architect, I would still only count the coders. My thinking for this is simple: if your team is staffed properly (that is, there are enough analysts to keep the coders busy and enough testers to completely validate what the coders are building), your coders become the critical path through the Scrum team. Of course, I mean no disrespect to the analysts, testers, writers, etc. (some of my best friends are analysts!). It simply works out pretty well that the number of coders has a significantly greater impact on velocity than any of the other roles taken individually.

For our hypothetical example, we can calculate the following developer loads for each module:

- Searching: 760 hours/2 coders = 380 hours developer load
- Purchasing: 320 hours/3 coders = 106 hours developer load
- Delivery: 320 hours/3 coders = 106 hours developer load

(Please note that I rounded the answer for purchasing and delivery; developer load is an approximation—the estimate would imply an accuracy that didn't exist.)

A Balancing Act

As you can see, the developer load for the searching module is over three times that of the purchasing and delivery modules. This means that, under the current staffing, it will take three times longer to finish the searching module's backlog than the other two modules in the project. If we wish to balance the backlog, we're going to have to find a way to (1) slow down the other modules, (2) speed up the searching module, or (3) both. We can most effectively do this by either hiring new employees to supplement the searching team, or moving coders from the other modules to the searching team. If we hire two new developers into the searching team, we could effectively lower their developer load to 760 hours/4 codes, or 190 hours developer load. If we move one each from purchasing and delivery, it would look more like this:

- Searching: 760 hours/4 coders = 190 hours developer load
- Purchasing: 320 hours/2 coders = 160 hours developer load
- Delivery: 320 hours/2 coders = 160 hours developer load

That looks better. Now that our modules are a little more balanced, we can schedule the project and get moving, right? Actually, I'm sure you may already be anticipating what comes next—the learning curve! In other words, in most environments, I can't just hire new employees or move employees from one team to another. There will be time needed for each new employee to learn the ropes (and time needed for some more experienced employees to provide the mentoring and training). How do we solve this? Well, that depends on whether we're just calculating developer load for *what if* scenarios or if we're definitely going through with some retraining to balance the backlog.

What if scenarios are just that: What if we did this? We don't want to spend a lot of time in calculation; we just want some high-level numbers to help us make some difficult decisions. If you're simply doing *what if* type calculations, you can adjust the developer load calculation by not counting two developers as two developers. For example, if we're just testing to see if we should move one coder each from the purchasing and delivery modules, we can count them in total as 1.5, or perhaps 1.25. What we're really saying here is that each new coder will produce approximately 60% of what an experienced coder would do during the same period. However (yes, there's always a catch), those coders are still equal to one when you remove them from their current teams. In other words, moving one coder each from purchasing and delivery will result in the following calculations:

- Searching: 760 hours/3.25 coders = 234 hours developer load
- Purchasing: 320 hours/2 coders = 160 hours developer load
- Delivery: 320 hours/2 coders = 160 hours developer load

Not as pretty a picture, is it? However, that's the reality of moving developers from one team to another. It hurts their productivity—a lot.

But let's also look at this if we were planning on balancing the backlog for real. We're not doing a *what if*; we're actually planning to do this. Our approach here will be a little different. Rather than estimating the reduction in a developer's productivity, the method for doing actual balancing is to determine what kind of training and coaching would be required, and then modifying the product backlog to incorporate the additional work. For example, the project planning team discusses moving one coder each from the purchasing and delivery teams to the searching team; we need to also discuss and estimate the following additional work:

- Training for the new team members—medium
- Coaching for the new team members—large
- Setting up new environments for the new team members—small

Using our worst-case estimates, when we add these new items to the searching module's backlog, we add 280 hours. However, when doing the actual calculation, we give the coders their full value (i.e., 2 rather than 1.25). So now our developer loads look like this:

- Searching: 1,040 hours/4 coders = 260 hours developer load
- Purchasing: 320 hours/2 coders = 160 hours developer load
- Delivery: 320 hours/2 coders = 160 hours developer load

Not too much different than when we simply counted them at sixty percent instead of one hundred percent. However, there's an added advantage here that the product backlog now contains items that will account for the additional effort needed to train our new team members. Having moved (or planned for the moving of) two employees from the purchasing and delivery modules over to the searching module, we still have an imbalance (260 hour developer load vs. 160 hour developer load). You could choose to hire an outside consultant for the project—that would improve your numbers (and your costs) a little more. How balanced you decide to make the backlog is completely up to you.

In fact, you might even decide not to balance the backlog at all. Balancing the backlog is an option when planning your project, but not a prerequisite for being successful. When your backlog isn't balanced, some of your teams will be done before the project is finished. Is that necessarily a bad thing? In my opinion: no. Those teams can do several things:

- Improve the test coverage of their portion of the application
- Continue to work on new backlog items for the next version of the product
- Provide testing assistance to the searching module team

In the end, what these teams do should be, in a large part, based on the product owner's direction.

In short, skill and product specializations will have a tremendous effect on your project planning. The number of teams that you can create may be constrained by the availability of specific skill sets. You might need to create four teams in order to get done on time, but only have enough of the needed skills to create two teams. Certainly, you can create more teams and work hard to cross-train, but your project planning will have to include extra time for training and coaching. Also, you'll have to plan on an overall decrease in team velocity as a result of our cross-trained employees.

Architecture Definition

Another impact on your scheduling and staffing is the state of your product's architecture definition. What I mean by architecture definition includes answers to the following common questions:

- How are authentication and authorization managed?
- How will your application read from and write to your database?
- How does your product communicate with other products?
- How are common functions and objects managed?
- How are reporting and archiving managed?

All of these questions, and many more like them, are generally answered by the product architecture. How (and if) your product architecture deals with these issues must be defined prior to the actual building of the architecture and feature development begins. If you attempt to do otherwise, you will likely end up with one or both of the following problems:

1. Your Scrum teams will be frequently blocked trying to determine if they are building something that should be part of the architecture. This can also lead to teams severely under- or overcommitting during sprint planning as a result of confusion surrounding what the architecture is supposed to do as opposed to what the application is supposed to support (e.g., who handles sign-on authentication, or who handles the print queues—the application or the architecture?).
2. Your product will end up with lots of redundant and inconsistently implemented functionality (e.g., differently formatted timestamps, logging and tracing functions that work differently, etc.).

At worst, you will experience an increased frequency of sprint failures[2] as teams are unable to make answer important questions and make proper design decisions about how to deal with architecturally significant features.

Unprepared Backlog Items

In order for a product backlog item to be usable by a Scrum team, it must be small enough that the team can easily translate the item into even smaller tasks. "Small enough" is generally considered to be an item that two or three people on a Scrum team can complete in less than a week; these items are called sprint-sized or right-sized. Reducing product backlog items to right-sized is done in an activity called backlog grooming.[3] In order to actually begin writing code, we need to have items that are right-sized, and to get there, we will schedule a number of backlog grooming work sessions during the first project sprint.

Getting Your Project Started

Throughout the course of this chapter, we've talked about determining your project budget, the challenges involved in staffing your teams, and building your project schedule. In this section, we will talk about putting all of that into actual practice in order to get our project started. Just as with all other aspects of our project, we will do this as a sprint.

There are two inputs to the first sprint of a project: a prioritized product backlog and the people that will be involved in this initial phase of the project. Those people include the following:

1. Project manager
2. Product owners
3. Scrum master
4. Subject matter experts
5. Other stakeholders, trainers, etc.
6. Release manager

These people make up your initial project team and will be responsible for the initial setup of the project (all of the topics we discussed earlier in the chapter, plus more). We will add more people and more teams as we move forward, possibly during this sprint, and definitely after.

Your product owners should have already prioritized the product backlog taken into the first sprint. In a small-scale situation, you should expect to have just a single product backlog. However, in a larger-scale scenario, you may be dealing with anywhere between two and ten product backlogs, each managed by a different product owner, and each product owner with his or her own specialized Scrum teams. Let's look at a complex, but common project organization, as shown in Figure 18.1.

In Figure 18.1, I've illustrated a project organization that begins on top with the business owner: the person(s) responsible for funding the project. Working for the business owner we have:

■ Project manager: Responsible for managing the overall project, creating the project charter and project schedule, setting the sprint length, coordinating assistance and support from other departments in the larger organization, and reporting project status to management in a consistent manner.
■ Product manager: Responsible for the overall vision and return on investment of the product; coordinates prioritization of product features with the product owners; ultimate arbiter of decisions across multiple product owner backlogs.

Next in the project organization comes the product owners, who each have responsibility for a product module. A product module, as we discussed in a previous example, is a semi-independent, functionally specific portion of a product. For example, in the case of the ticket purchasing web site we discussed earlier in the

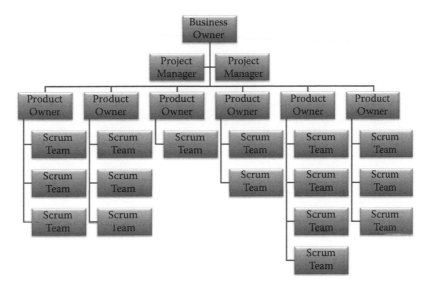

Figure 18.1   A large, agile project organization.

chapter, we used "Search for tickets," "Purchase tickets," and "Delivery of tickets" as modules. For each module and product owner, there may be one or more Scrum teams with necessary specialized skills.

Regardless of whether you have one product module or several, the first sprint of a project will have the following goals:

1. Create the release goals.
2. Create/update defined processes and policies.
3. Create/update DONEness definition.
4. Determine team staffing.
5. Prepare the product backlog for grooming.
6. Create the sprint schedule.
7. Begin backlog grooming work sessions.

During sprint planning, the team should focus on breaking down each goal into smaller steps. In the next sections, we will review each of these goals and how they can be achieved.

Creating the Release Goals

Release goals help define the purpose of the release.[4] They answer questions like:

■ What is the aim of the release?
■ What market segment(s) are we trying to address? Is it a particular market segment? Is it a venture into a new market?

- Are we just creating a release to fix a lot of previously reported problems and deficiencies?
- Is this a big release with lots of new, high-value features, or a small release with some reasonable improvements?
- When does the release have to hit the market?

Answering these questions, and perhaps many more, helps product owners prioritize the backlog, determine the value of various items on the product backlog, drive the creation of Scrum teams, and determine which portion of the product backlog includes "must haves" and which portion includes "nice to haves." By getting them defined up front, you can avoid a lot of misunderstandings and miscommunications later in the release planning and development effort.

The release goals do not have to be overly formal in language. It is, in fact, much more effective for the release goals to be clear and precise. For example, see Figure 18.2.

In this figure, the example release goals tell us that v3.0 of the flight management software is intended to be a major release targeting our largest customers. The major features are listed (which means that any product backlog items related to those features will be given the highest priority in the product backlog) and only the high and critical severity defects will be addressed. Finally, there's a desire from sales and marketing for the product to be ready by the third quarter of 2010. Of course, whether or not that's doable remains to be seen, but we can use that date as a target range for now and see what happens.

The target market segment is the very large-scale customer that has placed orders for new aircraft with multiple decks for passenger seating and for customers that are experiencing maximum load issues (or are expecting to experience load issues when they purchase the new aircraft).

Only high and critical severity defects will be addressed (lower-priority defects will be addressed in the 3.1 released).

This release is a major functionality improvement. The significant features are:

1. Support of multiple decks (for aircraft with seats on multiple decks)

2. Creation of "seat hopper" feature to more effectively match passengers with their seating preferences.

3. Improved scale-up capabilities to take further advantage of server visualization to gain improved end user performance

---

Figure 18.2 Sample release goals.

Sales and marketing wants to target the third quarter of 2010 (3Q10), just before the first planned delivery of the larger, multideck aircraft.

Once our Scrum teams are formed, we'll want to make sure that everyone understands the release goals and, particularly, that there's an understanding about not working on anything less severe than a high-severity ticket.

Create/Update Defined Processes and Policies

If you're in an organization where standards and regulatory requirements have mandated the creation of development processes and policies, you should also take advantage of the first sprint in your project to review the processes and policies and make sure that they are up-to-date and that the project team is fully aware of the applicable processes and policies. This is important, as processes and policies tend to fall behind the realities of the current situation and, when not regularly examined, often lead to things being done because "that's the way it's always been done."

One special item to consider when reviewing the organizational policies is the threshold at which defects, when discovered, are permitted to go directly to a Scrum team as opposed to being placed on a queue or on the product backlog for later prioritization. For example, assuming that your organization categorizes defects as critical, high, medium, and low, your project team might decide that critical and high-priority defects are passed directly to the responsible Scrum team to be diagnosed and corrected. If this causes the Scrum team to no longer be able to achieve their sprint goals, they must negotiate with their product owner to move some unfinished work back to the product backlog.

Create/Update the DONEness Definition

Absolutely all Scrum projects should have a definition of DONEness[5] that defines what developers have to accomplish in order to produce quality software. This definition, like the policies we spoke of earlier, needs frequent tuning in order to ensure that it remains current and relevant. When creating or updating the DONEness definition, you will likely want to plan to hold one or two work sessions that involve developers of a variety of different skills (e.g., application coders, analysts, architects, database architects, database designers, UI analysts, testers, etc.). Invite the participants to brainstorm on various aspects of DONEness. Keep your work sessions to ninety minutes or less, and hold as many as needed to get a comprehensive list of criteria that everyone can agree on. Be prepared for the DONEness definition to be quite extensive and for its length to be a source of concern for your Scrum teams. You will need to explain that the items on the definition must be done in order to ensure that the developers produce high-quality software. None of the items can be deferred without incurring additional costs and unwanted delays later in the project.

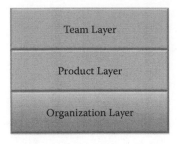

Figure 18.3   Layers of DONEness.

DONEness definitions tend to be defined in three comprehensive layers and with three complementary types. The layers describe how the definition is applied across the organization; the types describe how the definition is applied to different states of development. The three layers of DONEness are the organizational layer, the product layer, and the team layer (see Figure 18.3). These layers each represent a scope at which the DONEness definition is defined and applied.

In other words, the organizational layer of DONEness deals with the acceptance criteria for all stories, features, and defects completed by every team in every product in the organization. Criteria that are frequently defined in this layer include:

- Unit testing
- Functional testing
- Code and coding standards
- Compliance with Sarbanes-Oxley Act
- Designs refactored, meet standards, and are properly documented
- Code covered sufficiently by unit tests
- Code merged into the main development branch
- Designs and code are reviewed
- Baseline code builds work
- Acceptance criteria and tests are green
- UI testing is completed successfully
- Product owner accepts
- Internal documentation is completed, reviewed, and checked in
- Deployed to an internal acceptance server (a tightly controlled environment meant to, as closely as possible, duplicate a customer's environment)
- Compliance with documented UI standards
- Compliance with documented coding standards
- Compliance with documented design (possibly pattern) standards and usages
- Procedures to store all completed artifacts (internal software documentation, external user documentation, source code, training materials, review records, test summaries, etc.) in a document management system such as Rational Clearcase®, Subversion®, or Git

- Internal product documentation (generally defining what kind of documentation is required for every product)
- Requirements to use specific organizationally sanctioned development tools (e.g., configuration management tools, project management tools, source code archiving, defect tracking, etc.)
- Requirements to include specific organizationally mandated service marks, logos, symbols, copyright language, etc.

The next layer, the product layer, is defined "on top of" the organization layer and contains acceptance criteria *in addition to* (not in replacement of) the organization layer definitions. This layer describes the acceptance criteria for all stories, features, and defects that must, in addition to the organization layer, be completed by every team working on a specific product. Criteria frequently defined at this layer include:

- Additional standards or requirements specific to the product. For example, a product that is classified as a medical device may need to comply with ISO 13485 (for sale in the United States) or MDD (for sale in Europe) related requirements.
- Documentation of the product's data model in a specific manner and using a specific tool.
- Automated functional testing of the product's features using one or more approved tools.
- Unit test code coverage at or above a specific percentage.
- Requirement that certain functions of the product operate at or better than a specified level of performance.
- Compliance with documented architectural standards.

The final layer, the team layer, is defined "on top of" the product layer and contains acceptance criteria that are applied to stories in addition to the criteria defined in the product and organization layers. This layer describes acceptance criteria that an individual Scrum team has decided must apply to all stories, features, and defects that they complete during a sprint. Criteria frequently defined at this layer include rules that require:

- Peer review of certain modules or functions or a certain percentage of all code added or changed during a sprint
- Every completed story or defect to be independently validated by any team member not involved in the building or correction
- Every completed story to be reviewed by the product owner prior to sprint review
- All proposed database schema changes to be reviewed by the entire team prior to implementation

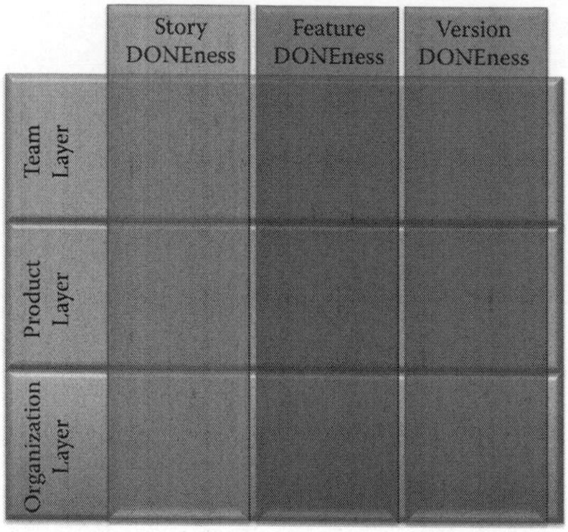

Figure 18.4 The DONEness types overlaid on the DONEness layers.

Spanning each DONEness layer are three more DONEness types: story, feature, and version. These types describe different stages of development at which different aspects of DONEness may apply. These types are shown in Figure 18.4.

Story DONEness involves acceptance criteria that must be adhered to when completing a story or correcting a defect. This is usually the most extensive type of DONEness containing all of the requirements for unit testing, functional testing, updating, and storage of internal documentation, among others. When a Scrum team plans out their approach to any story or defect, they use story DONEness across the organizational, product, and team layers to determine what must be done in order for the team to consider a story completed or a defect solved.

Feature DONEness involves the acceptance criteria that must be adhered to when a product feature is completed (either by virtue of finishing the last story in the feature or because the product owner has indicated that the feature is complete). This type of DONEness usually includes compliance with specific performance requirements, validation of the ability to install or de-install the feature, and completion of end user documentation (of any form, including written or web based). When a Scrum team plans to complete a feature during the sprint, they use feature DONEness at the organization, product, and team layers in order to determine what they have to do to consider the feature completed.

Version DONEness involves the acceptance criteria that must be adhered to when a product version is completed. This type of DONEness usually includes the completion of training materials and end user documentation as well as updating the product's installation and de-installation scripts and the solving and closure of some percentage of open, known defects (e.g., all critical and high-priority defects must be solved and validated, but some small percentage of medium- and low-priority defects may remain unsolved).

Determine Team Staffing

When staffing your teams, you want to consider how much imbalance is in your product backlog (i.e., if there are specialized teams that have considerably less or considerably more work to do than other teams on the project) and, of course, how many teams you need. If your teams are already defined, there's probably very little you will need to do. If, however, your teams have to be defined (some organizations rebuild their teams at the beginning of each project), you have a number of interesting, exciting options available to determine how to staff your teams.

Regardless of whether your teams are already formed or you need to create new ones, make sure that you create the teams that you need to respond to the highest-priority items on the product backlog first.

Let's review some of things that you can do to staff Scrum teams:

1. *Manager's choice*: This method is simplest, fastest, and the most de-motivating for the developers. In this method, the functional managers and product owners work together to determine team staffing. They then announce team staffing, probably during a project kickoff meeting, and let the teams get down to work. This method has the advantage of taking into account a combination of the project's priority requirements as well as, if the managers involved are well informed, the employee's career and professional needs. Managers should always make team staffing choices based on:
   a. Which individuals will likely work well together (or have worked well together in the past)?
   b. Does the team have the expertise it needs? Can the team afford less experienced employees that want the opportunity to grow?
   c. What does the employee want to do? What skills does he or she need to advance in his or her position or otherwise within the company?
2. *Draft*: This method has the advantage of allowing teams to form themselves. In practice, we start with all of the product owners and Scrum masters and a list of all employees involved in the project. The purpose of each team is defined (there's a Scrum master for each team and each team has a specific product owner). Over the course of what can be a lengthy meeting, the product owners and Scrum masters select (or draft) team members from the list of employees. Disadvantages: Since most developers are not involved, this doesn't provide much more motivation than manager's choice. Team members might be selected for the wrong reasons—personal friends of the product owner or Scrum master. In addition, selection to a team does not address the individual employee's career development and professional development hopes.

3. *Sign up*: This method is probably the hardest to employ and, in fact, you will often find yourself negotiating with some employees to get teams properly staffed. In this method, best done in a single large room (like an auditorium or large dining area), sign-up sheets are posted around the room with a team name, product owner's name, Scrum master's name, and a number of blank spots corresponding to the number of team members that the team is supposed to have. Then, with all project personnel present, the product owners take turns introducing their teams, what those teams will build, and who will be the Scrum master for each. Then, once all of the teams have been introduced, employees are invited to sign up for the team they would like to be on. While this method does an excellent job of giving each individual an opportunity to be on the teams they want to be on, it also has the disadvantage of leaving some unlucky employees no choice but to join teams that they would not consider joining except that there were no other available slots. In addition, this mode of self-selection, while it can be quite motivating, doesn't ensure that the right people end up on the right teams.

Your final selection of method to choose your teams, if indeed the teams aren't already chosen, will depend entirely on what you and the project management team feel is the best approach for your organization at that point in time. Methods that cannot work early in an organization's transition might be very feasible a year or two later.

Prepare the Product Backlog for Grooming

Though you may have completed a high-level estimation of product backlog when determining the overall budget, the high-level estimate won't be enough when your Scrum teams start building what's on your product backlog. At this point, it is important to give your Scrum teams a firsthand view of the portion of the product backlog targeted for the current project. By doing this, you can also create an opportunity for your Scrum teams to use their expertise to organize the product backlog to facilitate development. Try these steps to get your teams involved with the product backlog:

■ First, prepare the workshop by ensuring that all of the product backlog items targeted for the current release are recorded on 5 × 7 inch index cards. Make sure that each card contains a number that uniquely identifies the backlog item.
■ Using a large, open table space, the product owners lay their backlog item cards on a table in order, from highest priority to lowest priority (see Figure 18.5).
■ Invite your developers to review the backlog items looking for:
  – Dependencies with other backlog items and items that must be done in a specific sequence. When a dependency is suspected, the product owner

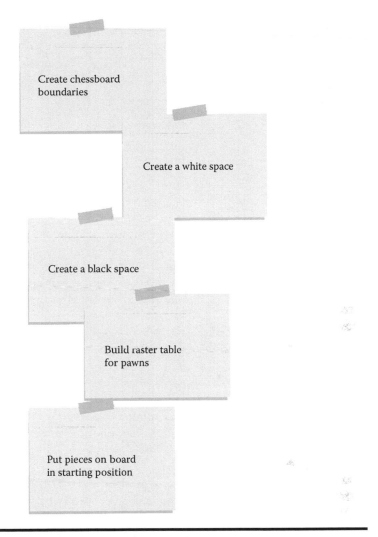

Figure 18.5   Backlog item cards laid across a surface.

should write down the dependency (by recording the ID numbers of the cards) for later discussion and investigation.

- Items that will require special handling because (1) the skills needed are in short supply in the organization or (2) information or assistance will be required from other departments in the larger organization. Product owners note these possibilities (by recording the ID number and the required skill or department) for later discussion and investigation.

Next, you will need to put your Scrum teams to work creating a baseline story point estimation that will give them a good starting point for backlog grooming

Table 18.7 Converting T-Shirt Sizes to Story Points

Any T-Shirt Size That Means a Duration/Complexity Less Than:	Or a T-Shirt Size of:	...is about this many story points
1–2 days	XS	1
1 week	S	2
2 weeks	M	4
1 month	L	8
2 months	XL	16
(More than 2 months?)	XXL	128

work sessions. The good news is that all of the work we put into the backlog during the budgeting process will come in handy right now. Your teams can directly convert t-shirt sizes to story points using a fairly straightforward scale, as illustrated in Table 18.7.

If you haven't done the budgeting step of creating high-level t-shirt size estimates, your teams can also use Table 18.7 to estimate duration and go right to story points.

The important things to remember when preparing the product backlog are:

1. Don't do this yourself, or let your product owners do this, or any select group of individuals. It's really important for your Scrum teams to become familiar with the product backlog before they start building features. Preparing the backlog gives them a chance to identify which backlog items should be assigned to their team (the team's product owner will drive this part of the process) and to look for connections or dependencies between the backlog items that, in some cases, only developers can identify.
2. Your teams should not be trying to be very precise at this point. There are so many unknowns that the more assumptions they make, the more likely they are to rely on a degree of precision that isn't really there. That's when the unpleasant surprises begin.
3. If the team feels strongly that the initial t-shirt size estimate is wrong, they should be encouraged to derive the story point estimate based on what they feel is the proper complexity. For example, if a backlog item is tagged as XS (a couple days) and the team feels strongly that the item will definitely take more than a week for two or three people on the team to do the job, the team should reestimate the item as four story points (medium).
4. Encourage your Scrum teams to not try to negotiate on the story points at this point in time. If they think the "right" answer is somewhere between

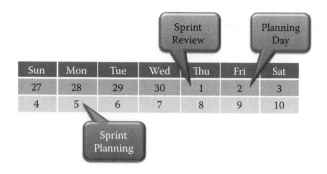

Figure 18.6 Starting sprints on the fifth day of the month.

four and eight, they should go with whichever value (four or eight) they feel is closer and move on to the next item.

Once this conversion (or estimation) effort is complete, you will have a product backlog that is ready for your Scrum teams to begin grooming.

Create the Sprint Schedule

Setting the sprint schedule has as much to do with your organization's experience with agile development as it does with the timing of your product releases. The first, most important item to consider is your product release date or dates. Shorter project timeframes will usually call for shorter sprints. Critical times during projects also tend to apply pressure toward shorter sprints. Another factor to consider is that less experienced Scrum teams will be more effective with longer sprints, while some of the best Scrum teams have no problem with sprints of only one week in length.

In general, sprints should be between one and four weeks in length. You should only plan one-week sprints in cases where you have very experienced teams that are already producing high-quality code. Because one-week sprints are only five business days in length and also have to include time for sprint planning, sprint review, and sprint retrospective meetings, only teams that are very experienced in agile practices will accomplish anything significant in so short a period of time. In addition, sprints should not be longer than one month. Sprints longer than one month tend to lose the productive pressure that a month-long (or shorter) sprint possesses. Most organizations transitioning to agile development find that sprints between three weeks and one month work best. My recommendation for your first project is to start with one-month sprints. As your organization matures, your teams accelerate, and quality improves, you can try shorter and shorter sprints.

Should all of your teams follow the same schedule? That will be completely up to you. While reporting progress across the project is simplified when all of the sprints are the same length and begin and end at the same time, it is also quite possible to determine project progress based on, for example, the condition of the backlog based on all sprints completed as of a specific date. In fact, one of the main drivers of the sprint schedule is the availability of the product owners. If one product owner has three or four teams working on the backlog, that product owner will have a difficult time attending three or four sprint planning meetings simultaneously. However, by starting some sprints, say, on Monday and others on Tuesday, the product owner will have a much easier time attending to his or her teams' needs.

One final recommendation for sprint scheduling is to try as much as possible to keep your sprints of the same length throughout the project. Scrum teams commit to work based on their experiences in previous sprints. When your sprints are of the same length, teams tend to get the same approximate amount of work done each month. This allows your teams to be more predictable; they can use that predictability to groom just enough of their backlog each sprint in order to be ready for the next sprint, and your project manager can use the team's predictability to better manage the project schedule, report progress, and make predictions regarding completion of features and the overall project. If you change the sprint length during the project, team performance changes in unpredictable ways and the predictability of the project likewise diminishes.

When establishing the sprint schedule, consider the following:

1. The experience level of your teams. Less experienced Scrum teams work best at three to four weeks or one calendar month. More experienced Scrum teams can work on one- or two-week sprints.
2. The anticipated length of the project. Shorter projects will work better with shorter sprints; longer projects with longer sprints. For example, while a six-month project will work quite well with three- or four-week sprints, a two-month project performs better with two-week sprints.
3. The complexity (inherent risk) of the project. Riskier projects will demand a greater visibility and flexibility during the development effort. Projects with backlogs that are more clearly understood can handle longer sprints.
4. How balanced is the backlog? An unbalanced backlog will leave one or more teams finished before other teams on the project. What will be your plan during those sprints? What will those teams do if they are still allocated to your project? If they are not, what is your plan of attack should something they write be discovered to contain a defect late in the project?

Sprint Schedules and Large Project Considerations

In some instances, when there are multiple modules (and thus multiple product owners) and a large number of teams (twenty or more, for example), you may discover that longer sprints allow time for the more complex interactions between product owners to take place. This is very important when product owners are dealing with backlogs that are complex and interconnected. Product owners will need a considerable amount of time each sprint to adjust to changing business realities and realign all of the affected product backlogs accordingly. Because of this, you may want to consider a sprint schedule with no fewer than three weeks per sprint.

In addition, when sprint reviews occur, each product backlog is affected by what the Scrum teams completed during the sprint. When you complicate this by adding multiple Scrum teams and multiple product owners, a situation develops immediately after the sprint reviews where the activity of all of the Scrum teams (items that are done, items that are not done and are to be returned to the product backlog) greatly affects the current condition of the product backlog. For that reason alone, it is often a good idea to allow a single day in between the sprint review and the sprint planning meetings. During this "planning" day, the product owners can, collectively, review the new state of the product backlog and make whatever changes they deem appropriate based on the outcome of the previous sprint and the goals of the project.

For example, let's take a situation where the sprints run for a calendar month, starting on the fifth of each month. In a complex situation such as we've discussed, the transition point between one sprint and the next might look like Figure 18.6 on page 221.

In Figure 18.6, we see that the sprint ends on the first of the month to allow for an extra planning day, during which the product backlog is reorganized based on the outcomes of the sprint reviews on the first. On the following Monday, the fifth, the next sprints begin.

Before we finish this topic, let's discuss a minor variation on this sprint schedule that helps when product owners are having a difficult time attending all of their teams' sprint planning meetings. But let's review the problem first. Product owners are a necessary attendee at Scrum team sprint planning meetings. However, when there are two, three, or more teams, the product owner has a harder and harder time getting to his or her teams' sprint planning meetings when they all happen

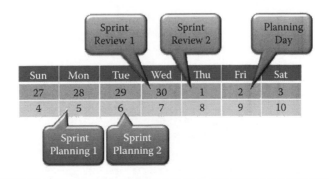

Figure 18.7   Setting up shifted sprints.

Figure 18.8 Placing a stabilization sprint.

on the same day. To mitigate this problem a bit, we can shift our sprints to give the product owners more options. You can see an example in Figure 18.7.

As illustrated in Figure 18.7, we have two sprint review days and two sprint planning days. The way we use this is by putting half of our Scrum teams on a schedule with sprints that begin on the fifth of the month, and the other half has sprints that begin on the sixth of the month, making sure that a product owner's teams are equally distributed across both schedules. With half of their teams doing planning on the fifth and the other half on the sixth, product owners have much more opportunity to attend sprint planning meetings. The disadvantage, of course, is that Scrum teams will find themselves between sprints for two days. However, the "pause" in their development activities can be a good opportunity to catch up on emails, technical reading, training sessions, and more.

The Unwanted Stabilization Sprint

As organizations transition to agile development, it is very common that the product under development is not properly covered with automated unit and functional tests. As development continues and portions of the product remain untested due to the lack of automated tests, a significant amount of "technical debt" is incurred. This means that some amount of work that should be done to the product to ensure quality is not done (in this case, continuous regression testing throughout the sprint). As this work accumulates, the risk of defects also increases. Many organizations deal with this problem by inserting a stabilization or "polishing" sprint at or near the end of the project (refer to Figure 18.8).

While the stabilization sprint can be a reasonable stopgap measure, it has many disadvantages:

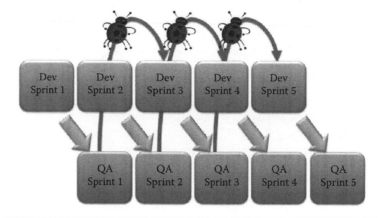

Figure 18.9   Using a QA team in step with development Scrums.

1. When a project ends successfully with the stabilization sprint, many in the organization will begin to accept the stabilization sprint as the "right way" to do a project, forgetting that the stabilization sprint is actually covering for a deficiency in the product development (i.e., the missing automated tests).

2. With a stabilization sprint at the end of the project being used to catch any accumulated technical debt, it becomes acceptable to simply assume that work that cannot be finished during a sprint can simply be pushed to the stabilization sprint. Unfortunately, there's no one controlling how much work is being shunted to the stabilization sprint, frequently resulting in a most unwanted surprise when the stabilization sprint nears its end, while there's still a considerable amount of work to do. By deferring work during the development sprints to the end of the project, the risk was also deferred to the end of the project, when there's no time to make any corrections without changing the project end dates.

3. The stabilization sprint provides an excuse for Scrum teams to not write automated unit and functional tests, assuming that the stabilization sprint will provide time for the necessary testing.

If stabilization sprints are to be used in your projects, make sure that the rules governing the use and purpose of the stabilization sprint are clearly understood by all development and management:

1. The stabilization sprint is for the testing of legacy code (i.e., code not covered by unit or functional tests) and, if applicable, the product UI.

2. Work that cannot be completed during a sprint is returned to the product backlog for reprioritization into another sprint. It cannot be deferred to the stabilization sprint.

3. Work not finished by the beginning of the stabilization sprint is removed from the product such that the stabilization sprint tests only the product that preexisted the project plus all of those features completed during the project.
4. No new backlog items may be scheduled for work during the stabilization sprint.

In addition to the stabilization sprint, there are other methods you can employ to help keep your product quality high when you don't have the automated test coverage you need to ensure quality throughout each day. We'll talk about these methods in the next section.

When the Automated Testing Isn't Sufficient

As discussed in the preceding section on the stabilization sprint, many organizations transitioning to agile development are affected by a significant amount of legacy code (i.e., code not covered by unit or function tests). While the stabilization sprint can be useful for some last-minute testing of the product before the project is finished, the major disadvantage is that, should anything significant go wrong, there's no time left in the project to fix it without delaying the project end.

There are three other methods you can employ in the project schedule to support earlier testing. The first method can be used when your development organization also includes quality assurance analysts and testers that are typically used to testing products *after* the project is finished. Instead, you can use the QA personnel to create a new Scrum team that tests the product in sprints that run in parallel with, but one step behind, the development sprints. As the development teams complete their sprints, the QA team goes into action testing the product that resulted from the development sprint.

As illustrated in Figure 18.9, developers build product during the development sprint (labeled as "Dev Sprint n"). When the first development sprint is completed, the development team moves on to the second development sprint while, simultaneously, the QA team begins a sprint (labeled as "QA Sprint n") to test the existing product, including what was added in the development sprint. Any defects that are found during the testing are opened in the defect management system and are addressed by the development team during the next sprint.

| Dev Sprint 1 | Dev Sprint 2 | Stabilization Sprint | Dev Sprint 3 | Dev Sprint 4 | Stabilization Sprint |

Figure 18.10   Interleaved stabilization sprints.

The advantage to this approach is that there is very quick feedback to product development. Since testing occurs immediately after the sprint, developers find out within days if the product they created had a significant number of undetected defects. The disadvantages to this approach are:

1. There may be a tendency for the developers to rely on the QA team to find the majority of the defects. When setting up an environment like this, make sure that your Scrum teams have a very rigorous DONEness definition and that the teams hold themselves responsible for completing every backlog item based on that definition.
2. This method requires a QA team to be dedicated to the project and to test the product repeatedly during every development sprint. Many organizations don't always have the personnel to dedicate to a single project.

The second method for getting proper testing done when the automated testing doesn't provide sufficient coverage is to interrupt the development sprints with a mid-project stabilization sprint. This differs from the stabilization sprint discussed earlier in that we aren't going to wait until the end of the project to make sure that the product is in good shape.

In Figure 18.10, you can see how the stabilization sprints are interleaved with the development sprints. After the initial two development sprints, focus turns to testing the product and ensuring that all known defects are solved and closed. Then, development begins again for two more sprints, followed by another stabilization. The advantage to this method is that the risk of not testing the entire product is deferred for only two development sprints—then the development staff stops developing new software and begins to test the existing software. Any defects discovered during the testing are immediately analyzed and solved. The testing process, when possible, repeats a few times during the stabilization sprint to ensure that

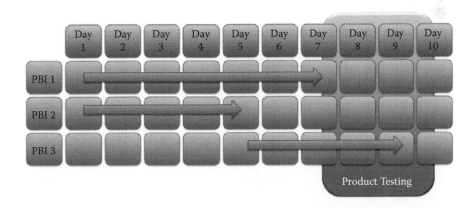

Figure 18.11   Product testing in a development sprint.

as many defects as possible have been found and solved. At the end of the sprint, the remaining defects are moved to the product backlog and prioritized with the rest of the development work.

The disadvantage to this process is that the development work has to be halted while the testing occurs. This can be hard to sell to management (although the alternative of developing to the end of the project and then trying to stabilize the product is a much greater evil!); however, the perceived delay can be mitigated by restarting development work during the stabilization sprint if no critical defects are found during testing (in other words, if the testing goes well, development can be restarted, during the stabilization sprint back into a development sprint). Improved testing during the development sprints can help make this a reality.

The third method for getting proper testing done when the automated testing doesn't provide sufficient coverage is to move the product testing into the development sprints. This method provides the best chance of developing high-quality software with few defects because it ensures that no product backlog item is considered finished unless the item passes a product test. In other words, the Scrum team coordinates instances of manual testing of the product to coincide with the completion of one or more of the Scrum team's goals for the Sprint.

In Figure 18.11, we see the first ten days of a development sprint. The highest-priority item in the sprint goals (PBI 1) is started by the Scrum team on day 1 of the sprint and is finished on day 7. The second item in the sprint goals (PBI 2) is likewise started on day 1 of the sprint, but is finished on day 5 of the sprint (the third item on the sprint goals, PBI 3, is started immediately after the completion of PBI 2). The Scrum team decides to do a complete round of product testing on days 7 through 10 of the sprint. This testing is then guaranteed to include the development work done on PBIs 1 and 2. Another round of testing, later in the sprint, will be scheduled to include work done on the product to test the remaining sprint goals. However, should any sprint goals fail the product testing at the end of the sprint, it is unlikely that the failed goal will be able to be fixed before the sprint review meeting, and will not be reviewable at the meeting.[6]

The advantage to this method is that, when the sprint ends, the product increment created by the sprint will have been fully tested in an integrated product environment, thus helping to ensure that the product increment is shippable to a customer. Another important advantage is that any defect will often be easier to find, rather than more difficult, because the developer will not be far removed from the coding effort that caused the defect. The disadvantage, similar to in the preceding method, is that the Scrum teams will complete fewer product backlog items during the sprint due to the additional manual testing.

When the automated testing for a product does not cover a sufficient portion of the product code (i.e., more than eighty-five percent), manual testing is the only alternative to ensuring that the product under development continues to be of high quality before delivery to its customers. Unfortunately, manual testing can be very expensive, requiring several personnel many hours to fully complete the testing. At the same time, however, the longer testing is deferred, the greater the risk that an error will be found that has profound effects on the project schedule. The methods reviewed in this section describe a practice for:

■ Testing at the end of the project—quite risky. The possibility for errors is substantial and the probability that one of those errors may impact the project schedule is high.

■ Testing during the project, in between development sprints—better, but more expensive. The possibility for errors is high but, except for the final round of testing at the end of the project, there will usually be time to correct significant defects in stabilization sprint or a development sprint.

■ Testing during the sprint—best, but very expensive. Testing is done once or twice per sprint, reducing how much work the Scrum team can produce, but also substantially reducing the possibility of defects at the end of the project and improving the chances that the project schedule will not be impacted.

Your organization will need to make a decision weighing the cost of repeated rounds of manual testing against the improved quality achieved by more testing closer to when development occurs.

More testing? Higher quality? Maybe somewhere in between?

Begin Backlog Grooming Work Sessions

With the teams staffed and the product backlog prioritized and estimated, we are finally ready to put our teams to work learning about the items on the backlog, slicing those items down into smaller, less complex pieces, and reestimating them. In the first sprint of the project, our goal is to ensure that there is enough work on the product backlog that, when we start the second sprint, the Scrum team will have enough properly sized stories to choose from that they can commit to as much as they deem possible. Knowing how much to prepare during the first sprint can be rather difficult, as not all Scrum teams will have enough of a history working together to accurately predict how much they can complete during a sprint.

During the first sprint of the project, your Scrum teams should be focused on preparing enough of the product backlog to carry them into the second sprint. The easiest way to do this is to keep a clearly visible running list (on a white board or large poster board) of everything that the team has successfully sliced down to the proper size and to encourage the team to continue this activity until they are all confident that there is more on the list than they could possibly commit to during sprint planning for the next sprint.

Some Scrum teams might also begin building stories that they have successfully reduced to a proper size, thus attempting to prepare the product backlog and finish some of the highest-priority items on the backlog simultaneously.

Starting with the second sprint, each Scrum team should spend between five and ten percent of their time in the process of grooming the backlog for the next sprint. Ideally, these work sessions should be scheduled at the same time each week during the sprint, allowing the team members to properly plan for the time away from the current sprint's backlog. My recommendation is to hold two work sessions each week in the morning or the afternoon. The goal of these work sessions is to prepare enough of the product backlog for the upcoming sprint, plus perhaps another twenty-five or fifty percent (just in case one or more stories are removed before sprint planning). Once that objective has been obtained, you can cancel the remainder of the grooming work sessions for the sprint.

Summary

Agile project management involves many different steps, from creating an initial estimate of the project's budget based on the portion of the product backlog that is targeted for completion to planning the deployment of Scrum teams, balancing around the product backlog's content, and creating the project's sprint schedule.

In a Scrum project, we deal with much of the planning and estimation during the first sprint of the project. In fact, the major goals of our first sprint can be rather extensive, and during this first sprint, it is not unusual at all to have a significant portion of the project team involved to prepare enough of the product backlog to start building the product while continuing to prepare the product backlog for the following sprint. During the first sprint, we want to make sure that the release goals are in place, that the product architecture is fully defined, that we've reviewed and updated any relevant corporate policies and processes (including the organizational and product DONEness definitions), set the sprint schedule, and begun grooming the product backlog preparatory to building software.

During this first sprint, we might also be taking time to determine how many Scrum teams we are going to create and how each team will be staffed. When doing this, we need to pay some amount of attention to specialization—the effect created when a significant number of product backlog items require skills that only a limited number of developers possess. When this occurs, we also have to be careful about balancing our Scrum teams so that we have enough of the right skills in the right place to ensure that the prioritization of the product backlog can be followed during the course of the entire project. Once you understand how to balance your teams, you can use a variety of methods for staffing them, from a traditional manager's choice to a more radical sign-up approach that allows employees to self-select for a team.

With all this in place, the project begins in earnest, moving from the first sprint, where we expect to see some kind of completed functionality, to the second sprint, when more teams are deployed, the product backlog is ready for another sprint, and the development effort ramps up to full (or nearly full) speed.

The key to agile project management is the same as the key to agile development. Too much reliance on up-front planning will result in a lot of plans and contingencies but no working software (and all, pretty much, for the same cost!). Plan your first sprint around the key people needed to determine the product backlog content, groom the backlog for the first and second sprints, and then go build software while the remaining Scrum teams are staffed and prepped. Done properly, you can finish the first sprint with a groomed product backlog, new Scrum teams, the original Scrum team with experience that can be passed on to the new Scrum teams, and some amount of working software to demonstrate to an eager audience of product owners and stakeholders. Not bad for one sprint's work, huh?

Endnotes

1. I have seen more sprints fail due to unfinished or incomplete architecture definitions than almost any other cause. Scrum teams need to know how the product architecture relates to the product application features prior to trying to analyze, design, and build those features; otherwise, the team often comes to a standstill.
2. Sprint failures are actually good things when they force the team to stop writing application features when the architecture definition doesn't support good decisions. Ideally, however, you can avoid most of these failures by ensuring that the architecture is properly defined before allowing application features to be built.
3. We will cover backlog grooming in Chapter 20.
4. Release goals provide the same information as the project charter (see http://en.wikipedia.org/wiki/Project_charter).
5. You can find more information on DONEness definitions at http://www.bigagiledevelopment.com/doneness.
6. Product backlog items that fail product testing at the end of the sprint are returned to the product backlog. When (and if) the failed PBI is committed to during another subsequent sprint, it is corrected and retested.

Chapter 19

Agile Project Management: Monitoring, Reporting, and Controlling

In this chapter, we will continue the discussion of the responsibilities of the agile project manager. In the previous chapter, we discussed the activities that the project manager performs to get a project started. In this chapter, we will assume that the project is already under way, and the project manager is now monitoring and reporting the progress of the project and, when needed, making changes to assert some control over the project.

1. *Monitoring and reporting progress*: While I won't campaign for collecting lots of metrics and measuring uncounted aspects of development, there is a need for some degree of monitoring and reporting the progress of development so that product owners and management have an ongoing idea of how much of the product backlog is completed and predicting how much might be completed during the next couple sprints.
2. *Controlling*: As the number of Scrum teams increases and the number of dependencies between backlog items increases, the possibility for moving from the edge of chaos to total chaos increases. There are steps that the release manager can take to help constrain some of the unwanted chaos.

We'll talk about each of these responsibilities in the following sections of this chapter.

Monitoring Project Progress

When monitoring project progress, we will focus on our project in terms of burn rate, accumulation rate, earned business value, and feature completion. These metrics will help us understand the progress that the Scrum teams are making through the product backlog and how much business value has been achieved during the course of the development effort. The goals of monitoring project progress is to provide the information needed by the business to make critical decisions that have a direct impact on the return on investment of the development effort. In other words, we try to provide the information that gives answers to questions like "When will we have enough value in the product that we can sell it?"

We will not, however, embark on an effort to measure Scrum team performance. Dr. Eli Goldratt points out in his book *The Haystack Syndrome* a rather interesting behavioral principle: "Tell me how you measure me, and I will tell you how I will behave." The same concept is also called the observer effect or reactivity. Simply put, individuals change their behavior when they know they are being watched. The same is true of Scrum teams. When you impose metrics on a Scrum team, their behavior is changed, often leading to wasteful dysfunctions, in order to respond or react to the collected metric. In order to avoid negatively impacting Scrum team morale and performance, Scrum teams (perhaps with the support of a functional manager) are expected to monitor and improve their own performance.

Let's define the measurements before proceeding:

1. *Burn rate* refers to the completion of product backlog items (which results in their removal from the product backlog and an overall reduction in the number of items left on the backlog; thus, the backlog is said to be burning down).
2. *Accumulation rate* refers to the addition of new items to the product backlog that occurs during the normal course of software development and requirements elaboration.
3 *Earned business value* refers to the sum of the value of the completed product backlog items. Often, projects earn a significant portion of the their total value during the first two-thirds of the project. Keeping a close eye on this value and how it changes can help organizations recognize when a product might already be ready for sale or production use.
4. *Feature completion* refers to the completion state of each of the major features in the release. By understanding the feature completion of the project, product owners can make intelligent decisions regarding when the key product features have enough value to permit use in a production environment.

Burning Down the Product Backlog

In many software development projects, whether the project is date driven or feature driven, a specific portion of the product backlog is expected to be included in the project and removed when completed. We can track the progress of the Scrum teams completing features by noting the change in the product backlog from sprint to sprint. By using the outcome of two or three sprints, we can even reasonably predict how long it will take to finish the portion of the product backlog to be included in the project.

For example, let's assume that we are three months into a project that is intended to be completed six months from today. The product backlog estimated at 10,300 story points at the beginning of the project was reduced by 500 story points during the first sprint and 1,800 story points during the second sprint. Using this information, and assuming the next six sprints will have similar results, we can track our progress to date and predict our probable completion date.

In Figure 19.1, by adding a linear trend line, we can see that the 10,300 story points in the project are predicted to be completed in sprint 10. The current burn rate, calculated as the average of the number of points completed each sprint, is 1,150 story points. Let's take this forward a few more months.

By the time we get to the eighth sprint (see Figure 19.2), the burn rate has continued to be fairly consistent (1,043 story points) and the project will still be finished if it is extended to a tenth sprint. However, we also have to consider the new backlog items that are added to the product backlog because new ideas that were not thought of when the project began are added during the project.

Let's look at what happens to our sample project when we allow for the addition of items to the product backlog during the project: Figure 19.3 shows what

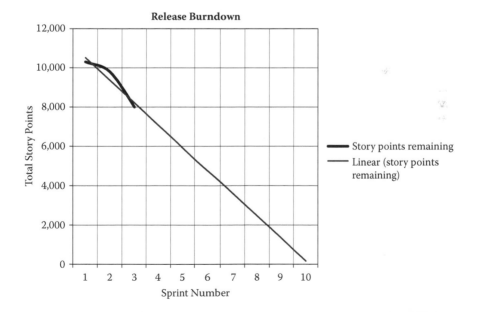

Figure 19.1 Simple release burn-down.

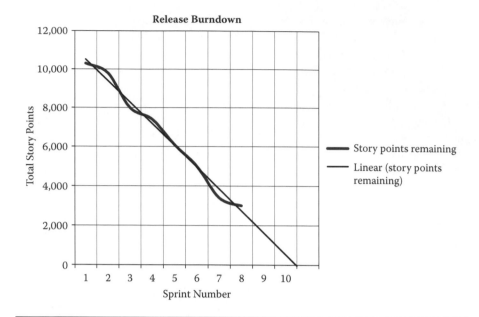

Figure 19.2   Simple release burn-down at sprint 8 of 9.

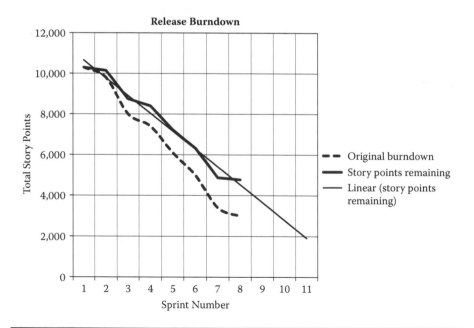

Figure 19.3   Simple release burn-down showing original burn and burn including added items.

happens when we include the addition of new backlog items during the project. Even though the same amount of work is being done, the effective burn rate has dropped to 790 story points. The problem, of course, is that the simple release burn-down tends to hide the difference between items being completed or removed and items being added. Also, because the impact of adding items to the backlog is incorporated into the impact of removing items from the backlog, it becomes much harder to determine if our Scrum teams completed less during a sprint or if there were simply a lot of new items added to the backlog.

For example, look at the difference between sprints 7 and 8 on the thick black line in Figure 19.3. At the beginning of sprint 7, there are about 4,900 story points left in the project. However, at the beginning of sprint 8, there are still nearly 4,800 story points left in the project. With an average burn rate of 790 story points, is it that our Scrum teams only completed 100 story points? Or, is it that our Scrum teams performed as per their average burn rate, but there were a lot of story points worth of items added to the backlog during this sprint?

Mike Cohn, founder of Mountain Goat Software, has suggested a modified release burn-down that separates the removal of product backlog items from the addition of new product backlog items. When applied to the example in Figure 19.3, it looks like what is shown in Figure 19.4.

In Figure 19.4, we've reproduced the same data used in the previous burn-down examples using the enhanced product burn-down format. In this view, the size of the original product backlog content is shown by how much the vertical bars extend above the x-axis (the zero line). Any items added to the product

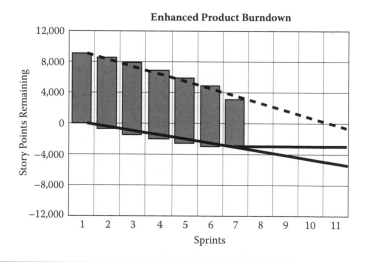

Figure 19.4 The enhanced product burn-down.

backlog are represented by how much of the bars extend below the x-axis. At the beginning of sprint 1, all of the content is original, so there's nothing below the x-axis and there are 10,300 story points of items represented above the x-axis. By the time we get to the beginning of sprint 6, even though the Scrum teams have burned the backlog down nearly 6,000 story points, there still seem to be more than 7,000 story points left on the backlog (about 4,300 story points above the x-axis and another 3,000 new story points added after the project started).

More importantly, look at the trend lines. The dotted trend line indicates the burn rate of the Scrum teams. This rate reflects *only* removal of product backlog items due to either completion of an item or deletion of an item. The solid trend line, on the other hand, indicates the accumulation rate and reflects *only* the addition of new items to the product backlog since the project began. To put it simply, the dotted trend line (burn rate) shows how fast we are removing items from the backlog and the solid trend line (accumulation rate) shows how fast we are adding new items to the backlog.

You can make some broad predictions by examining the trend lines and understanding that the intersection of the trend lines indicates that all of the work originally included in the project, plus all of the work added after the project began, has been completed. In Figure 19.4, you can see that the trend lines are slowly converging as each sprint is completed. However, the intersection of the two lines would appear to be several more sprints in the future. If, on the other hand, the dotted and solid lines are parallel or not converging at all, you can honestly say that the project cannot end unless the decision is made to begin pushing the lowest priority work to the next release. This is what the dark black line beginning at the bottom of the sprint 7 bar indicates: if the project management team decided to balance any new work with the removal of an equal amount of the lowest-priority backlog items, the bars would not descend any further below the x-axis. If you then look for the intersection between the dotted trend line and the *what if* line, you can determine when the current project might be finished. In the case of Figure 19.4, it seems like the dotted trend line and the *what if* line will intersect in sprint 12. The scenario indicated by the black line might be described by a project manager as:

> If we stop the backlog from growing by de-scoping the lowest-priority work when new items are added, we can finish the project in sprint 12.

If we were to allow the project to finish, pushing the lowest-priority work to the next release when new items are added, the final burn-down might look a little like that shown in Figure 19.5.

In Figure 19.5, we've followed the project manager's suggestion of pushing lower-priority work to the next release whenever new items are added to the product backlog. This means that the "new work" portion of the bars on the burn-down

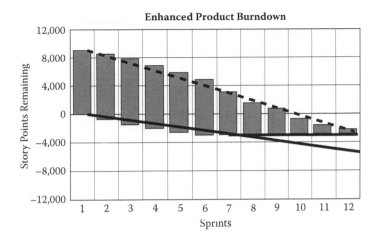

Figure 19.5   The completed project's product burn-down.

graph will not reach further below the x-axis and only the burn rate changes the backlog size from that point forward. As you can see, beginning in sprint 7, while the bars get shorter because of the efforts of the Scrum teams, the bars do not reach further below the x-axis.

But let's be very clear about this: this doesn't mean that new items aren't being added to the product backlog any longer. Doing that would imply that, no matter what good idea was thought of during the remainder of the project, the project team would not consider doing it. That's passing up on new opportunities and ignoring the natural uncertainty that is part of software development. In short, ignoring new ideas and new opportunities would be a shortsighted mistake. What the burn-down in Figure 19.5 represents is a decision to remove an amount of the lowest-priority work equal to the rough amount of new work added to the product backlog. In other words, if, during sprint 9, we come up with a fantastic new idea with a complexity estimate of about fifteen story points, we're going to have to remove the same (or roughly the same) amount of work from the bottom of the product backlog.[1] Fifteen new story points in, fifteen low-priority story points out.

Summary

In this section about monitoring project progress, we discussed how to show progress through the product backlog by using the *burn rate* and the *accumulation rate*. The burn rate reflects the rate (usually in average story points) at which backlog items are removed from the product backlog due to item completion and item deletion. The accumulation rate reflects the rate (also usually in average story points) at which new backlog items are being added to the product backlog as new ideas and new opportunities present themselves. We can show burn rate and accumulation rate on a variety of different graphs, but the enhanced versions (see Figures 19.4 and 19.5) provide the most useful information regarding both measurements. Using this information, the agile project manager can assess project progress and help the product owners to maximize return on investment.

The Release Plan

When reviewing the burn rate and the accumulation rate, the only aspect of the product backlog that we are considering is its size in terms of how much work the backlog represents. While this level of monitoring is useful from the project perspective, agile project managers are often called upon to help product owners understand not just *how much work* is getting done, but *what work*, in terms of actual features and backlog items:

- Finished by the Scrum teams
- Under way within the Scrum teams
- Coming up in the next sprint or two
- Likely to be de-scoped from the project (this item often being the most critical)

This requires the agile project manager to also have a clear idea of the state of the product backlog throughout the project. We accomplish this with the release plan, a view of the portion of the product backlog that is included in the project with separators indicating in which sprint each backlog item is anticipated to be built by a Scrum team. Let's consider a small gaming company with one Scrum team of seven developers and a fairly basic product backlog for building a chess game. Here's the initial product backlog:

- Collect the player's information (3 SP).
- Display an empty board (8 SP).
- Build all of the board pieces (10 SP).
- Put the pieces on the board in starting positions (5 SP).
- Allow player to move pieces (3 SP).
- Remove captured pieces (2 SP).
- Allow a player to indicate check (2 SP).
- Allow a player to indicate checkmate (2 SP).
- Allow a player to resign (2 SP).
- Allow both players to declare a draw (3 SP).
- Identify common legal vs. illegal piece moves (3 SP).
- Identify *en passant* pawn moves (3 SP).
- Identify king-side castle (3 SP).
- Identify queen-side castle (3 SP).
- Identify check condition without user's help (4 SP).

- Identify checkmate condition without user's help (7 SP).
- Support pawn promotion using captured pieces (4 SP).
- Support pawn promotion using any piece type (4 SP).
- Incorporate a game clock (3 SP).
- Provide a log of all moves in algebraic notation (3 SP).
- Provide a log of all moves in descriptive notation (3 SP).
- Playback the entire game using the move log (8 SP).
- Allow user to control playback speed (3 SP).
- Provide "forfeit on illegal move" option (2 SP).
- Support crusader-style chess pieces (7 SP).
- Support blitz-style game rules (4 SP).
- Allow users to select colors other than black or white (4 SP).
- Support new chessboard backgrounds (12 SP).

For the purposes of our CyberChess application, our release goals for version 1.0 are to create a basic game board; the players will be able to move their pieces fairly indiscriminately—the game will not be able to tell if an illegal move is made, nor will the game be able to detect a check or checkmate condition. The players will have to do that. The portion of the product backlog that we'll use in this project will include only the following backlog items:

- Collect the player's information (3 SP).
- Display an empty board (8 SP).
- Build all of the board pieces (10 SP).
- Put the pieces on the board in starting positions (5 SP).
- Allow player to move pieces (3 SP).
- Remove captured pieces (2 SP).
- Allow a player to indicate check (2 SP).
- Allow a player to indicate checkmate (2 SP).
- Allow a player to resign (2 SP).
- Allow both players to declare a draw (3 SP).

This small, low-tech release will give us a simple version that we can use to validate the concept, the hardware platform, etc. A quick review of the scoped product backlog shows that there are an anticipated forty story points in the content. If we assume from past experience that our one Scrum team can get about eight story points worth of work done in a sprint, we can slice up our product backlog along eight story point divisions like so:

- Sprint 1
  - Collect the player's information (3 SP).
  - Create board boundaries and outlines (2 SP) (from "Display an empty board—8 SP").

- – Create a white space (1 SP) (from "Display an empty board—8 SP").
- – Create a black space (1 SP) (from "Display an empty board—8 SP").
- ■ Sprint 2
  - – Compile spaces to create empty board (5 SP) (from "Display an empty board—8 SP").
  - – Learn how to use the rendering routines (3 SP) (from "Build all of the board pieces—10 SP").
  - – Build raster table for pawns (1 SP) (from "Build all of the board pieces—10 SP").
- ■ Sprint 3
  - – Build raster table for rooks and bishops (2 SP) (from "Build all of the board pieces—10 SP").
  - – Build raster table for knights (2 SP) (from "Build all of the board pieces—10 SP").
  - – Build raster table for king (2 SP) (from "Build all of the board pieces—10 SP").
  - – Build raster table for queen (2 SP) (from "Build all of the board pieces—10 SP").
- ■ Sprint 4
  - – Put the pieces on the board in starting positions (5 SP).
  - – Allow player to move pieces (3 SP).
- ■ Sprint 5
  - – Remove captured pieces (2 SP).
  - – Allow a player to indicate check (2 SP).
  - – Allow a player to indicate checkmate (2 SP).
  - – Allow a player to resign (2 SP).
- ■ Sprint 6
  - – Allow both players to declare a draw (3 SP).

The result of slicing up the product backlog along the lines of which sprint the items will be completed in is called the release plan. This plan gives us a basic idea of what's on the product backlog and when each item will be done. However, since we can't be sure what the Scrum team will actually complete by the end of the sprint, we will have to wait until the sprint is over and then reassess the plan. For instance, during the first sprint, the team ran into some difficulty displaying the board boundaries (the outline of the board). There were some unexpected problems with the rendering software being used by the application that resulted in some significant delays. So, at the end of sprint 1 and after the product owner approves the player information screen and the appearance of the white and black squares, the Scrum team completes five story points out of seven. We can now re-create the release plan by removing the completed pieces and keeping each sprint balanced at or near eight story points per sprint (we could take the team's velocity of five instead of eight, but one sprint is usually not enough to establish a pattern—the team decided to stick with eight story points for now). The updated release plan after sprint 1 looks like this:

- ■ Sprint 2
  - – Create board boundaries and outlines (2 SP)(from "Display an empty board—8 SP").
  - – Compile spaces to create empty board (5 SP).
- ■ Sprint 3
  - – Learn how to use the rendering routines (3 SP) (from "Build all of the board pieces—10 SP").
  - – Build raster table for pawns (1 SP) (from "Build all of the board pieces—10 SP").
  - – Build raster table for rooks and bishops (2 SP) (from "Build all of the board pieces—10 SP").
  - – Build raster table for knights (2 SP) (from "Build all of the board pieces—10 SP").
- ■ Sprint 4
  - – Build raster table for king (2 SP) (from "Build all of the board pieces—10 SP").
  - – Build raster table for queen (2 SP) (from "Build all of the board pieces—10 SP").
  - – Put the pieces on the board in starting positions (5 SP).
- ■ Sprint 5
  - – Allow player to move pieces (3 SP).
  - – Remove captured pieces (2 SP).
  - – Allow a player to indicate check (2 SP).
- ■ Sprint 6
  - – Allow a player to indicate checkmate (2 SP).
  - – Allow a player to resign (2 SP).
  - – Allow both players to declare a draw (3 SP).

The new release plan is still six sprints long (down to five now that sprint 1 is completed). We ended up rearranging the content of every sprint in order to keep each sprint at or near eight story points per sprint. Unfortunately, the last sprint, sprint 6, is already pretty full. This means that any more delays in the project may result in dropping a feature or extending the project. After a quick check with the product owner, we discover that he is fine dropping the lowest-priority story ("Allow both players to declare a draw") out of the release since players can accomplish the same thing by quitting the CyberChess program. At the same time, there is always a possibility that the Scrum team may finish an item faster than expected to achieve more than eight story points. In fact, we've overloaded sprint 4 with nine story points in case the team gains some velocity.

Let's jump ahead to the end of sprint 2. Our Scrum team was quite busy during the sprint. They got the board boundaries to work properly, but it took so much of the sprint that the story for putting all of the spaces together to make up the full board wasn't quite finished. The Scrum team achieved a velocity of two story points (although everyone agrees that they almost finished the other five story points). So, we rework the release plan again, but everyone agrees it would be OK to overload sprint 3 a little, since the "Compile spaces to create empty board" was almost finished:

- Sprint 3
  - Compile spaces to create empty board (5 SP).
  - Learn how to use the rendering routines (3 SP) (from "Build all of the board pieces—10 SP").
  - Build raster table for pawns (1 SP) (from "Build all of the board pieces—10 SP").
- Sprint 4
  - Build raster table for rooks and bishops (2 SP) (from "Build all of the board pieces—10 SP").
  - Build raster table for knights (2 SP) (from "Build all of the board pieces—10 SP").
  - Build raster table for king (2 SP) (from "Build all of the board pieces—10 SP").
  - Build raster table for queen (2 SP) (from "Build all of the board pieces—10 SP").
- Sprint 5
  - Put the pieces on the board in starting positions (5 SP).
  - Allow player to move pieces (3 SP).
- Sprint 6
  - Remove captured pieces (2 SP).
  - Allow a player to indicate check (2 SP).
  - Allow a player to indicate checkmate (2 SP).
  - Allow a player to resign (2 SP).
- On the chopping block
  - Allow both players to declare a draw (3 SP).

With sprint 2 completed and the release plan rewritten, we see the projected content for sprints 3 through 6. Unfortunately, I've also had to add a "On the chopping block" category to the end of the release plan. This early in the project, I don't usually just de-scope items that fall out the bottom of the release plan. You never know, a Scrum team may improve its velocity and, all of the sudden, you can bring a feature back into the release.

One more example: We complete one more sprint and, true to everyone's expectation, the Scrum team completed the empty board, learned the rendering routines, and completed the raster table for the pawns. They were also able to reach forward and grab the "Build raster table for rooks and bishops" story from the next sprint—a total of eleven story points. At this point, the release plan now looks like this:

- Sprint 4
  - Build raster table for knights (2 SP) (from "Build all of the board pieces—10 SP").
  - Build raster table for king (2 SP) (from "Build all of the board pieces—10 SP").
  - Build raster table for queen (2 SP) (from "Build all of the board pieces—10 SP").
- Sprint 5
  - Put the pieces on the board in starting positions (5 SP).
  - Allow player to move pieces (3 SP).
- Sprint 6
  - Remove captured pieces (2 SP).
  - Allow a player to indicate check (2 SP).
  - Allow a player to indicate checkmate (2 SP).
  - Allow a player to resign (2 SP).
- On the chopping block
  - Allow both players to declare a draw (3 SP).

However, we're faced with a little problem with this release plan—sprint 4 is undercommitted. As a team, the project manager, product owner, and Scrum team worked together to figure out a good arrangement of backlog items that promotes continued progress. The Scrum team suggested that we could move the "Build the raster table for king" item and the "Build the raster table for queen" item to another sprint (since we've built all of the other pieces at this point) and start putting all of the other pieces on the board. So, sprints 4 and 5 were changed to look like this:

- Sprint 4
  - Build raster table for knights (2 SP) (from "Build all of the board pieces—10 SP").
  - Put the pieces on the board in starting positions (5 SP).
- Sprint 5
  - Build raster table for king (2 SP) (from "Build all of the board pieces—10 SP").
  - Build raster table for queen (2 SP) (from "Build all of the board pieces—10 SP").
  - Allow player to move pieces (3 SP).

This allowed the release plan to put seven story points of items in sprint 4 and seven in sprint 5. Another advantage to this approach is that the team was able to begin putting pieces on the board in sprint 4 instead of waiting until sprint 5. By doing this, the team has moved a crucial step in the development of the application (that of displaying pieces on the board) to be done earlier instead of later.

Summary

The release plan is a very simple plan that lays out which features are planned to be built and when during the course of the project. For the project manager, the release plan provides information like:

- Which features are finished?
- Which features are in progress?
- Which features are coming up?
- Which features are in danger of being dropped from the project?

As each sprint is completed, the release plan is rewritten based on what the team accomplished and what their anticipated velocity (how many story points they are doing each sprint) is. The other advantage to the release plan is that it provides some visibility to what the Scrum teams are working on and in what order (better even than just looking at the product backlog). In some circumstances, project personnel might find more effective ways to arrange the work by finding better fits or even items that might be built more effectively in another order.

Feature Completion

In the previous sections, we discussed monitoring that helps product owners understand how much work is getting done (burn rate and accumulation rate). Then we discussed the release plan, which helps us to understand what specific backlog items are getting done. In this section we'll discuss how to actually understand how the completed backlog items relate to the major business features slated for introduction in the current project. For example, let's take another look at the CyberChess example used in the previous section. When I work with development teams planning out a whole new product or a new release of a product, I often use a simple group exercise where I draw a "cereal box" type figure on a flipchart or white board, like that shown in Figure 19.6.

I then invite the Scrum team (including the product owner) to decorate the box in a way that expresses the selling points of the product. Why would customers buy it? Where's the value? Were I to have the CyberChess development team work on this box, the result might look like that shown in Figure 19.7.

This exercise does a fantastic job of finding out how much about the product the Scrum team understands. Even if the product owner's involvement drives

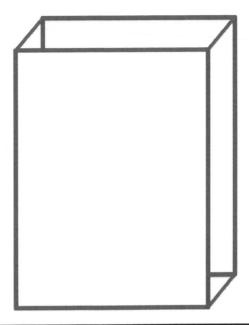

Figure 19.6   An empty cereal box.

Figure 19.7   The development team's version of the CyberChess product packaging.

much of the content, you might be surprised the number of times that the developers will find additional features that are key to product success. Looking at the box shown in Figure 19.7, we can see that the developers have identified the following major features:

1. Product runs on Microsoft Windows XP[2] operating system and Apple Mac OS® X
2. 3D chessboard rendering
3. Highly detailed chess pieces
4. Personalized for the players

As it turns out, if we were to review the portion of the product backlog tagged for the current release, we can see that most of the backlog items can be categorized under one of the major features.

As you can see in Table 19.1, we can categorize most of the project's backlog items under one of the major product features. For example, the "3D chessboard" feature contains the backlog items needed to create the board boundaries, the rendering of the white and black spaces, and the creation and display of the empty board. The "Highly detailed chess pieces" feature contains the backlog items to create the chess pieces and put the pieces in the starting positions on the chessboard. However, not all major features are accounted for and not all backlog items can be categorized. This is because of the following two exceptions when categorizing backlog items under major features:

1. Nonfunctional constraints: Some features don't actually describe things that the product does; these constraints describe how the product works. For example, in Table 19.1 we see that the "Product runs on Microsoft Windows and Mac OS X" feature has no backlog items categorized under it. This is because, in most instances, making the product work on one or more operating system platforms is a function of the DONEness criteria of each backlog item. In other words, making the product work on both Microsoft Windows and Mac OS X is something the Scrum team has to consider for every backlog item it builds—making sure that all of the tests and code they create work on both platforms.
2. Baseline support: Some features create the fundamental functions of the product. These features are usually not considered major; they aren't selling points. For example, telling CyberChess customers that the product supports playing chess is not only redundant, but it won't sell the product. Backlog items that describe the basic functions of supporting a chess game are considered a given and are not "exciters" from the customer's perspective, and therefore not a major feature.

Table 19.1   Product Backlog Categorized with Major Product Features for Version 1.0

Major Feature	Backlog Item
3D chessboard	• Create board boundaries and outlines (2 SP) • Create a white space (1 SP) • Create a black space (1 SP) • Compile spaces to create empty board (5 SP)
Highly detailed chess pieces	• Learn how to use the rendering routines (3 SP) • Build raster table for pawns (1 SP) • Build raster table for rooks and bishops (2 SP) • Build raster table for knights (2 SP) • Build raster table for king (2 SP) • Build raster table for queen (2 SP) • Put the pieces on the board in starting positions (5 SP)
Personalization	• Collect the player's information (3 SP) • Product runs on Microsoft Windows and Apple Mac OS X
Baseline support	• Allow player to move pieces (3 SP) • Remove captured pieces (2 SP) • Allow a player to indicate check (2 SP) • Allow a player to indicate checkmate (2 SP) • Allow a player to resign (2 SP) • Allow both players to declare a draw (3 SP)

Having categorized the backlog items into major features and baseline support, we can add up the story points within each category to get an idea of how big each feature is (see Table 19.4).

Using the information in Table 19.2, we can now begin to track the completion of the project's major features from sprint to sprint. Recall that, by the end of sprint 1, the Scrum team had completed the stories shown in Table 19.3.

If we look at the results of sprint 1 in terms of the major features, we can actually start to see development progress in terms of the selling features of the product. Take a look at Table 19.4.

Table 19.4 shows us the result of sprint 1 in terms of the completion of the project's major features. The Scrum team completed two story points of the total seventeen story points required to build the 3D chessboard. This means that the 3D chessboard is twelve percent completed by the end of sprint 1 and the personalization

Table 19.2   Major Feature Sizes

Major Feature Category	Size
3D chessboard	9 SP
Highly detailed chess pieces	17 SP
Personalization	3 SP
Baseline support	14 SP

Table 19.3   Backlog Items Completed in Sprint 1

Backlog Item	Category	Size
Collect the player's information	Personalization	3 SP
Create a white space	3D chessboard	1 SP
Create a black space	3D chessboard	1 SP

Table 19.4   Major Feature Completion after CyberChess Version 1, Sprint 1

		Sprint 1	
Category	Budget	Points Complete	% Complete
3D chessboard	9 SP	2 SP	22%
Highly detailed chess pieces	17 SP		0%
Personalization	3 SP	3 SP	100%
Baseline support	14 SP		0%

Table 19.5   Backlog Items Completed in Sprint 2

Backlog Item	Category	Size
Create board boundaries and outlines	3D chessboard	2 SP

feature is already finished. Unfortunately, none of the chess pieces have been built, and none of the baseline support has been completed to actually make the product capable of playing chess. Let's move forward to the end of sprint 2, where the Scrum team completed the backlog items shown in Table 19.5.

When we translate this into completion percentages, it looks like Table 19.6.

Our feature completion at the end of sprint 2 shows us that we're making good progress against the 3D chessboard feature and the personalization is finished. However, once again, we've made little to no progress against either the chess pieces

Table 19.6   Major Feature Completion after CyberChess Version 1, Sprint 2

Category	Budget	Sprint 1		Sprint 2	
		Points Complete	*% Complete*	*Points Complete*	*% Complete*
3D chessboard	9 SP	2 SP	22%		44%
Highly detailed chess pieces	17 SP		0%		0%
Personalization	3 SP	3 SP	100%		100%
Baseline support	14 SP		0%		0%

Table 19.7   Backlog Items Completed in Sprint 3

Backlog Item	Category	Size
Compile spaces to create empty board	3D chessboard	5 SP
Learn how to use the rendering routines	Highly detailed chess pieces	3 SP
Build raster table for pawns	Highly detailed chess pieces	1 SP
Build raster table for rooks and bishops	Highly detailed chess pieces	2 SP

or the simple rules for playing chess. Our product owners would have to agree unanimously—the product isn't ready to ship. Let's take a look at the result of sprint 3. The Scrum team completed the backlog items in Table 19.7.

Finally, our Scrum team has begun to work on the chess pieces. When we look at feature completion now (Table 19.8), we see some promising progress. Unfortunately, though, there is still no baseline support to allow players to move pieces, declare check or checkmate, or quit the game.

The project manager continues to review the feature completion with the product owner, looking for opportunities to improve the prioritization of the product backlog (which only the product owner can do) or somehow release the product early, maximizing the value while reducing the overall project cost.

If we assume that the Scrum team completes sprints 4, 5, and 6 as planned in the release plan (see Table 19.1), the feature completion looks Table 19.9 at the end of both sprints.

As sprint 5 ends, we can see that all aspects of the product are ready to go except for the baseline support (consisting of piece movement and end-game scenarios). Sprint 6 is therefore completely dedicated to getting as much of the baseline support done as possible. In fact, at the end of sprint 6, we have an important decision to make. The 3D chessboard is up and running, the chess pieces are ready, and the

Table 19.8 Major Feature Completion after CyberChess Version 1, Sprint 3

Category	Budget	Sprint 1		Sprint 2		Sprint 3	
		Points Complete	% Complete	Points Complete	% Complete	Points Complete	% Complete
3D chessboard	9 SP	2 SP	22%	2 SP	44%	5 SP	100%
Highly detailed chess pieces	17 SP		0%		0%	6 SP	35%
Personalization	3 SP	3 SP	100%		100%		100%
Baseline support	14 SP		0%		0%		0%

Table 19.9 Major Feature Completion after CyberChess Version 1, Sprint 6

Category	Budget	Sprint 1		Sprint 2		Sprint 3		Sprint 4		Sprint 5		Sprint 6	
		Points Complete	% Complete	Points Complete	% Complete	Points Complete	% Complete	Points Complete	% Complete	Points Complete	% Complete	Points Complete	% Complete
3D chessboard	9 SP	2 SP	22%	2 SP	44%	5 SP	100%		76%		100%		100%
Highly detailed chess pieces	17 SP		0%		0%	6 SP	35%	7 SP	76%	4 SP	100%		100%
Personalization	3 SP	3 SP	100%		100%		100%		100%		100%		100%
Baseline support	14 SP		0%		0%		0%		0%	3 SP	21%	8 SP	79%

personalization works. The only missing item originally planned for the product was the ability for the players to declare a draw. However, since the product owner has already indicated a willingness to ship the product without the draw feature, the product owner gives permission to go ahead and ship the product and the project ends at this point. The "Allow both players to declare a draw" backlog item is returned to the product backlog for possible inclusion in another release.

Summary

We learned in this portion of the chapter that feature completion helps our project manager and product owners to identify how much of the critical, value-adding backlog items have been completed. This is accomplished by grouping the backlog items under the major features that require their completion (understanding that not all features will have backlog items and not all backlog items will fit under a major feature) and then reporting following each sprint on how much of each major feature is completed based on a ratio of

$$\frac{\sum (\text{effort of completed items under major feature})}{\sum (\text{effort of all items under major feature})}$$

By calculating the feature completion after each sprint, we understand more than just which backlog items are finished and which are coming up. Feature completion tells us when our product reaches the point where there might be enough value to send it to its customers.

Controlling the Project

In general, agile projects do not require much in the way of specific controls. Each Scrum team is responsible for organizing around their work; Scrum masters help ensure that a working process is followed; Scrum teams ensure that development practices are continuously improved; Scrum masters and managers help ensure that obstacles identified by Scrum teams are corrected as quickly as possible. The product owners manage the product backlog, and the product backlog drives how work is taken into a sprint by the Scrum teams. However, there are frequently circumstances where a little additional control helps to bring a particularly complex or risky project to a successful conclusion. In this section, we'll discuss the following techniques:

1. Front-load your risk.
2. Shorten your sprints.
3. Manage interactions with nonagile development teams and providers.
4. Monitor scope-outs.

Front-Load Your Risk

Given the guaranteed uncertainty that comes with software development, every backlog item comes with a certain amount of risk. The Scrum team frequently determines whether the risk is low, high, or unacceptable during backlog grooming workshops. Of course, backlog items with unacceptable levels of risk are usually removed from the backlog and either dropped completely as not feasible or rethought and returned to the backlog as something with less inherent risk. However, the remaining backlog items with higher degrees of risk present a significant problem for the project. When the unexpected surprises occur, when the expected effort significantly increases, the impact to the project can be catastrophic. The best move is to give your Scrum teams as much time as possible to solve any unexpected problems.

To that end, the project manager should work with the product owners to encourage (1) Scrum teams to provide risk estimations[3] as well as effort estimations, and (2) product owners to review backlog item risk on a regular basis. In order to give the Scrum teams more time to deal with the unexpected obstacles that high-risk items tend to deliver, product owners should look for high-value, high-risk items and prioritize them higher on the product backlog in order to give Scrum teams more time to deal with unexpected problems. Of course, this has to be weighed against other factors in prioritizing the product backlog, but product owners need to be aware of the fact that you can't blame Scrum teams for surprises that occur too late in the project to be solved without delaying software delivery.

Shorten Your Sprints to Improve Visibility

As complex, risky, or critical projects draw toward completion, organizations have been known to get quite nervous about the progress of the final sprints in the project. During the early stages of the project, month-long or four-week-long sprints don't cause distress. Later in the project, however, the management team may want to have more visibility to what is happening during the development sprints. In these cases, it is very common to shorten four-week-long or one-month-long sprints to two weeks. By doing so, product owners and organization management get more opportunities to attend sprint reviews, see completed features, reprioritize the product backlog, and make critical changes to the project plan as the project nears the end.

As illustrated in Figure 19.8, a five-sprint project (where the sprints were either one month long or four weeks long) switches to two-week-long sprints for the final two months of the project. For logistical purposes, you can call these sprints 4A, 4B, 5A, and 5B. However, you can also just call them sprints 4, 5, 6, and 7—it makes little difference.

Once your sprints have been cut in half, the organization will have twice as many opportunities to review the result of the effort, approve or reject the results, and make whatever changes are needed before allowing the Scrum teams to

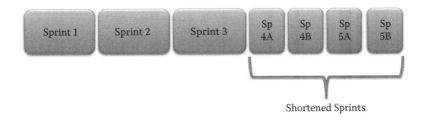

Figure 19.8   Shortening the sprints near the end of the project.

continue development. There are twice as many opportunities to see what has been completed, twice as many opportunities to make changes, twice as many opportunities to reprioritize the product backlog.

In general, it is a bad idea to change the length of your sprints during a project. Much of the predictability of a project (particularly with regard to the release plan) is based on Scrum teams achieving roughly similar velocities each month. By changing the sprint length, the pace that the Scrum teams are familiar with is changed and the predictability of the release plan may be seriously impacted. The effect of this change is minimized because the sprints are cut in half—most Scrum teams will be able to cut their typical commitment in half and be pretty close to accurate.

Manage Interactions with Nonagile Development Teams and Providers

There are very few organizations existing today that have completed a corporation-wide transition. This means that, in many cases, your agile project is going to need help from other, nonagile development teams and providers. This truly isn't difficult to manage in an agile project—since Scrum teams maintain their own impediments list, dependencies with other organizations can be recorded on the impediments list. Then, when the software or other service is provided by the nonagile team, the impediment is cleared and the backlog item can be finished. Let's look at an example.

CyberChess v1.0 was a fantastic hit in its market and the company was gearing up to produce version 2.0 of the game as quickly as possible. The orders for version 1.0 have been phenomenal, but many of the comments from satisfied and unsatisfied customers alike is that the game needs to support more advanced concepts, including the ability to recognize check and checkmate conditions without relying on the players to identify the conditions.

The content of version 2.0 was then selected from the remaining portion of the product backlog based on customer feedback and the priorities set by the product owner. The major features of this new version (including the product backlog items) were determined to be:

1. Advanced chess concepts (20 story points):
   a. Identify common legal vs. illegal piece moves (3 SP).
   b. Identify *en passant* pawn moves (3 SP).
   c. Identify king-side castle (3 SP).
   d. Identify queen-side castle (3 SP).
   e. Support pawn promotion using captured pieces (4 SP).
   f. Support pawn promotion using any piece type (4 SP).
2. Identify end-game scenarios (14 story points):
   a. Allow both players to declare a draw (3 SP).
   b. Identify check condition without user's help (4 SP).
   c. Identify checkmate condition without user's help (7 SP).
3. Create logging and replay capability (14 story points):
   a. Provide a log of all moves in algebraic notation (3 SP).
   b. Provide a log of all moves in descriptive notation (3 SP).
   c. Play back the entire game using the move log (8 SP).

With the proposed content for version 2.0 came another concern: at the rate that the CyberChess product was growing in complexity, and the development staff was likewise growing, there needed to be some additional infrastructure to support two Scrum teams. As a result, two new items were added to the top of the product backlog:

■ Implement source code version control software on a dedicated server (8 SP).
■ Implement an additional server for automated testing (4 SP).

Using the proposed content for Version 2.0 and these two new items, the project manager formed a release plan (based on two Scrum teams at an estimated total ten story points per sprint). One special note, though: The CyberChess procurement department handles the ordering of hardware. All that the Scrum team can do is identify the minimum requirements of the hardware.[4] So, the backlog items for ordering the hardware can really only be started by the Scrum team. Then it's in the procurement department's hands. Since the typical delay from ordering hardware to receiving and installing the hardware is twelve weeks, the project manager placed the install and implement backlog items in sprint 4.

■ Sprint 1
   – Select a source code control software vendor (2 SP).
   – Order the server hardware to be used for the source code control server (1 SP).
   – Order the server hardware to be used for automated testing (1 SP).
   – Order the source code control software (1 SP).
   – Identify common legal vs. illegal piece moves (3 SP).
   – Identify *en passant* pawn moves (3 SP).

- Sprint 2
  - Identify king-side castle (3 SP).
  - Identify queen-side castle (3 SP).
  - Support pawn promotion using captured pieces (4 SP).
- Sprint 3
  - Support pawn promotion using any piece type (4 SP).
  - Allow both players to declare a draw (3 SP).
- Sprint 4
  - Implement the source code control software and the server (4 SP).
  - Implement the automated testing software (4 SP).
  - Identify check condition without user's help (4 SP).
- Sprint 5
  - Identify checkmate condition without user's help (7 SP).
  - Provide a log of all moves in algebraic notation (3 SP).
- Sprint 6
  - Provide a log of all moves in descriptive notation (3 SP).
  - Playback the entire game using the move log (8 SP).

During sprint 1, the Scrum teams identified the source code control software they wanted and contacted procurement to place the software and hardware order. With the order placed, the backlog items are completed. However, there are now two backlog items—"Implement the source code control software and the server" and "Implement the automated testing software"—that are blocked because they cannot be done until the servers are delivered. As a result, the Scrum team responsible for the implementation backlog items adds two items to their impediment list:

- Cannot implement source code control software until the server is delivered
- Cannot implement automated testing server until the server is delivered

Listing the impediments in this manner keeps the issue of the receipt of the servers and the software foremost in everyone's minds. At each sprint planning meeting, the impediment list can be reviewed against the backlog items being considered by the team. If the needed servers haven't yet been delivered, the Scrum team (with the product owner's knowledge) can skip the blocked backlog item and move on to another that is not blocked. As soon as the servers become available, the Scrum master can remove the impediments from the list, effectively unblocking the backlog items that required the servers.

This method of using the impediments list for external dependencies works very well. As long as the Scrum master continues to work the impediment every sprint, you can be assured that there is always someone responsible for following up on these dependencies, making sure that problems are handled and backlog items are worked as soon as they are no longer blocked.

Monitor Scope-outs

As Scrum teams work on their backlog items, it is not uncommon for items to have to be returned to the product backlog. The problem, of course, is when another Scrum team needs the scoped-out backlog item and is counting on it to be available at the completion of the sprint. As a result, it is important that project managers be aware when a Scrum team removes a backlog item from the sprint. The project manager may need to get another Scrum team or another product owner involved in order to determine the impact of the scoped-out item.

A number of popular backlog management tools support the tracking of dependencies between backlog items and automatically alert the proper Scrum team and product owner when a predecessor item is committed to a Sprint and then returned to the backlog. These tools provide a means by which product backlog item dependencies can be tracked (which, of course, requires product owners and Scrum teams to identify and record dependencies between backlog items whenever new items are added or existing items are discussed or split) and usually also provide a means to alert product owners when a backlog item with one or more dependencies is threatened by another item being scoped out by another Scrum team.

When a potentially serious scope-out is flagged, the project manager does not need to become directly involved and, instead, should work to make sure that the proper product owners and Scrum teams are involved to resolve the problem. Prioritization of the backlog is a product owner concern, not a project manager's concern—except to get the matter resolved as quickly as possible. In a large organization, when product owners cannot agree on priority, they should discuss the prioritization as a product owner team, and should that fail to resolve the situation, they should escalate the issue to the "uber" product owner for final resolution.

Summary

In this chapter, we explored the concepts of monitoring and controlling an agile project. When we monitor an agile project, we focus on features and the value those features bring to the product. We want to know which features are completed, which are under way, and which are yet to be done. By combining that information with the estimated value of each feature, we understand how much value the project has created so far, and we can make good business decisions based on the desired value. We accomplish all of this by keeping a close eye on:

- *The burn rate and the accumulation rate*: This information tells us about *how much* of the product backlog we are moving through during the project. It helps us to understand the velocity of the Scrum teams and to predict when the project will be finished.

- *Release planning*: This information tells us *what* we are working on in the product backlog. It helps us understand which features are already finished, which features are being built, and in which sprint the remaining unstarted features will be done.
- *Feature completion*: This information tells us the condition of all major features included in a release by looking at how many of the backlog items that contribute to the feature are completed.

With this information, we not only have a much clearer understanding of how the project is progressing, but also can tell how much of what the customer will be looking for is finished and working. We will also be able to tell when enough of the project is completed that we might be able to cut the project short and release it to sales or internal customers at a reduced cost.

The monitoring and controlling of an agile project does not involve the monitoring and controlling of Scrum teams. A Scrum team is a very dynamic environment that is intended to be self-managing and, to a large extent, self-correcting. To the extent that Scrum teams need guidance, there is usually a manager responsible to some degree for assisting the team in improving their performance and helping to remove impediments. Most team measurements techniques, applied at the project level, become more of a hindrance than a help, causing unwanted behavior as the Scrum team, consciously or otherwise, adapts to the focus created by the measurement.

We also discussed controlling a project and the steps that a project manager can take to ensure that the project is a success. Sprints can be shortened to improve development visibility; risky product backlog items can be moved earlier in the project; impediment lists can be used to track dependencies with outside, nonagile departments.

Managing an agile project is all about helping product owners understand what is happening in terms of the product backlog and in terms of the value built into the project. We monitor the value created by the project, and when we achieve enough value to take the product to our customers, we do so.

Endnotes

1. Of course, if the fantastic new idea is still a lower priority than the lowest-priority items currently on the product backlog, we simply add the new idea to the product backlog for the next release.
2. Windows is a registered trademark of Microsoft Corporation in the United States and other countries.
3. See Chapter 20 for more information.
4. Of course, if a specific model is required, the Scrum team can request that, but they have to justify the additional cost of the server with proof from the vendor that only that model will work. Fun, huh?

Chapter 20

Agile Analysis

Agile analysis is probably not the best term to use to describe how analysis is handled during an agile project. Certainly, the analysis itself is not particularly agile when it is under way. We don't analyze features and requirements faster in agile development. There's no magic formula or novel exercise applied during agile analysis that causes user stories to "stand up" and divulge all their secrets. The same requirements elicitation techniques we learned preagile apply when we work with agile development. So, the term *agile analysis* is more a description of the steps that we take than the effort of analysis itself.

When we say *agile analysis*, we are referring not to an analysis technique, but rather a means by which we engage in requirements analysis throughout the agile project. Agile analysis[1] is probably most effectively described as "progressive elaboration." When we discuss agile analysis, we are really discussing:

1. *The timing of our analysis*: As with much of agile development, agile analysis is just in time. Our efforts to learn all of the details of a customer-desired feature are spread across the agile project and driven by the act of slicing large, complex features into smaller and simpler pieces of features; we obtain the final details when we begin to build the feature.
2. *The structure of our analysis*: In order to provide for a rapid exchange of ideas and ease of prioritization, we will build user stories that hold reminders of what we wanted to discuss, while separate artifacts will contain all of the detail.
3. *The order of our analysis*: We will focus on bringing the most value to the product as early as possible during an agile project. This means our analysis will not necessarily move functionally through a product (for example, we might schedule our work to complete all of the analysis for our customer registration requirements before moving on to our search requirements), but

rather will be done based on which user requirements provide the most value to the customer (and therefore to our organization).

We will cover all of these concepts in this chapter as well as:

1. Backlog grooming: How to break features into smaller, less complex pieces.
2. Estimation: How to quickly estimate the relative effort required to build a story.
3. Risk management: How to deal with features and stories that have an increased likelihood of causing problems during the project.

We will also, first, do a quick review of user stories and related terms, as the rest of the chapter will discuss the product backlog in terms of user stories.

User Stories and Related Terminology

The simplest definition for a user story is to call it a "reminder to have a conversation with your customer about something." User stories are intended to be no more information than you could, literally, fit on an index card. User stories can represent something that is quite large (e.g., "Build a ticket purchasing web site") or very small (e.g., "Allow the user to provide an airline preference for domestic flights"). Small stories are just that—stories. Large stories, however—those that can be further broken down into smaller pieces—are often called epics.

Believe it or not, that's pretty much all we need to discuss to introduce user stories. For a more complete review of user stories and how to use them, refer to *User Stories Applied* by Mike Cohn for more information.

The Life of a User Story

Probably the simplest way to describe agile analysis is in terms of the way ideas flow into our development system and how they are turned into actual working software.

Figure 20.1 illustrates, at a high level, the concept of a user story: starting as a customer's idea, stories are written and added to the product backlog, broken down into smaller stories, and finally handed off to the Scrum team for construction. We'll use this diagram as the basis for the rest of the discussion in this chapter. Let's start at the beginning.

The Next Great Idea

Ideas for products come from everywhere: customers, stakeholders, governments, product owners, and developers. When new ideas come to the product owner, they

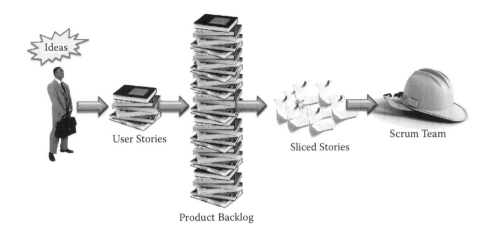

Figure 20.1   The life cycle of a user story.

are frequently (though not always) rewritten as user stories. Some ideas are perfect the way they are presented, for example:

> Update the architecture to support the latest version of the supported OSs.

In cases like this, we don't bother to rewrite the item, though we will still treat it just like a user story. On the other hand, some ideas are actually not ideas, but complaints, like:

> The performance of the customer registration pathway is too slow.

Interestingly, complaints are quite often actually two items in disguise. The first item is needed when research must be done in order to determine the cause behind the complaint. In other words, why is the performance of the customer registration pathway too slow? The second, of course, is based on the outcome of the first and describes what needs to be done in order to solve the problem. Neither of these items necessarily has to be written as a user story.

In many cases, however, customer and stakeholder needs are expressed in terms of either solutions:

> Please make the room reservation function support smoking and non-smoking rooms.

or needs:

> I want my nonsmoking customers to be able to reserve a non-smoking room.

In these cases, the product owner can rephrase the needs as user stories and add them to the product backlog. In my experience, the best way to phrase a user story is to follow a template introduced by Rachel Davies in 2002. Rachel suggested that each user story should be phrased in three pieces, as follows:

> As a <role>,
> I want <something>,
> so that <value or justification>.

This template has the distinct advantage of capturing not just the action, but who (role) and why (result) as well. These additions force the product owner to carefully consider who *uses* the story and why they would want it. The trap that many product owners fall into is writing user stories from the standpoint of themselves as the user. For example:

> As the product owner, I need the room reservation system to support smoking and nonsmoking rooms.

Within a short period of time, your product backlog is completely stuffed with items that begin with "As a product owner...." Stories written like this really aren't written from the standpoint of the user, and that could have a tremendous impact on how the function is actually written. When writing a user story, always consider who is going to use the story and what they really need it to do. For example, in the case of the room reservation system, it is our *nonsmoking customer* that wants the ability to reserve a nonsmoking room. With this in mind, we might now consider that a nonsmoking customer is, more often than not, going to want to reserve a nonsmoking room every time he or she makes a reservation. So, as we discuss the story further, we might also realize that our customer profiling capability needs to be extended to support smoking and nonsmoking preferences.

The product owner should also consider the value or justification for the story using Ms. Davies approach. Why does the customer want a nonsmoking room? Assuming this is primarily for comfort reasons, the resulting user story would look like:

> As a nonsmoking customer, I want to be able to reserve a nonsmoking room so that I can breathe comfortably within the room.

If the product owner is able to add any additional useful information to the user story at this point, he or she should do so. For example, the product owner may wish to ensure that the Scrum team considers the customer profiling functionality mentioned earlier.

Once the user story is written, the product owner should decide where in the product backlog the story belongs, effectively prioritizing the story for development. This is an activity that belongs singularly to the product owner. While the product owner may seek a number of opinions in order to prioritize or may be part of a committee that determines prioritization, the user story is placed somewhere on the product backlog that ultimately determines when the story will be built.

Grooming the Product Backlog

The product backlog represents a continuum of work targeted for a specific product. Items on the backlog represent additional functionality, changes to existing functionality (including making corrections and fixing defects), and (though somewhat rarely) removal of outdated functionality. In practice, the product backlog can be regarded as having a number of regions relative to the ongoing development effort. These regions help us to better understand which items on the backlog are:

1. Under construction
2. About to be under construction
3. In the near future and may be relevant to our immediate planning and marketing efforts
4. So far in the future as to be more strategic in nature

Of course, there are also items on the product backlog that are simply so far down the list that by the time we could build them, our customers will likely have found another way to solve the problem.

We can also describe these regions in terms of how they are engaged in agile analysis efforts.

During the course of an agile project, we want to have our Scrum teams engaged in agile analysis on those items with the highest probability of actually being built. In terms of regions, this would be the area in Figure 20.2 called "Next Up." Items in this region are likely to be built during the next sprint, and we need to ensure that the contents of the "Next Up" region are ready to be built by a Scrum team. If these items are not properly prepared for the Scrum team, they will potentially be too large and contain too many unknowns for a Scrum team to safely commit to completing them. When this happens, sprint planning takes too long (up to three or four days), and the team frequently overcommits as a result of the unknowns still hidden within each story. We ensure that stories are ready for Scrum teams through an activity called backlog grooming.

Backlog grooming is actually a series of workshops scheduled during the sprint where the Scrum teams stops what they are doing and focuses on gaining an understanding of the items in the "Next Up" region of the product backlog. These workshops are usually between two and four hours a week (between five and ten percent of the team's total capacity) and are best scheduled in advance and during the same days and times each week. For example, some teams schedule their backlog grooming workshops on Monday and Wednesday afternoons from 1:00

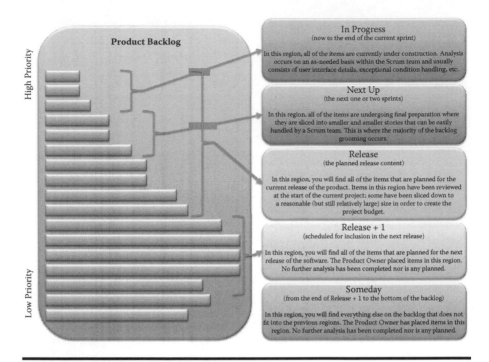

Figure 20.2   Regions in the product backlog.

to 3:00. Maintaining a consistent schedule helps team members to remember when and where the workshop will be held and also helps them to plan their days more effectively.

Teams spend the bulk of their time during these workshops talking with the product owner in an attempt to learn as much about the backlog items as they can. When the team is comfortable that they fully understand an item, they will decide whether or not to slice the story down into smaller pieces. The guideline I use is simple: if the story seems like it is more work than can be done by two or three team members in less than a week, it's too big and needs to be sliced into smaller pieces. For example, let's assume that we are building a web site to sell a variety of different kinds of merchandise. Our team is discussing the first story in the "Next Up" region. It reads:

> As a consumer, I want to be able to decide how I want the purchased item shipped so that I can have it shipped as quickly or as inexpensively as I wish.

This story, clearly, is quite large and will not be built by a couple people on the team in less than a week. So, after having discussed the story with the product owner, the team decides to slice the story into four parts, as follows:

> As a consumer, I want to ship my package overnight because I want it tomorrow.
>
> As a consumer, I want to ship my package via two-day air because I want it quickly.
>
> As a consumer, I want to ship my package by ground because I'm not in a hurry.
>
> As a consumer, I want to ship my package by the least expensive means possible because I want to maximize my savings.

Note that we did not slice the story based on development activities. In other words, there is no "Design the package shipment choices function." Likewise, there is no "Test the package shipment choices function." Stories built like this simply invite waterfall phases back into the development effort and are to be avoided.

After the slicing, the stories are much clearer and their scope much more limited, but still fairly complicated. In this case, we'll do even more analysis on each of the new stories by asking more questions of the product owner. For example, in discussing the fourth story (shipping by the least expensive means possible), our product owner has told us that this automatically means that we'll use ship-for-less for all of our domestic and international shipping and all that is needed are a valid destination address, a valid origin address, and the weight of the package. This is good, because now we can derive some new stories:

> Collect a valid destination address for ship-for-less shipping.
>
> Collect a valid origin address for ship-for-less shipping.
>
> Use valid postal codes and the weight of one item to determine shipping costs for ship-for-less.
>
> Submit the shipping order for ship-for-less shipping.
>
> Use valid postal codes and sum the weight of multiple items to determine shipping costs for ship-for-less.

Again, note that we did not slice the story into product layers like "Modify the UI to collect destination and shipping addresses" or "Update the items object to provide the weight of an item." Whenever we talk about user stories, we need to remain focused on actual, demonstrable, and complete function. For example, if we simply worked on a story where we modified the UI to suit the collection of new data, we could very likely end up in sprint review with nothing but updated screen shots. Screen shots don't work. You can't prove they do what they are supposed to do unless the data they collect end up used or stored somewhere in a manner that makes sense.

Our new stories slice the concept of shipping via the least expensive means possible and break the functionality down into pieces that are small, less complex than before, and can be demonstrated at sprint review. For example, the first of our new stories provides the capability to collect a valid destination address. When completed, we can demonstrate not only that the UI has been modified, but also that edit and reasonability checks are in place, and even that the information ends up in our database where it is supposed to be stored. In fact, this story could be further subdivided into the following:

> Collect the destination street address, edit it, and store it for ship-for-less shipping.
>
> Collect the domestic (U.S.) destination zip code, edit it, and store it for ship-for-less shipping.
>
> Collect the international destination postal code, edit it, and store it for ship-for-less shipping.
>
> Collect the domestic (U.S.) city and state, edit them, and store them for ship-for-less shipping.
>
> Collect the international region/province, edit them, and store them for ship-for-less shipping.

As before, each of these stories slices the prior story (collecting a valid destination address) into smaller pieces. Each of the new stories is independently demonstrable when completed. Each story can be proven to either reject the provided data for a specific reason or to place the data into the proper database location.

Avoiding the Waterfall User Story

When slicing user stories, it is important to think of each slice as an independent piece of a bigger function. Think about it in terms of application architecture. The typical application today is layered. Starting from the top, we often speak of the following (see Figure 20.3):

- User interface (UI): The screens or pages that the user actually sees.
- Business logic: Data validation and reasonableness checks, the "intelligence" of the application.
- Data access layer: An abstraction layer, separating the application from the database implementation.
- Architecture: The underpinnings of the application providing common functionality.
- Database: The storage layer of the application, usually a third-party engine, providing a means for data storage and retrieval.

Certainly we can argue from application to application whether or not these layers are present and, indeed, if additional layers shouldn't be included. Regardless of what layers your specific application includes, we want to avoid a typical mistake that inexperienced teams make when they slice stories along task lines, rather than functional ones. If we slice the stories properly, each and every story will be independently verifiable. In other words, when the team finishes building the "Collect the domestic (U.S.) city and state, edit them, and store them for ship-for-less shipping" story, you should be able to type in a valid city and state and

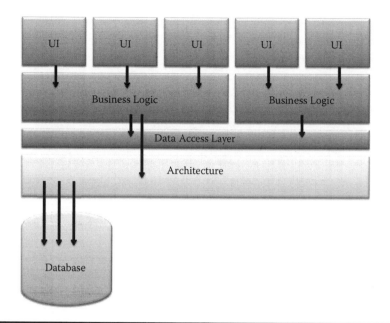

Figure 20.3 The typical layers of a client/server application.

then find them in the proper database locations. Whatever specifications need to be created to properly document this story can be written at the same time. This technique also has the advantage of allowing the developers to exercise every layer of the application immediately upon the building of the very first story. For example, if there is going to be a problem with the data access layer, we'll probably find out right away when we try to use it to store the city and state. Likewise, if there's a problem with the database access or the database server, or the database management software needs an upgrade, we'll find out immediately and we can address the problem right away rather than having to wait until all of the pieces are finished later in the project.

If, however, we incorrectly choose to slice the stories along task lines, we'll end up with stories like this:

Analyze the ship-for-less shipping option.
Design the ship-for-less shipping option.
Code the ship-for-less shipping option.
Test the ship-for-less shipping option.

Using these stories, we forfeit all of the aforementioned advantages and we reintroduce waterfall processes back into the sprint. When we complete the analysis story, there is nothing to show for our efforts except, perhaps, some documentation. When we complete the design story—well, more documentation. As we finally move on to the coding story (perhaps in the following sprint), we could discover that the way we planned to use the data access layer was completely wrong and, in order to adjust our code, we also have to rework our design.

Think of it like drinking a hot cup of coffee. If you sip a little at first, you can easily tell if it is too hot, too sweet, or too bitter without really subjecting yourself to an uncomfortable experience. However, take that same cup of coffee and make your first taste a nice big swallow and you could be in for a very painful surprise. Proper slicing of user stories accomplishes the same thing—little functional "sips" allow you to make sure that all of the pieces of the application are working before you put a lot of time and planning into writing a large, complex function.

Making Sure the Backlog Is Ready for Grooming

When you have one product backlog and a number of Scrum teams, you will need to make sure that every team knows which backlog items they will be working on and which will be completed by other teams. Ideally, you will want the team that builds an item to be the team that estimates and grooms it. In many cases, this is quite easy—when you have teams that are specialized, it becomes very clear which teams will work on which backlog items. However, in some circumstances, there will be items that are not clearly part of one team's specialization, or there are multiple teams in a single specialization. It this instance, it will fall, usually to the Scrum master and the product owner, to ensure that every item in the product backlog (at least for the next two to three sprints) is clearly assigned to a specific Scrum team. These assigned items become the list of items to be groomed by the Scrum team.

Scheduling the Workshops

When scheduling backlog-grooming workshops, it is better to schedule more frequent but shorter workshops than to schedule less frequent but longer workshops. I have experienced cases where Scrum teams planned their backlog grooming workshops for the last couple days of each sprint. Those teams initially felt that doing so helped them to avoid unnecessary interruptions during the course of the sprint caused by having to stop two or three times a week for grooming workshops. Unfortunately, each and every team learned that there were some significant drawbacks to this approach. First, they found that the last couple days of the sprint were often tied up with final touches, little surprises, and preparation for the upcoming sprint review. Being interrupted during this period to do backlog grooming was the last thing they wanted. Second, because the workshops occurred only at the end of the sprint, team members would often forget that the workshops were scheduled and would overcommit themselves to get work done. This led to some crucial team members missing their goals or missing the workshops—both of which led to very undesirable results. Even more importantly, however, is the effect on the innovativeness and imagination of the team when you give them only a couple days to get the backlog ready for the next sprint. The combination of long workshops (three to four hours per day) and the impending end of the current sprint results in the team settling for second-class solutions. There just isn't enough time to be imaginative. As one team member put it, "It's really hard to be innovative on a schedule."

My recommendation is that you schedule grooming workshops two times a week, anywhere between ninety minutes and two hours, and at the same time each week. I used to schedule workshops for Monday and Wednesday afternoons between 1 and 3 p.m. There are a number of advantages to approaching the workshops in this manner:

1. Because the meetings are short, they are over before team members start to get tired and lose concentration (when I teach classes or facilitate workshops, my rule is to take short breaks every 90 to 120 minutes; adults can only last that long before they start losing concentration).
2. Because the meetings are scheduled, team members get used to doing them on, for example, Monday and Wednesday afternoons and rarely commit to too much during those days.
3. Because the meetings are frequent, if the team isn't able to come to a conclusion on how to deal with a particular story during one workshop, there is always another opportunity just a couple days away to try again.
4. Because the meetings are scheduled across the entire sprint, they have little impact on last-minute work being done by the team at the end of the sprint.
5. Because it is clear at the beginning of the sprint that the workshops will consume up to ten percent of the team's total capacity, your team can plan for that ten percent when determining their total commitment at sprint planning.

One last advantage: when doing backlog grooming, your goal is to have enough stories ready in the product backlog so that the team can conduct a successful sprint planning meeting. Once you have achieved that goal, you can cancel the remaining workshops for the rest of the sprint.

Setting Up the Workshop

There are a number of methods for backlog grooming. In this section, I will outline a series of rules that I tend to use to create a clear understanding for the participants of what their role is and what is expected of them. For starters, I invite the entire Scrum team (including the product owner) to the workshop. This is a mandatory and very important meeting, so I ask all participants to try to ensure that they make no other commitments during the periods when the workshops are to be held. However, should the product owner be unavailable (which happens frequently due to the nature of the job), a business analyst should be assigned to "own" the item and must, prior to the workshop, discuss the item thoroughly with the product owner to ensure that the business analyst has the same clarity of direction and detail as the product owner.

Before the workshop, I prepare a table in the middle of the room with the following:

1. Index cards, each representing stories the team discussed and estimated in previous workshops, are stacked in estimation-specific piles on the table. There is a one-point stack, a two-point stack, a three-point stack, and so on. For the larger stories, around ten or so, I simply place a single stack of cards that are arranged in ascending point-size order (in other words, the first card in the stack might be a ten-point story, but as you flip through the cards in the pile, they get bigger).
2. A timer, used whenever a discussion exceeds a predefined ten- or fifteen-minute limit, to help ensure that the discussion is time boxed and does not take over the rest of the meeting.
3. Blank index cards, used to create new stories and upon which are recorded special notes and cost, value, and risk estimates.
4. A copy of the product backlog, used by the team to determine which stories need to be discussed and reviewed, looking for undiscovered dependencies.
5. A deck of planning poker cards, used for estimating effort and risk.
6. A flipchart page taped to the wall with the rules for the meeting.

In addition, I make available a digital camera for saving work done on a white board during the meeting and ensure the room has at least one white board and one or more flipcharts in it.

For new teams, we begin our first grooming workshop by reviewing the ground rules and goals (I will revisit the rules and goals from time to time, even with experienced teams, to keep everyone on the same page during future workshops). The rules are simple and negotiable, but they start like this:

1. Workshop attendees must decide how what is accomplished during the workshop is recorded for later use (who is taking minutes, recording design decisions, etc.).
2. The product owner or business analyst introduces the backlog item and then proceeds to answer any clarifying questions that the Scrum team may pose.
3. If a backlog item represents more effort to solve than two or three team members can complete over a period of one week, the item is to be sliced into two or more smaller pieces.
4. If a discussion about a backlog item continues for twenty minutes without the Scrum team being able to determine how to slice the item into smaller pieces, the team should agree to either:

a. Table the discussion until the next workshop

b. Continue the discussion for an additional five minutes and recheck to continue or table the discussion

5. When a backlog is sliced, it must be reestimated. If the item is still too large, the team should continue to discuss and slice until there are no more remaining items larger than what can be finished by two or three team members in less than a week (many Scrum teams that use story points for complexity estimation discover that appropriately sized items are no larger than three or four story points.

6. Once a backlog item is sliced to the proper size for inclusion in a sprint (i.e., the item can be completed by two or three team members in less than one week), discussion of the item ends and the team moves on to the next item on the backlog.

Again, I consider these rules negotiable for the team. So, for example, if the team wants to discuss one backlog item until they have the entire item sliced into appropriately sized items, that's their decision (they may prefer not to have their discussions time boxed, though, at the same time, I've often found that teams that don't want to time box their discussions do so because they aren't willing to keep their discussions focused as they should). Similarly, teams might decide that properly sized items can be done in less than two weeks, rather than one. Let your teams decide how to modify the basic structure of the workshop, but be sure to come back and address the workshops during the next sprint retrospective.

Discussing a Backlog Item

The goal of backlog item grooming is to understand enough about a backlog item that it can be easily sliced into smaller and smaller pieces. In the end, you want your Scrum teams committing to items that are clearly enough understood that they can be quickly reduced to tasks and that minimize the number of unexpected surprises that occur during the course of the sprint. To do this effectively, you may want to sit down with your Scrum teams prior to their first grooming workshop and start working out how they can be thorough in their discussions while, at the same time, avoiding unnecessarily long, drawn-out conversations.

Some of the items you will want your team to consider are:

■ Risk: Your Scrum teams can estimate risk in much the same way they estimate the problem space of the backlog item. This can be useful in sprint planning for helping the Scrum team recognize if the sprint is overloaded with too much risk; risk assessments can also be useful in helping the product owner with backlog prioritization.

Your Scrum team can consider many aspects of risk when deciding how to categorize an item's risk. Any of the following could significantly raise the risk of a backlog item:
- Does the team understand the technology?
- Does the team currently have all of the necessary skills to get the job done? Will those skills be hard to get? Will those skills have to be hired from outside the organizaton?
- Is this more research than development?
- Is there significant pressure from senior/executive management to get the job done (in other words, is this a high-visibility item)?
- Does this item require changes to a particularly error-prone portion of the application?
- If you have access to the end user of the item, has he or she bought into this item? Does he or she agree that the item is needed?
- Does the intent of the item seem to be fluid (i.e., when you discuss it with the product owner, is he or she unsure what's going to be needed)?

Items can be categorized in terms of 1 (greatest risk) to 5 (lowest risk). You can also try risk categories that also help you decide what actions to take next, for example:
- Low risk: No special action is required.
  - Medium risk: Item may require more slicing to isolate or mitigate risk.
  - High risk: Item should be sliced into an analysis item and a problem item. The analysis item must be completed before additional slicing of the problem item can proceed. Table the problem item and move on.
  - Unacceptable risk: Item should be removed from the product backlog and discussed with the product owner for appropriateness.
- Interdependencies: Your Scrum teams should always be watching for connections between different backlog items. These connections often force the product owner to reprioritize the product backlog to ensure that the right items get done in the right sequence. Understanding the interdependencies between backlog items is crucial to any Scrum team, as their progress can be completely blocked by an item that cannot be completed because another, lower-priority item needs to be completed first. In a large environment where two Scrum teams can exist that normally have little or no interaction, knowledge of interdependencies can help ensure that these typically independent teams coordinate on the order in which the items are built and can inform each other in the case of difficulties getting the items built. I have been asked to help in instances where a Scrum team finished a feature in a sprint only to find out that a related but required feature in the application's architecture had been scoped out of the project due to overruns.[2] It is vitally important to know the interdependencies between backlog items and to consider those dependencies during backlog grooming.

- Special constraints or conditions: Your Scrum teams should always be looking for unusual constraints or conditions that might affect how a backlog item would be built. Does the item require a tool that hasn't been installed yet? Does the item require knowledge that no one in the organization has?
- Nonfunctional requirements (NFRs): These can be very tedious to address, but are very important to deal with early. NFRs are requirements that your application must abide by in terms of, among other things, environmental and performance constraints. For example, you might be building a game that is supposed to be portable across various gaming platforms. In this case, just about every item on your backlog will be constrained by having to use only those functions and capabilities common across all of the applicable gaming platforms. In every case, your Scrum team will either have to build the item to work in all environments or (if permitted) have to slice the item into several items that will address each gaming platform independently.

You might also have to deal with performance constraints on an item (even when not specified, you can usually assume that there's a performance constraint on an item). Performance constraints usually take on the form "must perform/complete in less than x seconds y% of the time." Performance constraints drive nearly every aspect of the backlog item, from the type of solution employed to the final cost of the item.

The sooner nonfunctional requirements are known for each backlog item, the more effective a job the Scrum team can do in slicing the items and deriving the best solution for the circumstances. As I mentioned earlier, your Scrum teams will need to consider the nonfunctional requirements for each backlog item one at a time. The challenge is in ensuring that the team remembers to take the time to review each criterion against each backlog. Creating and posting a list of the common nonfunctional requirements in the room where you hold the grooming workshops can, in part, accomplish this. Teams should also make sure that backlog items have clear performance requirements. Where the nonfunctional requirements of a backlog item are not clearly specified, the team should be able to get clarification on the requirements from the product owner.

Backlog Items That Need Special Handling

In a large organization (and even in small ones), even though we want our Scrum teams to have all of the skills that they need to get the job done, there are always some specialized skills that are in short supply. Skills such as database architecture, database analysis, usability analysis, and even technical writing are frequently counted among those in short supply. When a backlog item is discovered that requires a specialized skill in order to be built, the item can be said to require special handling. Let's clarify this a little with a simple example.

Assume for a moment that you are managing the transition of an organization to agile development. You've launched a project that includes eight Scrum teams (roughly fifty or so developers). Supporting the development organization is a database designer, a technical writer (who is responsible for all of the documentation that accompanies your software), and a technical wizard who manages the server environments that your teams use to develop and test the product. As backlog grooming begins, a number of backlog items are discussed that require the creation of new tables in the product's database. Each item poses a problem for the Scrum team that would "own" the item, as they don't have a database designer as part of the team. These items require special handling.

For the purposes of backlog grooming, the important aspect of special handling is that the team recognizes that it is needed and that the item is "tagged"[3] as requiring a particular skill. Once an item is tagged as requiring special handling, teams can decide at sprint planning how to get the right skills on the team (for the sprint or just for a few days).

Remembering What We've Learned

Backlog grooming workshops have one main goal: to simplify the product backlog by reducing complex and large items into smaller items that are more easily understood. During the course of each workshop, we learn enough about various items on the backlog that we are able to slice those items into smaller and smaller items. However, what happens to the information that we acquire along the way about these items? Yes, some of that information is implicit in the existence of an item (for example, it's clear without additional information that if you have three items that provide for the use of MasterCard, VISA, and American Express credit cards in your product that your plan is to support those three cards).

As we discuss backlog items, we often review (and sometimes decide) how a particular item is to be constructed within the application or systems architecture of our application. We might discuss various aspects of the item design, or at least determine things to be careful of when the item is finally built.

What happens to all of that information after the grooming workshops?

Clearly, we don't want to have to rediscover this information later in the project. Having already discussed an item, we would ideally have this information available for later grooming workshops and for sprint planning when the item is finally reduced to tasks. Therefore, while we are slicing items into smaller items during the grooming workshops, we will also need to capture the information recorded on flipcharts, white boards, and in discussions somewhere. The simplest solution (and thus the one that appeals to me) is to capture the information in pictures and text on pages in a wiki, keyed to the backlog item number. In essence, we can create a wiki-based extension to our items (see Figure 20.4).

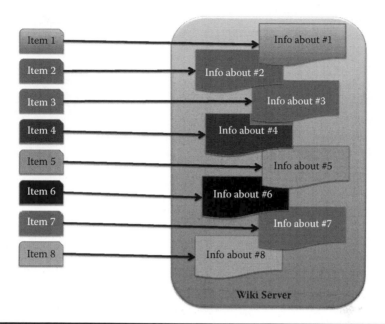

Figure 20.4   Extending backlog items with a wiki.

As each backlog grooming session ends, through a means decided upon by the Scrum team, the information collected during the workshop is added to the wiki. The backlog item ID is saved as part of the page number to facilitate easily finding the information later. The digital camera is used to capture drawings, and the images are stored on the wiki with the rest of the information.

When a backlog item is sliced into smaller pieces, you need only place links on the "parent" item page to the "child" items that were sliced from the parent (see Figure 20.5).

Using a wiki site in this manner allows the Scrum teams to save the result of all of their grooming workshop discussions in manner that allows for easy retrieval when needed again.

Another approach to saving the critical information we discover during backlog grooming is to build a series of documents based on the fundamental capabilities of the product. Let's go back to the ticket purchasing web site for an example. In that case, the fundamental capabilities were listed as follows:

■ Search for tickets
■ Purchase tickets
■ Deliver tickets
■ Other stuff

In this scenario then, as your Scrum teams discussed and sliced items related to searching for tickets, all of that information would be transferred to the "Search for

Figure 20.5 Using a wiki page to show child item information.

Tickets" document. Likewise, information related to purchasing tickets would be recorded in the "Purchase Tickets" document. This approach works well for small products, but as the number of items increases, this approach can become cumbersome. Indeed, as the number of personnel increases, this approach can create unnecessary obstacles when too many people need to access the same document.

One final thought on saving the outcomes of grooming workshops—be careful not to fall back into "big design up front" or "big analysis up front" patterns. In other words, don't try to make the aforementioned wiki pages or documents pretty, nor should you try to record every detail you can think of. These methods of extending the backlog item are not intended to replace the longer-term internal and external documentation that your organization needs with regard to its software applications. The information uncovered and discussed during grooming workshops and stored in the manner we've discussed is merely to ensure that the information is not lost or forgotten between workshops or before sprint planning.

Summary

This chapter covers (at a high level) the concepts surrounding the incorporation of ideas and requirements for a product, how to get those ideas and requirements onto the product backlog, and how to work the backlog in order to create easily understood, small items for our Scrum teams to commit to and achieve success while building. Agile analysis is all about the preparation of an inventory of ideas, slowly adding more and more information until the order, structure, and timing of our analysis makes each idea ready for construction.

The timing of analysis is important in an agile project. Our goal is to understand more and more about backlog items as our project progresses. From sprint to sprint, and from workshop to workshop, we learn more about the items that we are planning to build so that we achieve a complete and comprehensive understanding only just before we're ready to build the item. In addition to improving our knowledge of the item by giving us time to learn more about the item, we also reduce rework and risk by not spending a lot of time analyzing and making decisions about an item that might later prove to be completely different or removed from the project entirely.

The structure of analysis is also important. Rather than simply adding more and more information to an item as we learn about it, we slice items into smaller and smaller pieces, learning more about each piece every time we reduce its size.

The order of analysis is critically important to maximizing the value we bring to our product. Rather than just analyzing the intended features of our product in a random order, agile analysis forces us to focus on items in priority order. This allows us to build only what our product owner and customers want and helps us to avoid creating features and options that no one will use or even wanted in the first place.

Backlog grooming workshops, held frequently throughout every sprint in the project, help us to simultaneously build our product and learn more about our backlog. These workshops are short enough to ensure that our Scrum teams can be innovative and creative without being rushed or getting bored during the workshops. When discussing backlog items during backlog grooming, Scrum teams should consider the risk that the item poses, interdependencies with other items, special considerations that might add complexity to the item, and nonfunctional requirements that might apply to the item, further increasing its complexity or, at the least, constraining the possible solutions. The workshops also help us to not analyze more items during a sprint than we really need; once we have enough for the next sprint (plus a little extra, just in case), we can stop, further reducing risk and the possibility of rework and waste.

When product backlog items are analyzed, we learn more about them preparatory to slicing the item into smaller, less complex items. This information needs to be captured and stored, perhaps in a wiki, perhaps in a version-controlled document, in order to ensure that all of the information garnered during the backlog grooming process is not lost.

Agile analysis is about progressive elaboration; that is, we learn a little more each week about the product backlog items that we intend to work on in a future sprint. We do this in a progressive fashion because doing so:

1. Recognizes that the later we put the finishing details on a product backlog item before we build it, the more we know about how that item is supposed to work and appear once built.
2. Helps us to ensure that we do not spend a lot of valuable time on product backlog items that we can't be sure we are actually going to build until the Scrum team is actually ready to commit (and even then, there are possibilities).

By deferring decisions on backlog items until right before the Scrum team is ready to work on them, we also recognize the inherent uncertainty of software development.

Endnotes

1. You can find more information at http://www.bigagiledevelopment.com/agileanalysis.
2. Unfortunately, no matter what decision you make at this point (to remove the completed feature, to leave the feature in place but disable it in the application until later, or to find a way to get the necessary architecture feature built anyway), there's going to be a considerable expense incurred to deal with the situation.
3. Tagging a backlog item can be managed easily, regardless of how you manage your backlog. If you use cards, assign special colored cards to different specialized skills. For example, assign database design to red cards. Blue cards can be architecturally significant, requiring architectural changes and thus an architect. Yellow cards can be for items that require special attention from a technical writer. If you use software tools to manage your backlog, most tools provide the capability for tagging items or for applying themes to backlog items; themes are really just tags under a different name.

Chapter 21

Launching Scrum Teams

As the transition progresses, you'll find yourself forming and reforming Scrum teams on a fairly regular basis. Properly launched, Scrum teams can avoid many of the start-up difficulties that new teams face by recognizing the typical issues that new teams face and then finding ways to mitigate or eliminate those stumbling blocks as quickly and as early as possible. While every organization and culture is different, this chapter will review many good practices that you can employ to improve the initial start-up of Scrum teams. I also recommend reviewing the retrospective findings from new teams during the first three or four Sprints in order to get an idea of the typical types of problems that they are facing and amending your start-up procedures appropriately.

As with most small groups, Scrum teams typically follow Bruce Tuckman's model of group dynamics that includes the four phases forming, storming, norming, and performing. Dr. Tuckman observed that all small groups experience these phases in order, and that they can move in both directions through these phases when the team membership is changed and sometimes for absolutely no reason at all. A brief explanation of these phases, and steps to take with Scrum teams can be found in Table 21.1. We'll talk about all of these practices and more throughout the rest of this chapter.

Starting a New Scrum Team

When a new Scrum team is formed, it is a good idea to be proactive about bringing the team together before other less productive behaviors can set in. Even when the team is made up of experienced team members, be sure to go through the steps that follow in order to ensure a successful start to your team.

Table 21.1 The Tuckman Model and Scrum Teams

Phase	Definition	Scrum Team Steps
Forming	The team comes together with a new purpose. There is a lot of energy and excitement surrounding this new venture, but the team frequently doesn't know where to start.	• Establish team identity • Team building (icebreakers) • Define ground rules • Define DONEness • Prepare the product backlog
Storming	There's a lot of role confusion. Team members have repeatedly upset other members by doing or saying things they don't appreciate or understand. Cliques have formed within the team; there's an "us vs. them" feel within the team.	• Keep team goal focused • Continue to recognize and address conflict • Revisit and revise ground rules • Continuous learning
Norming	The team is feeling "burned" from the storming phase, but they are working through the major problems. There will be some tentativeness in discussions. There may be reluctance to take tasks that caused contention in the past. Team may be unwilling to assert action themselves.	• Use silence to encourage participation; don't lead as much as before • Continue to recognize and address team concerns • Revisit and revise ground rules • Keep team goal focused • Continuous learning
Performing	The team has found their own stride and are continuing to improve.	• Stay on top of obstacle resolution • Support the team as needed • Revisit and revise DONEness definition • Continuous learning

Establish a Team Identity

Sit down with your team and discuss creating a name and identity for your team. In one particularly interesting case, I worked with a team that not only identified themselves as a particular type of dinosaur, but they even had a seven-foot inflatable mascot in their team room. In addition to creating some team spirit, the mascot also served as a location marker for many other teams (i.e., "Go to the second team room to the left of the one with the big dinosaur"). Taking a picture of the team and posting it on the organization's wiki and even on the entrance to the team room also goes a long way toward establishing a team identity in the eyes of everyone else in the organization.

When creating a team name, try to avoid self-denigrating names (e.g., "The Losers" or "The Defects"). These names are initially intended to be funny, but they create a poor reflection on the team across the rest of the organization. In some cases, they even become self-fulfilling prophecies, causing good teams to fall apart for avoidable reasons.

Encourage some decoration of the team room, either in a way that reflects the team name and identity, or in some way that the team finds acceptable. Find out what is unacceptable or not allowed by your organization and communicate that in advance to your Scrum team. If they know what they can't do before they begin, they will be much less disappointed than if they decorate the room the way they like and then have to remove some portion of the decoration due to organizational policies or safety regulations.

Establish Team Ground Rules

Ground rules are very important when forming a new Scrum team. These rules become the basis for the Scrum master's ability to enforce the Scrum process and make sure that everyone is contributing to team success. In later sprints, if it should happen that a team member starts becoming habitually late to daily Scrums, or doesn't participate in backlog grooming, the Scrum master can review his or her concerns with the employee, reminding the employee of the ground rules he or she agreed to when the team was formed. If that doesn't work, the Scrum master can bring the entire team together under the pretense of revisiting and revising the ground rules since they no longer apply to everyone. This gets the problem out into the open in front of all the team members and creates a certain amount of pressure on the non-compliant employee to perform to the standards of the team. As with any practice, you also don't have to get it complete or perfect in the first try. Plan on revisiting the ground rules often during the first couple sprints and, even for very experienced teams, once every four or five sprints, just to keep it fresh in everyone minds.

I usually go into a ground rule workshop with a short list of items that I believe should be on the list. My starter set[1] is shown in Table 21.2.

During the discussion, I start by suggesting that most of our ground rules come from being a Scrum team. Therefore, I recommend starting the list with the descriptor "We are a Scrum team ..." and then let the team take it from there. Most of the first nine elements will usually get on the list in the initial discussion with just a little prompting from me. However, I usually have to suggest the tenth item ("When I no longer feel I can work with my team ..."). I call this the escape clause, and I will keep the discussion going around it until it has the basic form that you see in my example.

Table 21.2 My Initial Ground Rules

1. We show up for meetings on time (especially daily Scrums).
2. We keep our status updated on the team's task board.
3. We work together to complete stories.
4. It is everyone's responsibility to achieve our sprint commitment each month. No one says, "It's not my job" when being asked to work outside of his or her typical comfort zone.
5. We actively participate in sprint planning, backlog grooming, sprint retrospectives, and all other team meetings requiring team discussion.
6. We abide by the Scrum values of commitment, courage, focus, openness, respect, and visibility.
7. We will not call something done unless it is truly done, and we will not deliver "not done" software unless required to by the organization.
8. We work with each other to discuss and resolve conflict.
9. We will watch for better ways to build our product.
10. When I no longer feel I can work with my team, I will ask to be reassigned.

The escape clause is there to make sure that, should any team member in the future feel that he or she simply cannot stand being on the team anymore, he or she will specifically ask to be reassigned. I tend to require this ground rule whenever I do this because of the number of teams I've coached that were being dragged down by the deliberately poor performance of one team member who no longer wanted to be a member of his team. Frankly, I've never understood why people would rather be kicked off a team than asking to be removed. However, by making it clear up front that if a team member wants out he or she has an option other than just making everyone miserable, he or she usually takes the honorable way out.

As I mentioned earlier, ground rules do not reach their final state in one work session. Like the team itself, ground rules have to mature. For that reason, make sure your teams' Scrum masters plan to review the ground rules during the first three or four sprint retrospectives to "tune" them up. In addition, for teams that are together for a long period of time (i.e., eighteen months or more), plan on revisiting the ground rules once every four or five sprints to keep them fresh and up-to-date.

Establish Team DONEness Definition

There are fewer things more important to someone doing a task than a clear definition of what it means to be finished with a task. Architects know a building is done when they've finished constructing a bridge or a building and another engineer double-checks their work (inspection). NASA's space shuttle launches when the weather conditions meet a specific set of acceptance criteria and the onboard shuttle computers indicate that all other systems are ready; when all of this is done, the shuttle is cleared for launch. U.S. presidential elections are done (the 2004 Bush-Gore debacle notwithstanding) when all of the popular votes are counted and one candidate has a majority of the electoral votes. In the software development field, however, we have been very loose with our definition of DONEness. This has given us the ability to release incomplete software to our customers time and time again. Think about it: compare the number of building collapses caused by structural deficiency to software crashes caused by coding deficiencies. It's not pretty, and it makes software engineers look like a rather incompetent lot.

Therefore, following the establishment of ground rules, the team's next goal should be the creation of DONEness criteria against which every piece of code will be examined and weighed. Features that do not pass the team's definition of DONEness will not be demonstrated to the product owner at sprint review. Or, if the team is requested to demonstrate an incomplete feature, they will clearly state that the feature is not done.

When I sit down with new teams, I again walk in with a starter set of criteria that I bring into the team discussion if needed. As with the ground rules, I introduce items with the intention of getting the team to discuss and buy in. Nothing, even those items that I introduce, goes into the DONEness definition if the team doesn't unanimously accept the item. My DONEness starter set[2] has grown over the years and is shown in Table 21.3.

As with the ground rules, remember to revisit the team's DONEness definition every two or three sprints and definitely when the team has experienced a large number of defects in the previous sprint. Should this happen, the team should engage in some root cause analysis work to determine why a defect escaped the sprint and if it was from a deficiency in the DONEness definition or a deficiency in enforcing or proving that the software passed the DONEness criteria.

Preparing the Product Backlog: The Team's First Sprint

In some instances, a new Scrum team will be faced with a new product backlog. In others, the product backlog has already been groomed to some extent by previously existing teams. In either case, the next step for your new team is to begin grooming the backlog in order to (1) get some stories on the top of the backlog ready for construction and (2) become more familiar with the content of the backlog through discussing it. In a team's first sprint together, the team can follow a pattern that is similar to what most teams do in the beginning of a new project. The pattern works quite simply:

Table 21.3   DONEness Definition Starter Set

No software feature is finished unless the following is true:

- The software satisfies the acceptance criteria as defined by the product owner.
- All product source code (application code as well as test harnesses) is properly integrated into the code base and checked into source code control.
- All unit tests pass on an integrated environment considered reflective of a customer environment.
- All acceptance tests pass on an integrated environment considered reflective of a customer environment.
- The feature's performance criteria have been met or exceeded.
- The feature's sizing criteria have been met or exceeded. (Sometimes, the executing profile for a feature, which includes code and all in-flight memory usage, is not allowed to exceed a predetermined size to allow the software to fit in limited memory.)
- All internal documentation has been properly updated, reviewed, and checked in.
- All external (user) documentation has been properly updated, reviewed, and checked in.
- All training materials have been properly updated and reviewed or the necessary changes have been communicated to those who will update the training materials.
- All upgrade scripts have been completed and tested.
- All installation scripts have been completed and tested.
- All de-installation scripts have been completed and tested.
- All new or changed functions demonstrate a code coverage of at least 85%.
- All known stubs have been removed from the code.
- Code is refactored and meets all naming standards and coding standards.
- Designs are refactored and meet all design standards.

1. The Scrum master schedules backlog grooming sessions for the entire sprint. There should be four total hours of work sessions each week, separated across two days. I often go with Monday and Wednesday afternoons from 1 to 3 p.m.
2. The first two days of the sprint is backlog grooming (regardless of the work session schedule). The goal of these two days is to get enough backlog items down to size that, on the third day of the sprint, the team can start building one or two items.

3. From the third day of the sprint, the team continues to work on the initial backlog items and hold backlog grooming work sessions. When the initial stories are finished, the team continues to work from the top of the newly groomed backlog, taking and finishing as many items as they are able to manage.

By the end of the first sprint, the team will have groomed enough of the backlog to last at least one full sprint, they will have completed a considerable amount of work on the new groomed items, and they have a beginning velocity based on how much the team finished during the first sprint. The second sprint, of course, does not require any additional grooming workshops—four hours per week will usually be sufficient from that point forward.

Getting Ready for Sprint Planning

If you've worked with Scrum before, you are probably already aware of the basics of sprint planning and how it works. You've already learned commitment-based planning, where the team cycles through each backlog item—discuss, reach an agreement with the product owner, slice into tasks, commit—until they believe they can do no more during the sprint. You may also have experience with velocity-based planning, where teams commit to approximately the same amount of work completed in previous sprints. Most teams learn how to do their first sprint planning session as they do it. However, my recommendation is that, before the meeting, you or your team's Scrum master sit down with the team and explain the entire process with particular emphasis on the following points:

- *The focus of sprint planning is to determine how much work the team will do during the current sprint and how the team will do the work.* Many teams mistakenly assume that the main deliverable of the sprint planning meeting is the sprint backlog. This is entirely incorrect. The main deliverable of the sprint planning meeting is the team's plan and commitment to complete one or more backlog items during the course of the sprint. In fact, the sprint backlog is actually just a by-product of the team's discussion about what needs to be done in order to complete a backlog item.
- *Get as much information from the product owner as you can.* While there will still be time for details during the sprint, you can avoid significant over- or undercommitment by being thorough now. Also, remember to work out specific details regarding the acceptance criteria that the product owner has for the item. Nearly every Scrum team I've ever worked with (and, in fact, nearly every Scrum team simulation I've run in my classes) has revealed in a sprint retrospective following their first two or three sprints that they need to improve upon the acceptance criteria that they worked out with the product

owner. Lack of detail is a primary cause of delays in backlog item completion and in the rejection of items by the product owner at sprint review.

■ *Work together as a team to decide how each item will be built.* Sprint planning is an excellent opportunity to discuss how and where new code will be added or where existing code can be found. If the design is too complex to discuss in the meeting, schedule follow-up meetings to discuss it further.

■ *The sprint backlog is meant to reflect the decisions made regarding how an item is to be designed.* Also, include in the sprint backlog as much of the team's definition of DONEness that needs to be included to ensure that the definition is actually achieved during the sprint (e.g., updating all relevant documentation, getting that documentation reviewed and approved, writing all of the tests and verifying that the tests pass, installation documentation and scripts are completed, etc.). Less experienced Scrum teams and teams that have a history of not meeting DONEness criteria will usually create more and more detailed tasks to make sure that nothing is missed. More experienced teams tend to need fewer individual tasks to remind them of what to do.

■ *Remember that the product owner is concerned about what gets done and about how much backlog items costs.* Should an item prove to be considerably more effort than originally thought, the product owner must be consulted to decide if he or she still wants the item to be completed. This is because the effort estimate of the item as created at sprint planning is, in fact, a budget. For example, assume an item was estimated during sprint planning as costing 120 hours, but during the course of the sprint, the item grew to over 300 hours due to forgotten and underestimated tasks. In this circumstance, the product owner may decide remove the item from the sprint in favor of other items. Remember, product owners are responsible for return on investment. That means that both the cost of the item and the value of the item are a factor in determining if an item is to be built. Don't surprise your product owner after the fact with a sudden, substantial change in item cost.

■ *Tell the product owner immediately if you believe an item can't be finished during the sprint.* When backlog items are sliced during backlog grooming, teams are advised to stop grooming the item when it falls into an acceptable size[3] for commitment to a sprint. This means that there's still some room left for slicing if necessary. Therefore, if a Scrum team feels that a backlog item may not be able to be finished in a sprint, it is incumbent on the team to discuss the item with the product backlog as early in the sprint as possible to give the product owner as many options as possible, including slicing the problem item again, leaving the "important" part in the sprint and placing the remainder on the product backlog. Don't wait until the end of the sprint if you can avoid it—the later in the sprint you involve the product owner, the fewer options he or she will have to help you out.

▪ *Be conservative late in the project.* If your project is nearing the end, Scrum teams and product owners should consider being more conservative in their acceptance of risk in the sprint. Because timeframes will be limited late in a project, backlog items that introduce too much risk can end up costing Scrum teams unwanted delays and may even result in the team having to back out or remove code already added to the product, but there isn't enough time to finish the backlog item. Product owners should be careful to remove or de-prioritize risky features late in a project; Scrum teams should be willing to challenge product owners should they discover a highly risky item reaching the top of the product backlog late in the project.

Running a Successful Daily Scrum

The wonderful thing about daily Scrums is that, while they have very few rules, they are so incredibly powerful at making sure that everyone on the Scrum team knows what everyone else is doing and is more able to adapt their direction to the daily reality than any other kind of development team. A well-executed daily Scrum is over in less than fifteen minutes and allows the team to consider the kinds of conversations and decisions that need to be made immediately following the daily Scrum. Likewise, a poorly managed daily Scrum can become long (between thirty minutes and an hour each day), wasteful, and de-motivating for the Scrum team. The Scrum master is the key to a successful daily Scrum. Here are some things to remember when running that all-important meeting:

▪ *Start the daily Scrum at the same time and in the same place.* There are few times that are better than other times for having the daily Scrum. Some Scrum masters have discovered that holding the meeting at 11:45 in the morning keeps everyone motivated to end the meeting quickly (in time for lunch). Morning daily Scrums work out pretty well because they encourage each team member to consider what they accomplished the day before and to plan out their current day before it gets too late. Afternoon daily Scrums have the advantage of what's been done being fresh on everyone's mind. My advice is to leave it up to the team to decide when to hold the daily Scrum. The meeting is for them, after all.

▪ *Hold the daily Scrum every day.* Despite the fact that the name of the meeting—*daily Scrum*—answers the question, many people have asked me if they should hold the meeting every day. My answer is yes one hundred percent of the time. "But," they say, "what if very little changes from one day to the next and there's nothing new for the team members to report?" "Good," I reply, "your daily Scrum will be very short." All humor aside, you never know when the daily Scrum is going to turn up something important. Even if you feel that there isn't enough getting done everyday to make the daily Scrum interesting, the purpose of the meeting is to set the team up to make decisions about how to handle their current reality. Well, sometimes it's a good feeling just knowing that your current plan is the right plan. And that day you're surprised by something the team hadn't anticipated, you will be glad you had them together to discover it.

- *Announce the beginning of the Scrum.* Make sure everyone knows that the meeting is starting by saying something like "Scrum!" or "Stand up!" This gives team members an opportunity to gather together. This also gives non-team members an understanding of what is happening and why the team member they were talking with suddenly stepped away to handle another meeting. Announcing the beginning of the daily Scrum also alerts everyone that a specific set of rules are now in place—there are three questions to be answered, all other conversation should stop, and only Scrum team members are invited to speak.

- *Announce the end of the Scrum.* Just like the beginning, announcing the end of the daily Scrum provides a number of signals. First, it tells everyone that the daily Scrum is over and the rules surrounding who is supposed to talk and what questions are answered are lifted. In other words, the focused activity known as the daily Scrum is over. Second, it signals that the team members that need to gather to discuss decisions about what to do today should do so. Team members that don't need to participate in these "sidebar" conversations can return to work. Lastly, it tells any nonteam members in the team room that, should they wish to update the team with new information or ask questions of the team, they can do so before the team members break up to go back to their workstations or other conversations.

In addition, here are some dos and don'ts for your Scrum masters:

- *Do* be prompt and consistent about your starting times.
- *Do* be disciplined about the three questions; encourage your team to keep their answers brief.
- *Do* make sure to get more information on obstacles reported during the daily Scrum as quickly as possible after the meeting is over.
- *Do* answer the questions yourself as well; your team members want to know what you are doing too.
- *Do* encourage modifications to the style of the meeting, as long as the basic rules continue to apply (three questions, only team members speak, etc.).
- *Do* encourage your product owner to participate; your team members want to know what he or she is doing as well.
- *Do* encourage other team members to start, manage, and end the daily Scrum; just because you may be on vacation that day is no excuse for the daily Scrum to not be done.

- *Don't* take notes; this isn't a meeting that requires minutes. It's a tool for the team to figure out what's going on and whether or not they need to consider new information.
- *Don't* allow team members to show up late; if someone's late, discuss it with them immediately following the meeting.
- *Don't* tell team members what to do or give out assignments during or after the daily Scrum; that's their job, make them figure it out.
- *Don't* bring a laptop; there should be no distractions during the daily Scrum.
- *Don't* permit any nonteam members to contribute during the daily Scrum; ask them politely to wait no more than fifteen minutes until the meeting is done, then you'll give them an opportunity. Discuss this with them after the daily Scrum should they persist.

Before I finish the section on the daily Scrum, I want to give you a way to run the daily Scrum that has proven quite effective. Just follow the rules and dos and don'ts I gave you in the preceding paragraphs, and the following changes to the procedure:

1. Get your team used to starting the daily Scrum at the same time every day by encouraging anyone on the team that notices the time to call out the beginning of the daily Scrum. Right at 10 a.m., for example, someone should yell, "Scrum!" If necessary, the person who does it the most during a sprint can be given some kind of token award.
2. Have a stuffed animal or other token on the team's central table around which the team gathers when the daily Scrum is started. Whoever is standing closest to the token when the team gathers goes first.
3. The team member with the token goes by answering the three questions. When finished, the team member passes the token to any nonadjacent[4] person on the team who hasn't answered the questions yet.
4. We repeat step 3 until everyone on the team has answered the question. The last person announces that the daily Scrum is over.

The advantages of this practice are several:

- The meeting is self-starting; the Scrum master need not be present to run the meeting. This also has the added advantage of putting the Scrum master on the same level as the other team members. No special duties or privileges— sometimes being the one responsible for calling and running a meeting creates a false sense of authority. This practice defeats that.
- The team members don't have to argue about who goes first. The placement of the animal and how people gather around the table does it for them.
- Because the team members have to pass the token to someone who hasn't gone yet, everyone has to pay attention to make sure that they remember who answered the questions so far, and who hasn't. This keeps everyone engaged.

Getting Ready for Sprint Review

The ironic thing about sprint review meetings is that many teams spend too much time getting ready for the meeting, treating it as a formal demonstration of software functionality. When preparing your Scrum team for the first sprint review, you will save yourself a lot of excess worry and effort by remembering the following:

■ *The sprint review is an informal checkpoint*: Most people understand that the sprint review is about demonstrating to the product owner what was completed during the previous sprint. What many teams misunderstand, however, is that the sprint review meeting is meant to be informal. While you can schedule a conference room to hold the meeting, the best sprint reviews are done at a workstation in the team room, where the product owner can not only see the software, but also ask questions, make comments, and take notes. If the team has been working based on the DONEness definition (and that definition is fairly comprehensive), there is little to no preparation needed by the team to get ready for the product owner. While there is nothing wrong with an impending sprint review meeting causing a little last-minute pressure to get to DONE, energy should be put into achieving DONEness, not adding formality to the sprint review.

■ *Avoid discussions about metrics during the sprint review*: The sprint review is supposed to be about software, not how many lines of code were written or how many new tests were added to the test suite. This is good information, certainly, but the sprint review is the wrong time to discuss it. In one case that I'm aware of, a company created a standardized threefold brochure on which were placed all of their metrics. The brochure was handed out, but not discussed, during the sprint review. If anybody had questions about the metrics, they were welcome to ask questions *after* the sprint review had ended.

■ *Demonstrate only what is done*: During the review, demonstrate only that which the team agrees is fully done. One outcome you really want to avoid is demonstrating something that is almost finished and then coming under pressure to deliver the nearly completed item before it is ready. Unless your team is specifically asked otherwise, the only discussion of unfinished items should be about what's not complete and why.

■ *Be prepared to be challenged*: Part of the product owner's responsibility during the sprint review is to satisfy himself of herself that each item demonstrated is actually done per the item's acceptance criteria and the team's definition of DONEness. Be prepared to have your claim of DONEness challenged during the sprint review. Can you provide a list of test cases and results that show that all defined test cases worked properly? Can you produce a copy of the product user documentation that has been updated to reflect the changes you made during the sprint? Scrum teams that have failed to achieve DONEness (even accidentally) while saying that they were actually done should be prepared to offer additional proof beyond just saying that something is ready for sprint review.

Making sure your teams are ready for sprint reviews should be much more about making sure that your software is done than anything else. Keep your sprint reviews simple and informal, or they will assume a life of their own and will cost more and more each sprint.

Going to the First Sprint Retrospective

Much has been written about sprint retrospectives, and I will not spend much time in this chapter trying to review or somehow add to that body of work. Instead, there are just a few basic points that I would like to discuss in this section. Keep in mind that while the sprint review is all about the product that the Scrum team produces, the sprint retrospective is an opportunity to discuss how well the team worked during the sprint—what went well and what could be improved. Other than the daily Scrum, there is neither a more important meeting nor a meeting more effective at improving your application than the sprint retrospective meeting. It is therefore extremely critical that the sprint retrospective be managed properly.

I also recommend discussing the following important points with your team before they go to their first sprint retrospective:

- *Nothing worthwhile is ever painless*: The sprint retrospective can be a very difficult time for a Scrum team. A lot of anger and frustration can be voiced at the meeting that others in the meeting can take personally, whether it was intended to be so or not. However, it is always more important to deal with issues like these early, rather than letting them grow into bigger issues that can frequently bring a Scrum team to the point of total failure. Scrum team members need to be encouraged to attend the meeting and participate as much as possible.
- *Don't leave stuff "undone"*: Try not to end retrospective meetings with a lot of open issues. If there are conflicts or disagreements that need to be settled, settle them or agree on how they will be settled before you end the meeting. Carrying baggage from one sprint to the next will cause serious problems in the Scrum team and will result in reduced productivity.
- *Discuss every aspect of your development process*: Remember that the sprint retrospective is about all aspects of the development process, not just Scrum, Extreme Programming (XP), or stuff related to what the team worked on in the previous sprint. Encourage your team to discuss organizational standards and how those standards help or hinder your team's progress. How would

you improve on the organization's standards? Discuss any important training received during the past couple sprints. Was that training effective? Are you able to use what you learned? How would you improve the training?

■ *Don't try to "boil the ocean"*: Findings from retrospectives are almost always about changing behaviors—and behaviors do not change immediately. When I coach teams or teach classes, I recommend that they take one or two things that they want to continue to do well and one or two things they want to do differently, and then concentrate just on changing those things during the next sprint. Teams that try to change too much too fast are generally disappointed.

Removing Obstacles

Removing obstacles is one of the Scrum masters most important duties. In order to ensure that all Scrum team members remain as focused as possible on getting the tasks done on the sprint backlog, the Scrum master takes on impediments and obstacles and, after getting the obstructed developer back to work, takes it upon himself or herself to resolve the impediment as rapidly as possible. Simple examples of obstacles that the Scrum master would resolve while ensuring that the team member continued to work on something else in the meantime include:

1. *Getting time from the organization's expert*: Frequently, a Scrum team member is blocked when the expertise they need from the organization is not available or difficult to identify. The Scrum master's responsibility is to find out who in the organization can aid the Scrum team member, secure some time from him or her, and then get the Scrum team member and the expert together as quickly as possible.
2. *Hardware problems*: Very often, Scrum team members are impacted when their laptops or desktop computers develop hardware problems. In my experience, I've seen everything from display monitors with lines running through them to broken keyboards to crashed hard drives to CD/DVD readers that were jammed and would not open. After getting the Scrum team member working with someone else on the Scrum team, the Scrum master should seek out replacement hardware.
3. *Security/access problems*: The greater the focus on security (for good reasons), the more trouble we make for ourselves when developing software. This problem often surfaces when a new team member wants access to any file system or network resource or when an existing team member wants access to a new database or new network resource. The Scrum master can clear these hurdles while keeping team members focused on the sprint backlog.

When the impediment is beyond the Scrum master's scope or authority to resolve, he or she should involve management in whatever capacity required for solving the problem. For example, in the previous example regarding security and network resource access, it is often a manager who must step in to approve the security request or even bring enough pressure to bear on the security department to get the problem resolved more quickly than is typical.

Continuous Learning

President John F. Kennedy probably said it best when he said, "Our progress as a nation can be no swifter than our progress in education. The human mind is our fundamental resource." It would be hard to find a truer statement with regard to software development. As developers, we routinely take the imaginary and make it real. Every time a function is written, it is written for the first time. For that reason, it is critically important that Scrum teams embark on a journey of continuous learning during their sprints. In this section, I will discuss a way to ensure that Scrum teams can achieve continuous learning.

First, it's very important that the goal of continuous learning come from the organization's executive management. It is very easy to reduce the priority of educational efforts unless the directive comes "from the top" of the organization. With the importance of training established by executive management, the next step is to work with the Scrum team to determine how they want to manage continuous learning.

I start with reaching a consensus on how often the team wants to do the training. This decision also needs to be consistent with the senior management directive. In other words, holding the training too frequently or not frequently enough could cause problems for the Scrum team in the future. Most teams go with once a month, but I've worked with many teams that go with an hour every week or every other week. With the frequency determined, we can turn to the question of topics.

When I coach teams that have learning goals like this, I simply recommend starting by writing down as many topics as they can think of over the course of five or ten minutes and, using Post-it® notes, stick the topics to a wall. If there are a lot of topics, I'll ask the team to group the items in order to reduce the overall clutter. Then, I give every team member ten votes and have them use those votes for the topics they care the most about. With the list of topics created and prioritized (using the team members' votes), we have created a training backlog. Just like a product backlog, we can use the training backlog to look ahead at the upcoming training and decide:

1. Who on the team will own the training session? It is a good idea to make someone on the team the owner of the session. That way, no matter how the training is accomplished, there is a team member that coordinates for the team.
2. Who's going to do the training? There are many things the team can take advantage of, including:

    a. Let the team members provide the training.

    b. Let experts in the organization provide the training.

    c. Take advantage of a relationship with a consultant/coach.

    d. Use A/V materials already provided by your organization.

    e. Find something on the Internet.

3. What's the format of the training? Some of the common options include:

    a. Lunchtime session: Everyone brings their lunch and one or two team members provide a sixty-minute (or less) presentation to the team. These sessions are considered productivity-friendly as they use lunchtime for the session and result in no loss of productive time.

    b. Classroom: More formalized training provided in a classroom setting that may or may not include hands-on examples. Classes of this nature are usually either four hours (half day) or full-day sessions.

    c. Team room: Some training works well in the team room, where skills can be taught and then developers can use those skills immediately during the training on the code that they are (or will be) working on. These sessions take an hour or two to start, but the coaching continues throughout the day or even for several days (test-driven development is often taught this way—some intensive initial training and then coaching for one or more days until the team members completely understand it).

4. When should the training be scheduled? In general, the scheduling of the training has more to do with when the training can be ready than anything else. However, try to avoid scheduling the training on the same day as a backlog grooming workshop or late in the sprint when the team is likely to be focused on completing as much as possible.

Just like with the product backlog, don't try to put together a long-term training plan. Try to stay one or two sprints in the future. That provides enough time for the logistical planning of the course. Digging deeper in the training backlog has the same disadvantages of going too deep in the product backlog—you end up doing a lot of long-range planning that ends up having to be replanned or scrapped anyway.

Summary

Scrum teams are the key to success in an agile development. It is therefore critically important to give Scrum teams the best start you can. This starts with defining a clear team identity and setting the team's operating (ground) rules and definition of DONEness. With these in place, the team moves on to learning the best way to handle sprint planning and then gets their product backlog ready for development. This chapter also discusses good practices for daily Scrums, sprint reviews, and sprint retrospective meetings.

We also discussed the Scrum master's responsibility for removing team obstacles in order to keep the Scrum team focused on the sprint backlog.

Lastly, we discussed the concept of continuous learning and a way to create a form of a training backlog that can be used by the Scrum team to create a list of training topics. The Scrum team can then decide who will own the management of each training session as well as the format and source of each training session.

As with everything else in agile development, check back with Scrum teams during sprint retrospective meetings to make sure that the launch is working properly. Find out from your Scrum teams what they think worked and what didn't. Then, change your practices appropriately.

Endnotes

1. You can find more information at http://www.bigagiledevelopment.com/groundrules.
2. You can find more information at http://www.bigagiledevelopment.com/donenessdefinition.
3. As mentioned elsewhere in this book, I usually consider a backlog item sprint-sized when it can be completed by two or three people on the Scrum team in less than a week.
4. Yes, that means they can't simply hand the animal to the person next to them unless everyone else has gone already.

Chapter 22

Managing Scrum Teams

In the very first chapter of this book, I listed a number of factors that absolutely had to be present in order for an organization's transition to have any hope of success. Two of those eight factors discussed management support of the agile transition and management's involvement in the transition. In this chapter, we will discuss the relationship of management to Scrum teams and how managers can truly enable Scrum teams to achieve high performance. However, in order to first discuss management principles in this environment, we need to truly understand the science behind the environment in which agile development thrives.

The Edge of Chaos

First, it is important to explain that the environment created by Scrum and agile development and required in order to continue is not the typical work environment that we all grew up learning about and in which we worked. Since the eighteenth century, the manufacturing environment has matured into science around which successes may be repeated by following carefully prepared, clearly defined processes. Indeed, as the burgeoning software engineering industry took root in the mid-1960s, a 1968 North American Treaty Organization (NATO) conference defined software engineering as being similar to other fields of engineering in that there are clear processes and laws that can be followed. Since the formation of the first data processing (DP), management information systems (MIS), or information technology (IT) departments, businesses have tried repeatedly and with relatively few successes to manage application development as a clearly defined practice. However, recent developments in complexity theory and management practices have revealed some interesting facts about software engineering.

In response to the increasing complexities of organizations and the need to develop management practices to address today's needs, there has been growing interest in a field of study called *complexity theory*. While there is already a significant amount of writing done on the subject of complexity theory by rather prominent scientists, I will attempt to provide a brief description. Consider first the concept of stable and unstable systems. A stable system, when affected by some outside interference, quickly returns to its stable state once the interference is removed. A great example of a stable system is how our moon orbits the earth. The moon orbits the earth once every 27.3 days and repeats its phases (due to something called the synodic period) once every 29.5 days. The moon has stuck to this schedule, despite thousands of meteorite collisions, for a bit over 4.5 billion years. On the other hand, an unstable system moves farther and farther away from stability until it stops due to some overriding constraint. Imagine someone riding a bicycle on an icy road. When the bicycle crosses an unexpectedly slippery patch, the cyclist goes down.

In between the stable system and the unstable system is a form of system that is called *chaotic behavior*. However, this version of chaos is different from the common definition of "a state of total confusion and disorder." Chaotic behavior describes a system that, while it has certain regularities, defies prediction. Consider the weather. Despite years and years of information and some of the most detailed computer models in existence, today's meteorologists still cannot predict the weather with any real success. Still, however, the Nile doesn't freeze and Toronto doesn't experience monsoons.[1] A chaotic system sits in between the stable and the unstable system and exhibits characteristics of both. Software development fits the description of a chaotic system; anyone who needs proof of this need only look as far as the original 1994 CHAOS survey[2] that brought light to the fact that 83.8% of software development projects were either being cancelled, delivering less than promised, finishing significantly overbudget (to the tune of 189%), or were both overbudget and short of delivery targets.

Further scientific research has yielded some additional principles that sum up what is being experienced across the entire software development industry. We know these principles today as:

- *Ziv's uncertainty principle in software engineering*:[3] Uncertainty is inherent and inevitable in software development processes and products.
- *Humphrey's requirements uncertainty principle*:[4] For a new software system, the requirements will not be completely known until after the users have used it.
- *Wegner's lemma*:[5] An interactive system can never be fully specified, nor can it ever be fully tested.

Software engineering clearly does not behave as a stable system. The aforementioned principles prove through modeling and empirical evidence that there is a considerable degree of uncertainty in software engineering. This inherent uncertainty makes impossible the concept that we could define processes that we can follow and be successful time and time again. The software engineering industry cannot derive a "magic process formula" that will provide greater success in writing software applications.

Software engineering is also not an unstable system. After all, we have been successful in creating applications over the years. Even when our projects are set back by unexpected changes and the massive uncertainty that Ziv's, Humphrey's, and Wegner's principles describe, we are still able to regroup, replan, and finish some of our projects. So, we are left somewhere in between stability and instability. As mentioned earlier, the space in between these systems is the edge of chaos.

Management in a Chaotic System

Though the field of complexity theory and how it applies to management practices is still quite new, the recognition that conventional management practices do not work well in a chaotic system has been embraced successfully by large, modern corporations. For example, consider the web portal giant Google. This is an organization that has a business vision and mission like more conventional organizations, yet how it manages its personnel truly reflects an understanding of complexity theory and work in a chaotic system. Some of the behaviors that make Google different are:

1. When developers are hired, they are given time to review the projects and the teams that currently exist. They then "apply" to join a team by producing an original "new" feature for that team's product. If the team appreciates the developer's work, he or she is invited to join.
2. Should a developer tire of a team and need a change, he or she needs only communicate the desire and is quickly moved from one team room to another.
3. Developers are encouraged to spend a portion of their time, every week, working on something that has nothing to do with their current project.
4. Google's philosophy is that they it doesn't tell developers what to do. The development teams decide what to do and how to do it.

Google's management style reflects some of the basic lessons to be learned about management in a chaotic system. We'll discuss these lessons in terms of how they apply to Scrum teams and an agile development environment.

Continuous Learning

In a chaotic system, we generally understand that, while our organizations have a direction and a purpose (a mission and vision), much of what we are going to encounter is unknown to us at the outset. We can try to analyze ourselves out of the corner and prepare for every contingency, but there's only so much we can learn by analysis, and the effort itself is costly and doesn't guarantee success. Even worse, the analysis can tend to paralyze the organization while the analysis is under way and the organization convinces itself that it is safe to move forward. Management and software development in an environment such as this requires that there be a continuous learning cycle under way at all times.

Retrospection is generally employed in an agile environment to understand what worked and what didn't during a period of time. Questions are asked not only about practices and methods, but also about skills and training. At the end of every sprint, Scrum teams and management teams alike should be looking at what they achieved during the previous sprint to evaluate their performance and decide how they can improve. In many cases, items will surface during these discussions that require the team to acquire or improve upon some important skill. Teams should be encouraged to identify these needed skills and take steps to improve upon those skills as quickly as possible.

In addition, the organizational culture itself should be focused on continuous learning. Employees (including managers) should have personal learning goals for spending a specific amount of time each week or each month on professional and technical skills improvement (don't set yearly goals—they always end up waiting until the end of the year). In my experience, however, the choices made for training by many employees just end up being a list they put together at the last minute based on a generic job description of their next title. To improve upon the decisions made for training goals, your employees should work with teams to determine, as a group, what training would most benefit the organization and, starting with that list, develop individual training goals.

Encourage Change and Chaos

Organizations that seek out stability and define themselves by their rigid structures generally find themselves seeking out fewer and fewer innovations and, instead, "stick with what works." In fact, a great way to describe such organizations can be found in the motto: "If it ain't broke, don't fix it." If everything in the corporation works well enough to get the job done, there's no incentive to get better and to get the job done in more innovative and revolutionary ways. However, software development being as uncertain as it is, the better motto might be: "If it works, break it and see if you can make it better." I've made the point several times in this book that organizations hoping to become agile have to be willing to make mistakes and, indeed, that a motto of agile developers is to "fail fast and fail often"—embracing the concept that real improvement comes from learning what doesn't work because once we find something that does work, we tend to stop looking. Management complexity theorists emphasize the importance of openness to accident, coincidence, and serendipity. Strategy is the emergent result.[6]

Think of it like refactoring at the organizational level. I often teach my students that a close look at Da Vinci's *Mona Lisa* shows there may be up to thirty layers of paint on parts of the famous painting. In fact, the painting itself seems to have taken the genius nearly two decades to finish. Da Vinci knew that the first pass at the painting would not be the best, and he continued to improve both the painting and his methods from the painting's beginnings somewhere between 1503 and 1506 CE and its completion in 1519 CE. Likewise, finding a "right" way to accomplish a task in an organization doesn't mean you found the *best* way. Chaotic systems keep looking and keep changing.

Fluidity of Structure

One of the principles of Scrum teams is that they should have the skills that they need in order to get the job done. This usually means that we look at what needs to be done, and then form the proper team (which is the right way to do this). Unfortunately, it also frequently means that, once a team is formed and becomes productive, we subordinate the work to the team. In other words, we will change or reassign the work to another team rather than look at the current team and decide if the reason that the team was formed is still valid.

In a chaotic system, management is encouraged to facilitate the spontaneous creation of informal structures, made up of people from across the organization, in response to the problems that the organization is currently facing or to take advantage of opportunities that the organization wants to seize. These structures must be self-organizing and capable of redefining or extending their charter, rather than being bound by a fixed definition.

Likewise, having formed Scrum teams to contain the proper skills to address specific needs, there should be a constant reevaluation of the team's purpose and capabilities. After any given sprint, the team should decide:

1. *Does the opportunity or problem that caused the origination of our team still exist?* If not, the team must seriously consider disbanding and finding other teams to work with. Without an opportunity to take advantage of or a problem to solve, the value of the team has diminished. Don't keep the team around longer than necessary.
2. *Has the opportunity or problem changed in such a way that the team's skills are no longer a match?* In some cases, this may simply require a rebalancing of skills to the problem or opportunity. Can the team take on a new member? Does the team need to give up an existing member whose skills are no longer needed?

Chaotic environments provide ways to address problems and take advantage of opportunities in a manner that taps into the individual skills and interests in your employees—skills and interests that can remain hidden, unknown, and untapped in more conventional management strategies. Senior management's part in all of this is to help ensure a balance between traditional methods of managing a stable system (analysis and planning) and more unconventional methods of managing a chaotic system (learning and fluidity). Too much enforced stability and the organization stagnates and loses to its competition. Too much chaos and the organization descends into anarchy, becoming incapable of achieving even its short-term goals.

Management in an Agile Environment

We discussed in preceding sections that software development is an activity fraught with uncertainty at every turn. We don't know all of the requirements we need to know until after we've built our product and, in fact, we concede that we can't ever completely test our own interactive software. In embracing these realities and with a growing understanding of complexity theory and chaotic system, agile development methods were created. But what are the management practices that work best in an agile environment? Using some practical experience and the information reviewed previously in this chapter, we'll discuss management in an agile environment.

In general, management in an agile environment, a chaotic system, is all about maintaining a balance between stability and chaos. We need our organization to be stable so that it can operate in today's business environment. The business needs to be able to define its vision and mission and then make the large-scale business decisions based on those tenets. The organization's accounting practices need to be stable and, in most countries, abide by very specific guidelines regarding how the organization's accounting is to be done. At the same time, the same organization needs to recognize that software development activities are more chaotic. There may, in fact, be closely tied combinations of stable and chaotic systems; for example, while the accounting practices need to be clearly defined and followed (stable), the accounting department itself may be more flexible and innovative by following practices that are more chaotic (agile). The most difficult aspect of any manager's job will be to understand the true difference: When does the organization benefit from stability and when does it benefit from chaos?

The Front-Line Manager

Let's start with the front-line (or first-line) manager. This manager is usually the administrative supervisor of the developers (including analysts, testers, coders, etc.) that participate on Scrum teams. The first-line manager has more direct exposure to the Scrum team than any other manager in the organization and will be involved in most staffing decisions regarding the team. The manager is sometimes a technical resource, sometimes a leader. In other cases, the first-line manager is an obstacle, a de-motivational force that can quickly take good teams and make them entirely ineffective. The best description I've heard so far talks about the first-line manager as a sheepdog, continuously moving around the Scrum team, keeping everyone focused and together, and handling defects and obstacles that interfere with the progress of the Scrum team. We'll take a look at a first-line manager's responsibilities in the following paragraphs:

- *Help resolve impediments*: In many instances, Scrum masters are either overwhelmed by obstacles reported by their team or lack the authority to resolve some of the obstacles that they've inherited. In these cases, the first-line manager should frequently check with the Scrum master to ensure that no obstacles go unaddressed for lack of authority.
- Scrum teams, to help mediate or resolve arguments between Scrum team members, may call upon first-line managers for their assistance. These arguments can be about the product (a disagreement about a design approach) or about a personality conflict. In either case, the manager should attempt to respect the team's self-managing responsibilities while still trying to guide the disputing parties to a reasonable solution. In other words, in the case of most disagreements within the team, the manager's job is to help the team help themselves.
- *Support individual development*: While developers need to continue to be responsible for their performance plans and career development plans, managers are the people that can help provide the ideas, the structure, and the support. If the organization uses employee performance plans, the manager needs to ensure that the plans are an appropriate combination of team goals and organizational goals. If the organization also employs career development plans, the manager needs to ensure that the employee has the information and input he or she needs to make appropriate decisions.
- *Help filter organizational "noise"*: The typical organization is a very busy place. New employees are being hired; others are transferring to new positions or leaving the organization entirely. News from other parts of the organization is announced and discussed. Of course, there are also the escalations, the upset customers, the visiting executive, and so on. All of these events create noise, which is pervasive throughout the organization. It is critical for the manager to support his or her Scrum masters in organizing the noise so that the Scrum teams hear what they need to hear at the right time. That doesn't mean keeping information from the team, but rather keeping the team from being interrupted every ten minutes when something new is learned by the organization's grapevine.
- *Handle administrative responsibilities*: Of course, a manager in an agile environment still has all of the typical responsibilities he or she has to deal with on a regular basis—status reports to be written, meetings to attend, organizational strategies to help plan.

While performing all of the aforementioned responsibilities, the first-line manager also has to learn and master a very difficult skill. As Scrum teams are supposed to be self-managing, that management responsibility has to come from somewhere. The first-line manager must learn how to delegate much of his or her responsibilities to the Scrum team. This means that the manager, other than supporting the Scrum team, will have to learn to how to leave the decisions on what the Scrum teams commits to at sprint planning and the decisions they make during the sprint; the outcomes of sprint reviews and the decisions made during sprint retrospectives must be managed by the Scrum team. While it certainly is not unheard of that a manager might make a suggestion or two to a Scrum team, managers must be very careful not to provide too much coaching to their Scrum teams as they risk making their Scrum teams dependent upon them. Coaching of Scrum teams should always be aimed at helping the teams to find the solution themselves, rather than having a solution handed to them.

In addition to delegating responsibility to Scrum teams, managers also have to learn to trust their Scrum teams. This means that managers will have to trust their teams to make good decisions and, on some occasions, to make poor decisions and learn from the consequences. In one story, a team attempting to implement continuous integration practices failed four sprints in a row while their manager watched and waited. This manager knew that forcing the team to implement continuous integration in a specific way would create skeptics on the team that might never completely embrace the value and concepts of continuous integration. By allowing the team to make mistakes and learn from those mistakes, the team learned the value of continuous integration and how to properly implement it. While the delays the organization experienced as a result created a hardship, the Scrum team had not only internalized the practice of continuous integration, but had become continuous integration's biggest proponent in the organization. Managers must also avoid micromanagement, allowing the team to make decisions without the manager, and even more importantly, the temptation to assert control over the team during a crisis.

Lastly, the first-line manager may also be faced with the fact that, unfortunately, not everyone will appreciate working in a team environment where everyone works together. Managers will frequently be faced with the question of what to do with team members that do not know how to work with others, do not want to work on the team any longer, or have angered their team members so fully that they have requested the removal of the problem employee from the team. Managers in these situations have very little time to make the right decision. Leave the wrong employee on a team long enough and the entire team will become demoralized.

General Management Responsibilities

While the first-line managers have significant interactions with Scrum teams, managers in general (including middle management and executive management) share some other important responsibilities in an agile environment:

- *Be accessible to your employees*: Agile development will raise a lot of issues in your organization. Employees will want to express both their concerns and their ideas to executive management. They want to know that their executives understand agile development, and they need to know that while they are dealing with the impediments, executives are willing to deal with the bigger problems in the organization. Sometimes doing nothing more than listening and showing concern for your employees is all that's really being asked for.

■ *Show your commitment to the transition to agile development*: Several years ago, Ken Schwaber noted that seventy percent of all transitions to Scrum ended in failure. More recently, another survey conducted by IBM concluded that sixty percent of projects aimed at achieving business change did not fully meet their objectives,[7] and seventy percent of respondents indicated that honest and timely communication is important in project success. Transitioning to agile development is much more than a change in development process; it will affect nearly every aspect of your business and, at a very basic level, will have a tremendous impact on your corporate culture as well. Employees will need to know at the beginning and frequently during the transition that the organization's management (particularly executive management) completely supports the transition, even when mistakes and missteps occur.

■ *Communicate your vision*: Make a point of explaining your business vision and that your organization's product reflects and supports that vision. Do it every opportunity that you can. Repeat and expand upon your vision so often that your employees know what you are going to say before you say it. Make it how you open and close every meeting and every presentation. Visit your Scrum teams frequently and relate your vision to what the Scrum teams are doing. What's their role in achieving the vision?

■ *Lead from behind*: Managers who have delegated their authority to the Scrum team must learn to lead by coaching from the sidelines. This requires managers to ask leading questions, rather than simply suggesting solutions or courses of action. More importantly, managers need to see themselves as supporting their teams rather than talking about teams that "report to them."

■ *Let the teams decide*: Get the Scrum teams to decide on standards and practices and make sure that you discuss these standards and practices, as well as problems caused by the standards and improvements made to the standards, in terms of what "you [the team] decided" and "the decisions you made." When you discuss standards and practices in terms of "we decided" or "they were decided upon," you remove responsibility from the team and place it on the organization. Keep your teams in the driver's seat.

Helping to Improve Team Performance

As self-managing and self-organizing teams, Scrum teams are expected to evaluate and improve their own performance on a regular basis (usually starting through sprint retrospective meetings). However, a good manager will always be watching for opportunities to help his or her Scrum teams excel. Most Scrum teams, after a while, tend to reach a point where their performance plateaus. They've solved all of the low-hanging impediments and there are few known obstacles left for the team to address. By looking closely, however, many managers will see that the team has created practices that circumvent rather than solve other issues. For example, Scrum teams frequently ask me for advice on how they should handle defects that are reported during the sprint. The usual plan is to set aside a certain percentage of the team's availability at sprint planning for defect diagnosis and solution. For example, many teams start by setting aside thirty percent of their time during sprint planning, so that the team doesn't overcommit. While that's a reasonable question,[8] it is sometimes troubling the number of teams that don't also couple the desire to plan for support with a plan for reducing the number of defects being found in their code. In other words, the major concern becomes planning for the defects, while too little thinking goes into reducing the defects in the first place.

In observing Scrum teams while evaluating team performance, managers must be very careful not to commit either of the following sins:

1. *Tampering*: Scrum teams are intended to be responsible for their own performance and for the improvement of that performance. Managers charged with evaluating Scrum team performance and helping the team improve their performance must be very careful not to tamper with the teams, i.e., not to make changes to the Scrum team's practices.
2. *Micromanagement*: By being too involved in the daily activities of a Scrum team, the team's own self-management will tend to dissipate under the close supervision, and the team will revert to relying on the manager to provide direction and solve problems.

Managers trying to search for a way to challenge their Scrum teams to higher levels of performance should review team activities looking for practices that support agility. It is not uncommon for teams to decide to give up or ease off on important practices that eventually make the teams ineffective. Some of the things you can look for[9] are:

- ◼ Sprint planning:
  - Are your teams' sprint planning sessions effective? Do they set a commitment for the sprint, determine how they are going to complete each backlog item committed to, and derive a sprint backlog that supports the commitment?
  - Is DONEness a key element of determining how to complete backlog items?
  - Is the entire Scrum team (including the product owner) present at the meeting?
  - Is the product backlog prioritized, sized, and ready for the Scrum team prior to sprint planning?
- ◼ Sprinting
  - Is the sprint longer than thirty-one days?
  - Is the sprint ever extended to allow team members to "finish up"?

- Does anyone other than the Scrum team modify the sprint planning commitment?
- Does anyone other than the Scrum team cause the sprint planning commitment to be modified?
- Is the sprint backlog updated daily?
- Do the sprints end with working software?
- Does the team produce documentation that no one uses?
- Does the Scrum master work to protect the team from outside interference and noise?
- Is the Scrum master always actively working on getting rid of obstacles?
- Are the team's committed backlog items and tasks located somewhere that everyone can see them?

■ Daily Scrums
  - Is the daily Scrum held every day?
  - Does everyone participate in the daily Scrum?
  - Is the daily Scrum finished in fifteen minutes or less?
  - Does anyone other than the Scrum team participate in the daily Scrum?
  - Does everyone stick to the three questions?

■ Backlog grooming
  - Are backlog grooming sessions held throughout the sprint?
  - Does the entire team participate (including the product owner)?
  - Does the team continue to slice backlog items until they are small enough to fit into a sprint? Do they then stop and move on to other backlog items?
  - Does the team get bogged down in lengthy conversations that do not provide value? Do they have a means for checking where they are and deciding whether or not to continue the discussion?
  - Does the team stop when there's enough groomed items on the product backlog (plus a little more) for the next sprint?

■ Sprint reviews
  - Are reviews primarily about demonstrating software?
  - Does management attend sprint reviews?
  - Sprint retrospectives
  - Does your Scrum team hold a retrospective meeting after every sprint?
  - Do retrospectives result in improvements in team practices, and do the team decisions focus on root cause or just the aftereffects?
  - Do retrospectives end with a list of three or four things to continue to do or to do differently?

■ About the Scrum team
  - Is the Scrum team too big (more than nine people)?
  - Does the Scrum master tend to tell team members what to do?
  - Do any managers tend to tell team members what to do?
  - Where do team members look for answers to questions? To themselves or others outside the team?

- – Does the Scrum team have a clear definition of what it means to be done?
- – Does the Scrum team first evaluate problems from a standpoint of how to deal with the problem or do they focus on who caused it?
- – Does the Scrum team look at mistakes and failures as an opportunity to improve, or a reason to be more conservative?
- – Does the team focus on spreading skills horizontally, or do they continue to become more and more specialized?
- – Is everyone on the team participating in discussions? Are all opinions heard, or do one or two opinions dominate the decisions?
- – Does the team have the skills and knowledge they need to get the job done, or do they constantly have to wait for the information they need to finish their work?
- – Does the team seem willing to take risks and make mistakes, or do they tend to avoid trying new things?
- – Does the team tend to pass responsibility for correcting organizational decisions and problems back to the organization, or do they see themselves as empowered to make decisions? Do they complain about the problems, ignore the problems, or fix the problems?

■ About development practices
  - – Is the team writing unit tests that support what the code is supposed to do, or what the code already does?[10]
  - – Do team members work together to write code and tests, build UIs, and update documentation at the same time, or are they handing work off to one another?
  - – Does the team build their product several times a day to make sure that nothing they have done in the past couple of hours broke the build?
  - – Does the team test their product several times a day to make sure that nothing that they have done in the past couple of hours broke the application?
  - – Does the team engage in frequent refactoring of their code in order to improve the supportability of the code itself?
  - – Does the team engage in any kind of peer review of the code written or changed during a sprint?

While working with Scrum teams to help them improve their performance, remember that it is unwise to compare one team's performance to another's. While we can classify teams into various categories (e.g., forming, storming, norming, and performing[11]), it is equally true that, like fingerprints,[12] no two Scrum teams are alike. Scrum teams are made up of people, not resources, and each team must be evaluated on its own merits. For example, I will never coach an organization that its Scrum teams (assuming they are all roughly the same size) should all achieve a velocity of at least twenty story points. This is effectively the same as saying that all Scrum teams should be able to achieve the same result, despite the fact that they are all working on different software, are solving different problems, and are made up of different personalities and different skill sets.[13] With all the uncertainty of software development and the differences introduced by personalities, what cause is there to suppose that different Scrum teams would perform identically? The actions taken by a manager must be independently determined by the actions and the decisions of the Scrum team itself.

Endnotes

1. Rosenhead, Jonathan. *Complexity Theory and Management Practice*. http://human-nature.com/science-as-culture/rosenhead.html.
2. The Standish Group. *The Standish Group Report: CHAOS*. 1995. http://net.educause.edu/ir/library/pdf/NCP08083B.pdf.
3. Ziv, Hadar, and Richardson, Debra J. *The Uncertainty Principle in Software Engineering*. University of California, Irvine, CA: 1996.
4. The concept of calling this Humphrey's principle seems to have been coined by Jeff Sutherland and is a reference to Watts Humphrey's paper, "Some Programming Principles: Requirements." http://www.sei.cmu.edu/news-at-sei/columns/watts_new/2003/1q03/watts-new-1q03.htm.
5. Wegner, Peter. *The Paradigm Shift from Algorithms to Interaction*. Brown University, October 14, 1996. Also, for those of you in the same boat I was in when I saw this, a *lemma* is a proven statement used as a way of proving another statement.
6. Rosenhead.
7. *IBM Global Study: Majority of Organizational Change Projects Fail*. http://www-935.ibm.com/services/us/index.wss/summary/imc/a1030548?cntxt=a1000401.
8. My answer usually is not to bother planning for support at all. If the team is properly calculating velocity as the sum of the story point sizes of completed backlog items, is using that value to groom enough for the next sprint, and also uses that value to determine their likely commitment for the next sprint, then there's no reason to plan specifically for support—using velocity allows the team's commitment to self-correct.
9. You can find more information at http://www.bigagiledevelopment.com/watchlist.
10. This is the fundamental difference between writing unit tests and writing them using test-driven development. For more information, I recommend looking at Scott Ambler's web site: http://www.agiledata.org/essays/tdd.html.
11. These are categorizations of group dynamics as proposed by Bruce Tuckman.
12. Fingerprints can be classified in ways that describe their appearance (i.e., whorl, loop, and arch) as well as the mode of the fingerprint itself (i.e., visible, latent, and impressed).
13. It also tends to cause Scrum teams to modify their story point estimations to ensure that they are hitting the expected goals.

Chapter 23

Agile Product Management

Product management in an agile environment is very similar to product management in any application development environment. Much of the work of product management centers on understanding what features will make your product valuable to the eventual users. This requires a clear understanding of development constraints and timeframes and a delicate balancing of market and customer needs, business needs, and an endless variety of competing limitations and requirements. In agile development, specifically when using Scrum, we more fully enhance the product manager role by giving a more appropriate title of "product owner" and, from the perspective of the development teams, limiting the authority to prioritize and interpret requirements solely to the product owner. In this chapter, we will review the major responsibilities of the product owner, how the product owner uses and maintains the product backlog, and how defects affect the product backlog.

The fundamental responsibilities of the product owner make the person in this role accountable for the success or failure of their product. We'll start by discussing these responsibilities and then move on to how product ownership is often managed in a larger organization. The product owner's responsibilities include the following:

- *Understanding the needs of your customers*: While this should be a clear-cut description, the reality of understanding your customers' needs actually requires the product owner to understand the difference between a customer's wants (what they say they need) and a customer's needs (what they actually need). A good product owner must be able to detect when solutions (wants) are being given to them by their customers and must know how to work with the customer to reinterpret those solutions as actual needs.

313

Market segmentation tends to make the problem even more difficult—a product with a number of customers will find that those customers often have competing if not completely opposing needs. This happens when your product is sold to customers that are in the same industry but have completely different business drivers. Typical market segmentation occurs within industries where there are both for-profit and not-for-profit players in the industry at the same time. A third segmentation occurs when there are government-subsidized businesses in the industry as well. This occurs frequently in the healthcare industry, where you might have hospitals run by for-profit organizations, hospitals run by charities (e.g., Shriners), and hospitals run all or in part by the national government (e.g., Veterans Administration). You can find similar segmentation in education with schools at all levels of education occurring in for-profit (private schools and colleges), not-for-profit (religious schools), and public schools managed by state and local governments.

Complicating the product owner's job still further is that he or she needs to possess an excellent ability to predict events up to three, four, or even five years in the future, and how those events might change the needs of the customer so that the product can be ready (or nearly ready) at the same time that substantial pressure for a resolution to the need begins to surface.

- *Represent your stakeholders*: The product owner is the voice of the customer within the organization.[1] The product owner must represent the priorities, needs, and opinions of customers, government regulators, and executive management alike. By constantly representing the stakeholder in everything that the product owner does, the product is built with the features that provide the greatest value to the customers. Additionally, good representation of stakeholder needs will help produce a product that works the way customers would wish it to work and is customizable within the parameters set by the needs of the largest part of the customer base.

- *Maximize your product's return on investment (ROI)*: While evaluating which features to put in the product and which to leave for another day, the product owner is expected to maximize the return on development activities. In other words, the product owner is supposed to get the greatest value for the least cost from every single feature added to the product. This puts intense pressure on the product owner and the development teams to minimize defects (because defects lead to having to work on the same feature more than once for the same initial value or less) and carefully balance customer-valued functionality with architectural improvements that do not provide direct functionality but are necessary nonetheless.

- *Prioritize the work*: The product owner drives what his or her Scrum teams develop by prioritizing the product backlog. Scrum teams take their work from the top of the product backlog and are required to obtain permission from the product owner to do any item out of the defined order. While anyone

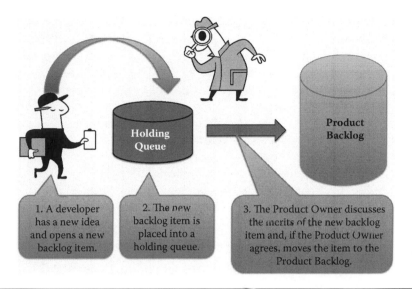

Figure 23.1   Using a holding queue with the product backlog.

is allowed to add items to the product backlog, these items are usually added to the bottom of the product backlog or, alternatively, into a holding queue pending review by the product owner. Only the product owner is allowed to prioritize the product backlog or to remove items from the product backlog (see Figure 23.1).

■ *Translate backlog items for development teams*: No matter how product backlog items are written, the product owner is the final authority on what they mean and how the product should behave when the item is completed (e.g., features that the customer can see, that includes what the customer sees and how the UI works as well as how any formulas work, search criteria, whether or not data is optional, and even the performance characteristics of the feature—that it should run in less than 1 second 95% of the time under normal load conditions). For architectural items, the product owner could communicate that the architectural change should not be visible to the customer in any way unless the customer activates a specific option. Product owners accomplish most of this communication during backlog grooming workshops, sprint planning, and the sprints themselves. In general, many details are discussed and documented during backlog grooming sessions and are further developed during sprint planning. During the sprint, the product owner is frequently involved to answer very detailed questions as the features are actually being built.

■ *Achieve and sustain a maintainable development pace*: I teach all of my product owners that there is one basic and unavoidable truth in agile product management: your Scrum teams will never complete as many features during their sprints as you want them to. I suggest that, as product owners, if they can't accept that truth, they reconsider being product owners in the first place. It is an unfortunate reality, but product owners are always focused on completing as much value as they can for as little cost as possible. That will always have the product owners focused on getting their Scrum teams to produce more and more every sprint, even if the teams are not prepared to do so. A good Scrum team will know when to say no to the product owner, drawing the line at the point where they produce the best-quality software at a pace that they can sustain for several consecutive sprints. The product owner needs to be very careful to push his or her Scrum teams just enough to keep them motivated and challenged and to help them find that maximum sustainable pace. Push too hard, and if your teams don't push back (and many won't, if they fear reprisal), they will begin to both produce lower-quality software and work at a pace that cannot be sustained for long.

■ *Understand the needs of multiple teams*: The product owner is the beginning point from which new product ideas are introduced to the product backlog and, indeed, to many other potentially nonagile portions of the larger organization. Product owners have to understand how the following teams are affected by changed and additions to the product backlog and need to ensure that the right steps are taken by the right people at the right time:

  – Development teams: Of course, our development teams are where the items have to be built, and product owners must work directly with the development teams (with or without business analysts) to break down items into work that the development teams can understand and complete within a sprint.

  – Sales: Product owners have a delicate balancing act to do with the sales teams. While it is crucial to keep the sales teams prepared for what is planned for development, the product owner must also keep lines of communication open to ensure that the sales team does not release information to customers or the press that the product owner is not certain will be finished in time for the product release. Communication regarding the availability of features has to be very clear and always up-to-date.

  – Technical marketing: Product owners need to be able to communicate to technical marketing how new features will be added to the product, the effect those features will have on the overall product, and what if any architectural changes may be made as a result. Some of this information won't be available until after the development teams begin grooming the related items or building the feature—the product owner should ensure that he or she or a business analyst or a Scrum team member handles the ongoing communication with technical marketing to keep them up-to-date as the feature construction continues.

  – Education services: Product owners need to be able to communicate to education services teams how the planned changes to the product will affect training materials and even training schedules. As the creation of new materials and updating of existing materials usually lags behind the actual development activity, it is critical that the product owner keep the education services teams as up-to-date as possible.

- Customer service/technical support: All too often, technical support personnel are not considered in the development of new features or the changes made to existing features. Ideally, technical and customer support personnel should be involved in the development of new features as those features are planned. Product owners, often through their business analysts, must get technical support personnel involved in how items are added to the product, what the technical support requirements are of those changes, and help get the technical support personnel ready to provide support for the new features and product changes.

■ *Plan for your beta testing*: No matter how good a job you do with agile development, building and testing your product every day, you will still need to install your product in one or more actual customer environments in order to ensure that your product is tested under the most production-like circumstances possible. The product owner needs to plan for one or more betas, solicit potential customers, manage the delivery of the beta software, collect bugs reported by the customers, and ensure that the bugs are actually diagnosed and fixed.

With all these responsibilities, reaching outward to customers to understand their needs, reaching inward to Scrum teams to help explain the product backlog, the product owner in a large organization often has to be more than just a single person.

Large-Scale Product Ownership

In a larger organization, the product owner is often part of a team of product managers and business analysts that work together to accomplish the responsibilities of the product owner. In these larger teams, one or more product owners support complex pieces of a large application by working directly with stakeholders and customers and prioritizing the product backlog. Several business analysts, working closely with the product owners, support the Scrum teams during backlog grooming, sprint planning, and throughout the sprint. Two common organizations are shown in Figure 23.2.

In Figure 23.2, we see an example of a small product owner arrangement. In this example, we have a single product owner. While this product owner is still wholly accountable for the success of the product, this product owner will focus primarily on outward facing responsibilities—meeting with customers, meeting with management, and attending industry conferences. Working closely and frequently with the product owner are four business analysts. These analysts learn as much as they can from the product owner about each and every backlog item on

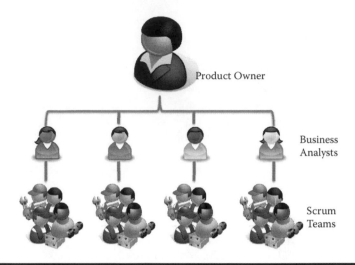

Figure 23.2 A small product owner arrangement.

the product backlog in order for them to properly represent the product owner's desires. The business analysts work directly with each Scrum team, fulfilling most of the product owner's responsibilities for the Scrum team. The business analysts participate in backlog grooming workshops, sprint planning meetings, and assist the Scrum teams during the sprint.

In Figure 23.3, we see an example of a much larger product owner arrangement that helps us to deal with a much larger and more complex product. In this scenario, our product is so complex as to require us to have several product owners. Each product owner is responsible for some major portion of the product (e.g., student registration, class scheduling, billing for college management software or patient registration, patient orders, billing for hospital management software). As with the small group arrangement, each product owner has one or more business analysts working directly with him or her to help communicate and coordinate with the Scrum teams. However, in this arrangement there is one more product owner, an "uber" product owner that has overall responsibility for the entire product and delegates his or her authority to the "unter" product owners. Together, the product owners share responsibility for prioritizing their backlogs, though the uber product owner drives the overall product priorities.

On a regular basis, but at least once per sprint, the uber product owner should be sure to bring all of the product owners together to compare business needs and current opportunities. At this meeting, the product owners should:

1. Review the outcomes of the previous sprints (what was finished, what was returned to the backlog) and adjust accordingly.
2. Review the current project status to ensure that all product backlogs reflect the organization's priorities and needs.

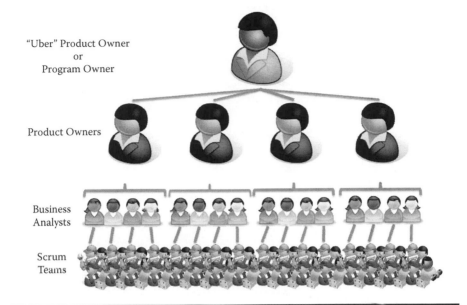

Figure 23.3 A large product owner arrangement.

3. Negotiate with other product owners to resolve any issues caused by dependencies between the backlogs.

4. Identify new opportunities and challenges and update the product backlogs accordingly.

Let's talk a bit about how this works. For example, let's assume we're responsible for a large software package that manages all of the flights and the booking of seats on our customer's airlines. Every passenger's reservation, no matter how they book their flight, ends up in our system. Of course, our software handles everything for our customers for every flight, including:

- Seat reservation: Who's in which seat?
- Seat availability: Which seats are available? Remember, some stay unavailable until twenty-four hours before the flight.
- Seat location: Is this a bulkhead seat (the seats in the front of each cabin with nothing but a wall right in front of them)? Is this seat in an exit row?
- Meal preferences: No preference, vegetarian, kosher, gluten-free?
- Gate assignment at each airport: From which gate does the flight leave and at which does it arrive?
- Seat pricing: How much does it cost to reserve the seat? Many airlines now have multiple levels of economy/coach, then business class, and then first class.
- Seat juggling: This is a special function provided when a party (usually a family) all books together and wants to sit together. This function tries to get

everyone in the party as close together as possible while honoring as much as of the affected passengers' preferences it can. Priority, of course, is given to those who booked first.

■ Customer status: Some customers have preferred status due to their frequent flights with our customers. So, these customers can be automatically upgraded, when available, to the next class of seat. Of course, when the upgrade occurs, other passengers' preferences are also taken into account, causing a cascade of reseating to put everyone where they most prefer to be.

Having created this basic outline of functionality, let's also assume that we have three product owners that work with an uber product owner to manage the ongoing development of our flight management software. Responsibility across the product breaks down like this:

■ Paul: The uber product owner; has been with the company for twenty years and knows the product and the customers inside and out. His guidance has brought our product to a leading position within the industry.

■ Linda: Knows the fare calculations like no one else in the industry and is responsible for the seat pricing, location, and availability functions. Since no one else seemed to want it, Linda handles the gate assignment capabilities as well. Linda's been with the company for a little less time than Paul. The team tends to defer to Linda if Paul isn't available to help solve a problem or answer a question.

■ Jody: Has a hotel management background and came to our company as a result of an interesting gambit to see if her training could help us create a better experience for our customers' passengers. Jody handles the meal preferences and customer status capabilities and is responsible for looking for ways to improve repeat ridership on our customers' airlines.

■ Bill: The newest member of the team; brought onboard when the company decided to add some new capabilities to differentiate us further from the competition. There were a growing number of passenger complaints about their seat assignments being changed from "window" to "aisle" or "aisle" to "center," and there was a concern that passenger loyalty was being directly affected. Bill came onboard to create the complex seat juggling capabilities that, given passenger preferences, would continuously reseat passengers until two hours before boarding, always trying to achieve a balance that satisfies as many passengers as possible. Bill also handles the architectural aspects of the product, being more familiar with the technical details of the product than his peers.

The unter product owners, Linda, Jody, and Bill, all have between two and five business analysts working with them to assist their Scrum teams in understanding and building the items on the flight management system's product backlog. They meet regularly (at least once per sprint) to discuss the direction of the product, the newest flight regulations from the FAA,[2] press releases and information from the competition, new customer requests, and information coming from the industry. Based on their discussions, the product backlogs managed by product owners are modified by adding new items, deleting unnecessary ones, and reprioritizing the items.

In fact, in one meeting, Paul (the uber product owner) decided it was time to begin discussing the new fleet of Airbus A380s that the company's customers were beginning to place orders for. By considering the impacts of this new aircraft early, Paul was considering all of the opportunities for product promotion that the company could take advantage of if they could start thinking about what the A380 would mean and getting some of that work prioritized and into the hands of the business analysts and the Scrum teams as soon as possible. The Airbus A380 is a two-deck aircraft that seats 525 passengers with improved galley facilities. The aircraft is also much larger than previous versions and requires a larger and higher jet way and more room to taxi and park.

During the course of the meeting, the product owner team decided to add the following items to their product backlogs:

- Architectural
  The team knew this was coming eventually—the current architecture does not support multiple decks on an aircraft. However, since our customers are placing orders for an aircraft with two decks, we've also got to make extensive database and architectural changes to support upper and lower decks. The team agreed that this item would have to get attention right away— pretty much nothing else related to the A380 could be done until this was under way. Bill and Linda's teams will need to work closely together to figure out exactly how the extensions to the architecture should affect the application code.
- Seat reservations/pricing/availability/location
  Need to add the A380 seat configuration to the software. With the architectural changes, this item shouldn't be extensive, but the team agreed to review with their customers how the decks might be divided into different classes of seating to see if there could be a more extensive impact.
- Gate assignment
  The team agreed, at Paul's urging of course, that the product would have the ability to flag when an A380 has been assigned to a gate that cannot support the size of the aircraft. Seeing this might be useful in the future as aircraft become larger and airports become older, Paul felt this might be a good time to introduce this capability.
- Meal preferences/customer status
  With the increased galley capabilities, Jody decided to follow up with some customers to see if they might increase their food offerings to passengers.

Jody had recently become familiar with a growing need for gluten-free foods and wanted to see if this might be when the airlines would begin introducing that option.
■ Seat juggling
   With the architectural changes, the seat juggling routines should not be affected, but the team agreed that it may be necessary to create more test cases for the juggling routines based on the increased complexity created by 500+ seats and two decks. Bill's teams will have to work closely with Linda's teams to figure out the new test cases.

   Because Paul was very concerned about getting the architectural changes under way (they were clearly key to completing any of the rest of the code), some features previously planned for the next quarter were pushed a little further down the product backlogs of the various product owners in order to allow some room for the architectural work and the collaboration needed between several teams to ensure that the architectural changes truly supported the application functionality. Immediately following the meetings, the product owners met with their business analysts to discuss the new items and the prioritization changes.

   At the daily Scrums of the Scrum teams, the product owners introduced, at a high level, the new items and why they were being added to the product backlogs. It was left to the business analysts to go into details during backlog grooming workshops.

   The preceding example illustrates how a product owner team functions in a large organization. While the uber product owner drives overall product direction, a team of highly qualified unter product owners provide the ability to evaluate market trends, industry changes, and customer needs, turning those influences into backlog items for grooming and development and into decisions to speak with customers about future needs and opportunities. The product owners are also responsible for communicating all of these decisions and concepts to the business analysts, enabling the business analysts in turn to speak with the Scrum teams.

   However, as in the example, I recommend that product owners speak with Scrum teams directly about what is going on with the product, why decisions are being made, why prioritizations are changed, and how those changes will improve the profitability of the product and the value it provides to the customer. Don't use your business analysts as a "go-between" with your Scrum teams. It is good advice for all product owners to always maintain an open line of communication with their Scrum teams—don't use others to transmit important information about changes to the product backlog.

The Extended Product Backlog

As the product owner defines more and more of the product that he or she wishes to have built, the information takes partial shape in the product backlog. However, as

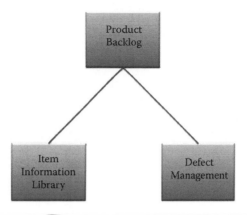

Figure 23.4 The extended product backlog.

more and more information is uncovered and defined, it becomes clear that, while the product backlog defines and orders the work, there is much more to the product backlog than simply the list that we call the product backlog. As backlog items are discussed, analyzed, and sliced into smaller and smaller items, information is uncovered and documented, and that information needs to go to some kind of permanent storage. As software is built and tested, defects are found. Information about those defects is placed into a defect tracking system just as the defects themselves often end up on the product backlog as defect numbers or brief descriptions. This concept of an extended product backlog, consisting of the product backlog, an item information library, and defect management software, is illustrated in Figure 23.4.

Let's discuss the pieces in a little detail:

1. *The product backlog*: This piece of the extended backlog has been discussed thoroughly throughout this book and most literature about Scrum. We needn't go into more detail on the backlog here.
2. *The item information library*: The library portion of the extended backlog is a storage area for all of the information gleaned from the various conversations that the Scrum team has regarding the backlog item. Information stored in the library can include (but certainly is not limited to):
   - Flowcharts
   - UI mock-ups
   - Database schema designs
   - Test case definitions
   - Any other information that the team finds useful
3. *The defect management system*: The defect management portion of the extended backlog contains information regarding defects found in the product after the Scrum team has decided that the software feature is done. Defects are found

by other developers, testers, and customers (among many others), so the real importance of a defect management system is that it can collect important and necessary information about the nature of the defect from a variety of sources and can categorize defects to facilitate easy searching, prioritization, and reporting. When defects are added to the defect management system, the product owner can choose to put placeholders for the defects in the product backlog, prioritized relative to other work on the product backlog, to ensure that the defect is analyzed and solved by the Scrum team.

We'll use the aircraft management example from the previous section to illustrate a little more fully what this means. Let's assume that there's an item on the product backlog to add multideck support to the aircraft management system's architecture in order to allow the application to support aircraft with passenger seats on multiple decks. The item description itself will reflect the most basic, general decisions about the enhancement. For example, we can assume that Paul, the uber product owner, has already confirmed that the team need not consider more than two decks. Paul may have also allowed the team to limit the number of seats on the aircraft to no more than 999 (the maximum seating capacity of the Airbus A390 is only 525 passengers, so this constraint didn't seem very limiting to Paul). The resulting backlog item might look more like this:

> Modify the architecture to support aircraft of one or two decks and less than 1,000 seats.

However, as the team continues to evaluate and analyze this backlog item, information related to the design is created that doesn't fit on the backlog item and has to be stored somewhere. The team builds tentative schemas for the "aircraft" and "seats" tables and also starts constructing a list of code modules and reports that will be impacted by the changes. Further discussions lead to agreed upon modifications to existing internal application interfaces to support the new database and the new functions. None of this information really belongs on the backlog itself, but it's important to retain the information for future discussions and reference during the actual building of the items during a sprint.

In addition, during the detailed discussions, one of the architects identifies two bugs in one of the routines supporting the "seats" table in the database and adds those defects to the defect management system for tracking. Bill, the product owner for this portion of the application, decides that the defects will be made critical by the planned changes and therefore decides to put the defects IDs of the new defects on the product backlog.

As a result of discussions regarding this single backlog item, all three pieces of the extended product backlog are modified: the product backlog itself, the item information library, and the defect management system (see Figure 23.5).

Figure 23.5 illustrates how discussion concerning a single backlog item (**number** 100) creates new information in the library storage tool about the "aircraft"

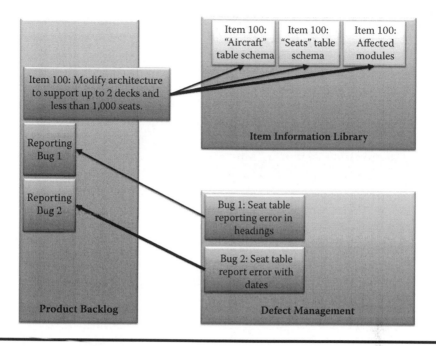

Figure 23.5 How the extended product backlog works.

table schema, the "seats" table schema, and a list of modules affected by backlog item 100. In addition, the discussion yields information on two new defects, **bug 1 and bug 2**, which are not only opened in the **defect management** tool for tracking, but also responsible for the creation of two new items in the **product backlog** that allow the **product owner** to essentially schedule the correction of the defects.

All three pieces of the extended product backlog, therefore, work together to help ensure that the product owner and the Scrum teams have all of the information they need to understand, estimate, plan, and finally build the product as the product owner envisions it.

The Product Backlog

The real challenge of the product backlog is making it visible to everyone in the organization, making it easy to access and understand, making it easy to rearrange and prioritize, and yet, at the same time, restricting access so that only the product owner and the business analysts can add and update information and only the product owner can prioritize the items. It is the reporting and security needs that usually drive organizations to select specialized tools to manage the product backlog rather than using a spreadsheet. The most common tools for managing the product backlog are:

- Excel (http://www.microsoft.com/office)
- ScrumWorks (http://www.scrumworks.com)
- XPlanner (http://www.xplanner.org)
- Rally (http://www.rallydev.com)
- VersionOne (http://www.versionone.com)

Other than the spreadsheets, most of these tools provide some degree of security to protect the backlog and utilities to support the viewing, modification, and prioritization of product backlog items. Most of them also provide features that simplify the slicing of items into smaller "child" items. One unique feature of ScrumWorks Pro by Danube Technologies, Inc. is its ability to print backlog items on cards, which can then be used by Scrum teams to populate their story walls.

The Information Library

The information library, holding all of the information that supports the content of the product backlog, needs to be able to hold many types of information and must also allow Scrum teams to easily organize the content of the library around the product backlog items. In other words, users of the information library must be able to easily see what backlog item the information supports. Team collaboration tools often provide all of the capability that a Scrum team needs—the biggest concerns are keeping the information organized relative to the product backlog and keeping the information up-to-date. Organizations that I have worked with in the past have used the following tools to support this capability:

- Sharepoint (http://www.microsoft.com/sharepoint)
- Basecamp (http://www.basecamphq.com)
- Lotus Notes (http://www-01.ibm.com/software/lotus/)
- Wiki (http://www.mediawiki.org)

While some of these tools are more about document management than team collaboration, all of them support the ability to tag documents (providing the ability to associate a document with a backlog item number) and, more importantly, can be configured to allow appropriate access to the information in the library. My personal preference for the information library is to use any modern wiki application; with some very simple naming and usage standards, a simple wiki application can manage a significant amount of complex information.

The Defect Management System

The third component of the extended product backlog is the defect management system. The defect management system needs to be able to store all of the information needed to help developers understand, diagnose, and solve defects that have been found in the application software. There are no special agile needs for a defect management system that nearly all currently available products do not provide. Some common, easily used, and mostly free products that will work fine in this environment are:

- BugTracker.NET (http://ifdefined.com/bugtrackernet.html)
- Bugzilla (http://www.bugzilla.org/)
- Mantis (http://www.mantisbt.org/)
- GNATS (http://www.gnu.org/software/gnats/)
- Redmine (http://www.redmine.org/)

The key with the defect management system is to use it like the library system—an extended pool of information about problems in the product. However, there are two views on how to approach the solving of defects. We'll review both approaches later in this chapter.

With the concept of the extended product backlog defined, we can move on to discuss how to put information on the product backlog in the first place and what kind of information should accompany each item.

Adding Items to the Product Backlog

As mentioned earlier in this chapter, the product backlog represents the means by which the product owner defines what he or she wants in the product and in what order. To that end, the product owner must be vigilant in ensuring that *anything* he or she wants for the product ends up on the product backlog. This includes items like:

- *Features*: Of course, most of the product backlog contains items that describe "stuff" that the product owner wants his or her product to be able to do.
- *Architectural needs*:[3] Common printing and reporting routines, queue management, list management, event management, authentication and authorization, common UI rendering routines, etc.
- *Technical debt*: These are items of "DONEness" that were, in fact, not done by the developers when the feature was built. This list can be quite extensive as the organization begins a transition to agile development, and should (if the organization properly enforces the definition of DONEness in determining whether or not a feature is actually ready for production use) diminish rather rapidly during the first two years of agile development. These often include items like:
  - Incomplete refactoring
  - Writing missing unit tests
  - Writing missing acceptance tests

- Checking all product artifacts (code, documents, etc.) into source code control
- Fixing the code to pass all unit and acceptance tests
- Completing quality checks required by your quality system requirements
- Completing artifacts and other documentation required by the regulations that govern your product's development
- Updating internal specifications
- Updating product documentation

■ *Infrastructure items*: These items don't actually contribute features to the product, but they do *directly* support the developer's ability to build the product. These items can include things like:
- Building or fixing a continuous integration server
- Researching, installing, implementing developer tools

Now that we've defined some of the many types of items that can be on the product backlog, let's take a closer look at some of the information we might want to add to the item that helps us to make sure that our Scrum teams build the right product.

Adding Defects to the Product Backlog

As the completed software moves from the Scrum team to additional quality assurance teams, other development teams, and customers, defects in the software operation will be found. In most organizations, newly opened defects are categorized based on their severity and impact to the customer: low, medium, high, and critical. Low and medium defects usually indicate problems that can be worked around or ignored; high-severity defects require some kind of a solution within a specific timeframe; critical-severity defects require immediate attention.

When defects are discovered, they are recorded and tracked in the organization's defect management system. From that point forward, defects are often handled as follows:

■ Defects rated as critical go directly to the responsible Scrum team to be immediately addressed. The Scrum team will need to determine how the defect will affect the current sprint and discuss with the product owner how to modify the sprint commitment.
■ All other defects are assigned to a Scrum team and then handled in one of two ways:
- The defects are added to the product backlog and prioritized with the rest of the work. In some cases, only the high-severity defects are added to the product backlog; the medium- and low-severity defects are added during project planning for a subsequent project.

– Scrum teams save a little capacity every sprint and solve defects in their queue in priority order. The Scrum team should negotiate with the product owner on an ongoing basis to determine how much capacity should be set aside for defect resolution.

Setting Up Your Product Backlog Items for Success

Items on the product backlog drive the creation of the product. Therefore, it follows that when the Scrum team starts building an item, the more clearly defined it is, the more successful the Scrum team can be. In this section, we'll discuss many ideas that you can use with your Scrum teams to provide good and useful information to assist both with their building of the item and with the product owner's prioritization of the item. The important thing to consider when deciding which of these approaches to use and which to skip is the value that each piece of information provides. Doing something simply because it is suggested herein leads to spending time on process steps without getting any value in return. Since the product owner's job includes maximizing the return on investment (ROI), the product owner must be careful not to implement zero-value-adding steps in the development process.

One more item before we review some of the information you might want to include with your backlog items. Items in the product backlog "mature" through a process of progressive elaboration. In other words, when the item is added to the product backlog, we may know nothing about it except that the product owner wants it. As the Scrum team (and the business analysts) more fully considers the backlog item during backlog grooming workshops, the amount of information about the backlog item grows. This means that none of the information discussed in this section need be part of the backlog item at the time that the item is created. Information can and should be added over time, culminating only at the time that the item is finally under construction by the Scrum team. So, no matter what type of information your product owners decide to add to their backlog items (and not all items will need all of the same information), it should be expected that this information would collect over time, not all at once.

So, other than a description of the desired feature itself, what other types of information might your product owners and Scrum teams want to include on a backlog item? Following are some common examples.

Estimation of Problem Complexity

This, of course, is the typical estimate of the backlog item and should be present on every item on the backlog. The Scrum team that will build the item is responsible for an item's estimation (the product owner should never provide an estimate on his or her own). Whenever a new item is found on the backlog during backlog grooming, the Scrum team should be sure to put at least a high-level estimate on the item. Whether this estimate is in hours, ideal person-days, ideal team-days, or (my preference) story points, it is best if a consistent approach to estimation is a part of the grooming process from day 1.

Acceptance Criteria

Acceptance criteria help define what it is the product owner wants an item to be able to do. Typically, these items are written as if the phrase "When finished, if you do <x>, the result will be <y>" was used as a template. In other words, the acceptance criteria help the Scrum team to define DONEness for the backlog item by laying out the conditions that must be satisfied for the item to actually be considered done. Product owners and business analysts define acceptance criteria. The Scrum team can also contribute ideas for acceptance, but the product owner owns these criteria. It is recommended that *all* backlog items have acceptance criteria before the Scrum teams attempt to build them.

Risk

When we discuss the risk of an item, we are generally talking about the risk of building the item. In other words, how likely is it that an item may cause significant difficulty during or after being built? By doing a quick assessment of a backlog item's risk, the Scrum team can decide whether or not to consider the possibility of encountering significant obstacles during sprint planning and, as a result, increase the complexity estimate of the backlog item.

When assessing an item's risk, the idea is to avoid lengthy evaluation unless specifically called for. We want to keep the ROI on this activity high; since the value returned by risk assessment is somewhat directly proportionate to the risk of building the item, it pays to avoid detailed analysis of an item's risk unless that initial assessment indicates that the risk is inordinately high. Therefore, there are some statements you can consider about an item to obtain a quick evaluation of its risk, before deciding whether or not to do additional, deeper, analysis. Respond to each statement on a scale of 1 through 5.

1. Rate the team's understanding of the technology, algorithms, and concepts needed to build the item (1 = completely understood, 5 = no understanding).
2. Rate the clarity of the product owner's understanding of the feature (1 = completely clear, 5 = constantly changing).
3. Rate the team's ability to work well together (1 = very good, 5 = very poor).
4. Rate the team's overall level of experience with the product (1 = multiple senior developers with years on the product, 5 = mostly new team members with no more than one senior developer with experience).
5. Rate the stability of the application being modified (1 = very stable, 5 = very unstable).

By considering each of these statements (the team can "vote" on their answers to each statement with a rock-paper-scissors approach using between one and five fingers), you can add all of the answers together to derive a basic concept of the risk. The team can either negotiate to come to a single answer or just average the answers together and round the average off. Either way, they can reach a quick evaluation of the risk as follows:

- Minimal risk (total is less than 10): The backlog item is probably fine as defined and the team needn't consider taking any steps with regard to the risk of the item.
- Moderate risk (total is between 10 and 14): The Scrum team may wish to reestimate the complexity of the item (they don't have to change it, but they may want to rethink it).
- High risk (total is between 15 and 19): The product owner may want to consider spending a little bit more time gaining some clarity on the item. Additionally, the Scrum team may want to reestimate the complexity of the item and do some additional work understanding how the item might be built in a way that might reduce the risk. By digging a little deeper than normal, it is possible that the team, working with the product owner, can isolate and mitigate some of the risk inherent in the backlog item.
- Unacceptable risk (total is greater than 19): The product owner should strongly consider removing the item from the backlog (or drastically lowering its priority) until any or all of the following are true:
  1. The item is understood more fully.
  2. The Scrum team is better prepared to build the item.
  3. Technology exists that make the item a less risky proposition.

As the Scrum team gets better at estimating risk, they will often learn how to use previously assessed backlog items as examples in order to assess the risk in a single estimation. In other words, rather than considering the five statements listed above, team members will be able to simply assess the item as minimal, moderate, high, and unacceptable.

Value

Of course, no backlog item should be on the product backlog without some indication of the value of the item from the product owner. This piece(s) of information helps the product owner to prioritize the backlog properly and also assists in determining the ROI of the item, allowing the product owner to more objectively assess individual backlog items.

Assessing the value of a backlog item is the sole responsibility of the product owner. Just as the Scrum team owns the *complexity estimation*, the product owner owns the value estimate. What unit the product owner chooses to use, however, is up to him or her, as long as the unit is used consistently across the backlog. The product owner can use actual monetary amounts (although this can be quite difficult to do across the entire backlog) or other custom-defined units (e.g., on a scale of 0 to 10, high/medium/low, $/$$/$$$, etc.).

One approach that I have seen implemented very successfully is a method that actually uses two numbers in order to determine the overall value of the item. In this approach, we define two kinds of value as follows:

1. *Benefit*: This is a value from 0 to 20 that reflects the benefit to the customer of building a particular backlog item. A benefit of 0 indicates that the product's customers will not recognize the item as providing any value to them whatsoever. Setting the benefit to 20 means that the product won't sell without the feature represented by the backlog item.
2. *Penalty*: This is also a value from 0 to 20 that reflects the penalty or harm that may come to the product or the organization if the feature represented by the backlog item is not built. A penalty of 0 means that no harm will come to the product or organization if the feature is not built. On the other hand, a penalty of 20 indicates the likelihood that the organization would suffer near irreparable harm if the feature represented by the backlog item was not built.

The brilliance behind the penalty concept is that many backlog items represent features that are either architecturally significant or mandated by government regulations or industry standards. Items of this nature are either completely transparent to the customer or are merely baseline functions that customers will not be excited to have, but will probably not purchase the product without.

After calculating both the benefit and the penalty, the item's business value is then said to be the sum of the two values. For example, a backlog item with a benefit of 15 and a penalty of 7 would have a value of 22. Referring back to the example used earlier in the chapter, let's look at the backlog item added to the product backlog to adjust the aircraft management system's database to handle aircraft with two decks (see the "Large-Scale Product Ownership" section above).

Initial discussions of the backlog item to adjust the database schemas and several affected modules clearly demonstrated to the product owner that the architectural changes were required for the application to handle aircraft with multiple decks. While the developers made it clear that the application could be modified to support multiple decks without changing either the architecture or the database, they also made it clear that they would have to "fake out" both the database and the architecture. When the product owner asked what it meant to fake out the database, the developers responded that they would have to "force the database to do stuff it wasn't intended to do." With that reassuring thought sitting in the back of Bill's (the product owner) mind, the penalty was set to 15. At the same time, changing the architecture and the database schema would, by necessity, have absolutely no impact on the customer's view of the data or use of the application (in fact, customer transparency was one of the acceptance criteria for the item). Therefore, Bill set the benefit for the item to 3 (it would have been 0, but one of the developers mentioned that some customer would see "lower deck" on their passenger listings; assuming that there would probably be other such dubious "improvements," Bill set the benefit to 3).

Items thus valued can now be compared with other items and their complexity estimates to aid the product owner in effectively prioritizing the product backlog. Of course, you should not assume that value is the only information needed to do a proper prioritization of the product backlog. In fact, value is only one piece of all of the information needed. Product backlog prioritization is a very subjective process.

Performance Constraints

One of my major concerns with how modern software is developed (yes, even software developed using agile practices) is how little attention is given to the performance of the system until extremely late in the development effort. When I coach product owners, I suggest to them that, when they create a new item in the product backlog, they should consider the required performance of the item from the perspective of the customer. Does the item need to run nearly instantaneously? Will the customer care if the item took three or four seconds to complete? What about twenty or thirty seconds? Will the customer even notice the performance of the item (i.e., does the feature run behind the scenes or at night)? By adding performance characteristics to the backlog item, the Scrum team can derive acceptance criteria that reflect the performance requirements and, by writing automated acceptance tests that prove the performance criteria are met or exceeded, can ensure that system performance continues to be, at minimum, acceptable throughout the development effort.

For example, let's assume that the flight management software we've discussed throughout this chapter (again, for more information see "Large-Scale Product Ownership") had backlog items completed many months before regarding the recording of a seat reservation on one of the customer's flights. The performance characteristic for the original backlog item indicates that every seat reservation had to be completed within 1.5 seconds. When the feature was originally built, the Scrum teams created acceptance tests that validated that the 1.5-second limit was met under various conditions (first seat booked, last seat booked, etc.). Because the developers employ continuous integration and testing, the test that verifies the performance of the seat reservation function runs several times every day. As work begins on the architecture and the database schema to support multiple decks on an aircraft, the test will continue to execute and, should the seat reservation function performance degrade, will alert the developers at the first sign of a problem.

One method for indicating performance criteria on a backlog item is for the product owner to initially specify a relative value that will later, during backlog grooming, evolve into more detailed criteria. By adding the high-level relative value early, the Scrum team has a reasonable idea of the product owner's expectations and can evaluate the complexity of the item appropriately (i.e., the complexity of building a search capability that can search over 1 million seat reservation listings for a specific passenger in less than ten seconds can be considerably less than that of a function that has to do the same thing in less than one second). Product owners can set relative performance criteria with a very simple system, like this one:

- B (for *batch* or *background*): This feature will run overnight or in the background and won't affect the customer experience at all. In general, features in this category will run at least five minutes.
- S (for *search*): This feature will likely be a long-running search that will take up to five minutes to execute. It is expected that the feature will include a notification to the user that the search may take a while, some kind of progress bar or indicator that the system is indeed working, and a means for the user to cancel the search.
- C (for *commit*): This feature will likely be the completion of a complex workflow and the user should expect a short delay while all of the unsaved data are committed. The feature may take up to fifteen seconds to complete. It is expected that the feature will include some kind of progress bar or indicator that the system is indeed working.
- F (for *fast*): This feature will not include screen updates/flips that take longer than three seconds to complete.
- VF (for *very fast*): This feature will not include screen updates/flips that take longer than one second to complete.

Once a Scrum team begins grooming a backlog item, the item is usually sliced into smaller and smaller pieces. As backlog items are sliced, the performance characteristics of the original backlog item have to be carried forward to the smaller items.

As illustrated in Figure 23.6, we start with a "search for flights" item with a three-second performance constraint. As the item is sliced down into "searching by city" or "searching by an airport code," the three-second performance constraint remains. Then searching by an airport code is sliced into the original item and additional items to limit the search by dates, the number of stops, the time of day, and the display items. However, as the "search by airport code" item is sliced into smaller pieces, its performance constraint is lowered to allow time for processing the search limits and the display capabilities in the other items. In other words, if a user were to:

- Search for a flight by airport code (2.6 seconds), plus
- Limit the search to the first through the third of the next month (0.05 seconds), plus
- Limit the search to nonstop flights (0.05 seconds), plus
- Limit the search to flights that leave before noon (0.05 seconds), plus
- Display the results as an abbreviated listing (0.2 seconds)

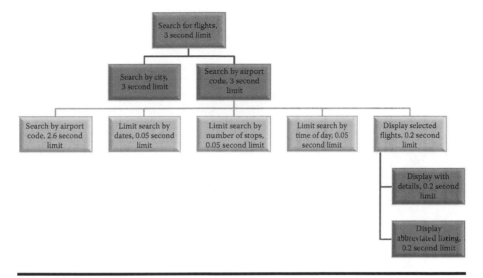

Figure 23.6   Splitting an item with a performance constraint.

The end result, if all of the performance constraints were obeyed, must be finished within 2.95 seconds (the sum total of the performance constraints of all of the affected items).

Specialized Skills

In many organizations, Scrum teams work on backlog items that frequently require skills that the team does not have and the organization has only in short supply. This leaves the time struggling to find the right people in the organization and then hoping to get enough of their time during the sprint that the backlog item can be completed in time. I frequently see this happen with limited skills such as:

- Database architect
- Database analyst
- UI usability analyst
- Technical writers/user documentation writers

In order to allow the Scrum team additional time to identify the skills they need and get a commitment of time from the proper resources before the sprint begins, Scrum teams can flag backlog items that required specialized skills. By doing so, the Scrum team can, one or two Sprints in advance, see the flagged item (see Figure 23.7) and make the necessary arrangements so that when the Scrum teams commits to the backlog item, the proper individuals can be involved.

The many preceding sections detail a number of different types of information that your product owners and Scrum teams can choose to include on their backlog

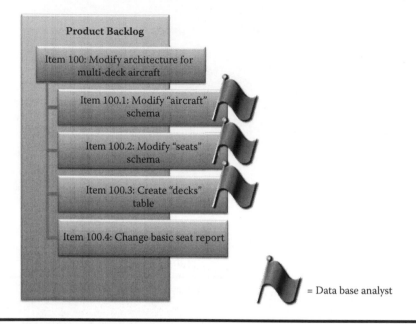

Figure 23.7 Flagging product backlog items.

items. My recommendation is to use these only when the organization feels strongly that their use will bring some positive value. For example, the preceding example of flagging backlog items that required specialized skills should probably not be implemented unless Scrum teams are suffering from lack of contact with the needed expertise. A possible plan for implementing these practices is suggested as follows:

- Implement immediately
  - Complexity estimate: This helps the Scrum teams understand how much they can get done each month (velocity) and also helps limit the backlog grooming done during a given sprint.
  - Acceptance criteria: Absolutely essential for every item, acceptance criteria help the Scrum teams understand how to build the item.
  - Value estimate: This helps the product owner maximize the return on investment during the course of the project.
- Implement as needed
  - Risk: Should your Scrum teams experience a number of unexpected complications during their sprints, implement a risk evaluation during backlog grooming. This extra thinking about complexity before building the item will reduce the number of unwanted complications.
  - Performance constraints: If your development process does not include enough performance testing until too late or if your application is very

dependent on performance, implement performance constraints on your backlog items.

- Specialized skills: If your Scrum teams are frequently finding that they can't complete backlog items because they don't have the necessary skills (but the organization does), implement backlog item flagging.

Prioritizing Items in the Product Backlog

With the product backlog filled with items that are constantly being reviewed and sliced, the product owner has the difficult job of continuously prioritizing and reprioritizing the backlog items. And there's no simple formula for prioritizing! There are many different approaches for prioritizing, and if your organization is estimating value, risk, and complexity on all of the backlog items, you'll give your product owner some information to start with. However, prioritizing the product backlog is a completely subjective experience. Here are some ideas your product owners can use to help them prioritize:

- *Which items provide the greatest business value?* By comparing the backlog item value to its complexity estimate, a rough business value can be calculated.[4]
- *Which items cost less if done earlier or in combination with other items?* Some backlog items are less expensive to complete if done early in the development of a product. For example, making significant changes to a product's database schema makes is easier to do before adding a number of new tables to the database. Adding authentication and authorization capabilities is also much easier when the product is initially built than adding the capability later. Similarly, some backlog items are easier done in combination with other items, rather than separately.
- *Which items may be riskier if done later?* Some backlog items become harder and harder to build as the product gains features and thus complexity. For example, auditing and logging capabilities become more and more risky as functions of this sort tend to require modifications across the entire product.
- *Which items add excitement, but wouldn't be asked for unless it was suggested?* Customers don't initially think of some features but, when present, those features tend to add excitement to the product and gain customer interest in it.

There are no perfect prioritizations, and the conditions that drive the order of items on the backlog change constantly. A good product owner keeps his or her eye on the current opportunities and organizes the product backlog to take advantage of them.

Managing System Constraints

We've spent most of this chapter talking about the product backlog and backlog items that help Scrum teams to understand what it is they are supposed to build. Before I close this chapter, I also want to discuss what to do with *system constraints*. Whereas the items on the product backlog tell us what we want the application to do, system constraints (also frequently called nonfunctional requirements) tell us the characteristics of the application. System constraints generally occur in two "flavors":

- *Operational characteristics*: These describe how the application is supposed to operate. On which operating systems is the application supposed to execute? How portable is the application supposed to be? What kind of database management systems is the application supposed to work with? What kind of security applications is the application supposed to support?
- *Structural characteristics*: These describe how the application is supposed to be built. There can be many kinds of structural characteristics to consider, including:
  - Maintainability: Is the application and the code itself easy to understand and make changes?
  - Scalability: How well will the application scale up (support and use additional CPUs or memory) and scale out (support and use additional nodes, like a new server in a distributed application)?
  - Testability: How well does the application support testing? Can all of the pieces of the application be tested?
  - Portability: How portable is the code? Can the code be easily moved from platform to platform without changes?

In general, structural characteristics need to be built into every Scrum team's definition of DONEness, though many of them should and will be defined at the product or organizational level. In other words, the structural characteristics of an application apply to the entire application, not just the work done by a single Scrum team. Therefore, the organization may, for example, define *maintainability* in terms of very clear coding standards that detail rules for writing code, commenting the code, and avoiding overly complex code. Each Scrum team, however, is responsible for determining how they will ensure that all of their code meets the standards mandated by the organization.

Operational characteristics, on the other hand, constrain how Scrum teams build features. Each and every backlog item, as it is being discussed, analyzed, and estimated, must be considered with respect to every operational characteristic. For example, consider the impact of an operational characteristic like this:

The application will support version 3.0.1 SP 4 of MyDatabaseManager.[5]

Unfortunately for the Scrum teams, version 3.1 of MyDatabaseManager comes with some fantastic sorting and selection routines that really speed up data table access. As the Scrum teams review the backlog items, every time they come across an item that requires reading a significant number of records from the database, they realize they are constrained to use the older selection routines and they have to be much more concerned about functional performance.

When the list of operational characteristics is fairly short, Scrum teams can consider these constraints during backlog grooming and sprint planning and note the impacts. When this is true, print the operational constraints on a large poster board and place them in the Scrum team's room and wherever backlog grooming occurs, if not the team room. However, since the list of operational characteristics can sometimes be extensive, it may sometimes be difficult to ensure that each and every backlog item is reviewed with respect to the operational constraints. Under these circumstances, consider this alternative. During backlog grooming, when a backlog item is sliced into smaller items, someone on the Scrum team takes responsibility for reviewing the new item against the operational constraints to look for any impacts. While this seems like a lot of work (and frequently it is), once an original backlog item is reviewed against the operational constraints, the "children" items that are sliced from the parent are impacted in much the same way.

Summary

In an agile environment, the product owner handles product management by populating, prioritizing, and explaining the product backlog. The items on the product backlog are defined through the product owner's contact with business management, customers, stakeholders, and developers. The product owner's primary responsibilities are several and include:

- Understanding the needs of his or her customers
- Representing the needs of the stakeholders
- Understanding the needs of multiple teams (including development, sales, technical marketing, education services, and customer service teams)
- Maximizing the return on investment of developing the product
- Prioritizing the work on the product backlog
- Translating backlog items into details for the Scrum teams
- Helping the Scrum teams to achieve a sustainable pace of development
- Planning the product beta

In large organizations, the product owner may be supplemented with business analysts to help him or her keep on top of his or her responsibilities. In these instances, the business analysts support the Scrum teams while the product owners handle the prioritization of the backlog as well as working with customers, stakeholders, and management to understand their needs. In larger projects with complex applications, the product owner is often part of a group of product owners, each with responsibility over a portion of the overall product (or, each with responsibility for a single smaller product in a family of products). In these instances, an uber product owner leads the product owner team and also sets the direction for the entire product. Product owner groups work together to coordinate their backlogs, resolve dependencies between the product backlogs, and discuss how to take advantage of new opportunities.

The product owner is responsible for the content and prioritization of the product backlog. In many organizations, the product backlog is actually made up of three pieces: the backlog itself, which contains the items that describe at a high level what needs to be done to the product; an information library into which the details of each backlog item are placed; and a defect tracking system into which information is placed that describes the defects found in the application software. The product backlog contains high-level descriptions of features to be added to the product, architectural features to be added to the product, technical debt that helps Scrum teams finish pieces of the product that had not been previously finished, and infrastructure items that help the Scrum teams to build the product. The information library and the defect tracking system support the product backlog by containing the important details needed when the Scrum team is ready to build the item or solve the defect. In this chapter, we reviewed a number of tools that many organizations use to manage their product backlog, information library, and defects.

When the product owner adds items to the product backlog, and as those items are analyzed and discussed by the product owner, the business analysts, and the Scrum team, information is added to the backlog items that can be crucial in helping the product owner to prioritize the backlog, the Scrum team assess risk, and even the Scrum team get the right expertise at the right time.

With all this information on the product backlog, the product owner is responsible for prioritizing the backlog to maximize the value of the product to his or her customers. Unfortunately, there is no good formula for helping a product owner prioritize the backlog except to keep in mind the needs of the business, stakeholder, and customers—and then to keep trying to improve the product backlog through more research, more discussion, and more prioritization.

Endnotes

1. Even in cases where actual customers support the Scrum teams, those customers have been selected by the product owner to assist the Scrum team in building features that the product owner has defined for the Scrum team.
2. FAA is the abbreviation for the U.S. agency that is responsible for the advancement, safety, and regulation of civil aviation. This is similar to the Civil Aviation Authority in the United Kingdom and Germany's Bundesministerium für Verkehr, Bau und Stadtentwicklung (Federal Ministry of Transport, Building, and Urban Affairs).
3. One particular note about architectural items: I prefer to handle architectural needs from the standpoint of application needs. In other words, are there any Scrum teams working on the application that actually need the architectural changes proposed by the item in question? Granted, some architectural changes are needed to support newer frameworks, newer operating systems, and newer hardware. These changes should be considered as part of the product direction.
4. ScrumWorks Pro, by Danube Technologies, Inc., supports the unique ability to calculate relative business weight based on the total complexity and total value in the product backlog.
5. Yes, this is a fictional product—I'm making it up.

Chapter 24

Incorporating ISO 9001 into the Agile Transition

One of the most significant concerns when implementing agile development in an organization is how to ensure that the organization can obtain or keep its ISO 9001 certification while still remaining agile. These concerns usually come from (1) the organization's quality and process managers who are concerned that agile development is too undisciplined to be successfully combined with a quality management system (QMS) and (2) developers and managers who feel that agility's strengths are threatened by being forced into a structure that allows it to work with a QMS. Fortunately, the reality is that agile development does work with a QMS and it can remain effective at the same time.

We must discuss two important points before continuing, so that you understand the focus of this chapter:

1. Implementing ISO 9001 requires expertise in the standard. If there is no one in your organization who both understands the standard and is familiar with how the standard is interpreted, hire someone to help you. Many organizations adopt the ISO 9001 standard not because they feel the need, but because their industry requires that they become ISO 9001 certified in order to sell to their market. Going about the adoption of ISO 9001 in the wrong manner will result in a lot of useless processes and bureaucracy that accomplishes nothing except slowing down your developers.
2. This chapter only covers a small portion of the ISO 9001 standard. We will discuss portions of the following:

- Section 4: General Requirements
- Section 4.2: Document your QMS
- Section 5: Management Responsibilities
- Section 5.2: Customer Focus
- Section 5.6: Management Review
- Section 6: Resource Management
- Section 6.2.2: Competence
- Section 6.3: Provide Necessary Infrastructure
- Section 6.4: Provide Suitable Work Environment
- Section 7: Product Realization
- Section 8: Measurement, Analysis, and Improvement

There is a considerable portion of the standard that will be left unreviewed by the end of this chapter that you and your organization will need to review and decide what to do about.

Implementing agile development creates a fascinating paradigm in the organization that is the root of both aforementioned, but needless, concerns: that agile is too chaotic and that agile development is weakened by structured quality management systems. Agile development can, in fact, be chaotic, but that chaos encapsulates the collaborative, creative process of knowledge creation that occurs within the development teams. Scrum builds "containers" for this chaos (sprints) that have clearly defined entry and exit points (sprint planning and sprint review meetings) and, as we have discussed elsewhere in this book, clearly defined exit criteria known as a the DONEness definition. We can focus our processes toward clarifying the exit criteria and, thus, driving quality into the sprint without having to define our processes *through* the sprint. Let's look at a few examples of DONEness definition items:

- All code within critical modules (defined by the organization) must be reviewed.
- All preexisting tests must work at the end of the sprint as they did at the beginning.
- All code must achieve unit test coverage of 90%.

The first item helps ensure that code reviews are done when the organization's most critical (or perhaps most brittle) modules are modified. Of course, whenever there's a *must* defined in the process, the Scrum team will have to prove that the proper code reviews were done. That will require a code review record that identifies what code was reviewed, who participated in the review, and what was the outcome of the review (including steps taken based on the review findings).

The second item requires that all preexisting tests work at the end of the sprint as they did at the beginning of the sprint. That will require that the team acquire the outcome of the regression test run just prior to the beginning of the sprint and at the end of the sprint (or run the tests themselves) and provide those at the sprint review.

Similarly, the third item also requires proof, generated by a tool of some kind, that the total unit test coverage of the application is still at or above 90%. This can only be demonstrated by running the tool at the end of the sprint and providing the proof during the sprint review.

By setting these criteria into the organization's DONEness definition, we drive quality into the sprint without creating additional and unnecessary process steps in or around the sprint at the same time. The Scrum team still has the flexibility to build the product as they see fit, within the bounds of the organization's standards for quality. While this does mean that the Scrum team will need to show proof that the DONEness criteria have been adhered to during the sprint (which means the creation and collection of records and signatures from time to time), we're really not doing anything more than asking for evidence that the work that they say is done is actually done (this is part of the team's responsibility for self-management). We ask no less from a contractor that puts a roof on our house or does electrical work in our office buildings. We would certainly not dream of asking less from our physicians and surgeons.

In short, we allow the chaos of the sprint, but we protect the rest of the organization from that chaos by surrounding it with controls like:

- DONEness criteria: These help the Scrum team, whenever they build a product backlog item, incorporate all of the activities that are proven to improve product quality.
- A product backlog, groomed and ready: A groomed product backlog has been reviewed and discussed many times by the Scrum teams. When it comes time for sprint planning, the Scrum teams are already very familiar with the content of the product backlog and can easily break the items down into tasks.
- Continuous build and testing: By continuously rebuilding and retesting the product, the Scrum teams can be alerted immediately when the product suffers a failure of any kind.
- Product owners: By enforcing the DONEness criteria at sprint review, the Scrum team gets repeated reminders to use the DONEness criteria and, more importantly, software that isn't done won't be released into the final product.
- Scrum master: By enforcing the DONEness criteria during sprint planning and throughout the sprint, there is a force throughout the development process ensuring that good development practices are followed and quality is programmed into the product, rather than being added on later.

There's a standard mantra around ISO 9001: "Say what you do and do what you say." In other words, the whole point behind ISO 9001 is to take something that works and to ensure that it continues to work by documenting the processes and ensuring that those processes are repeated. However, ISO 9001 is not prescriptive—it instructs you on what needs documentation, but you and your organization have to decide on the content of the document. If you can deliver good, high-quality code most of the time, ISO 9001 will help you do it all of the time.[1] The real key to ISO 9001 and agile development is to step your way through the standard one slice at a time and not to try for perfection (you'll end up creating big, fat processes that you don't need and you'll drive a wedge between your Scrum teams and your quality managers). Develop your processes a bit at a time, taking time during sprint retrospectives to correct, enhance, and improve your processes as needed.

Setup

There are several steps that you'll have to consider during the implementation of the ISO 9001 standard, but it primarily boils down to:

- *Document*: In order to get anyone to review, provide feedback, or even learn and follow procedure, you have to give your organization something to read. Thus, all of your development procedures will need to be documented.
- *Communicate and train*: Your Scrum teams will want to understand why you are implementing the ISO 9001 standard. Many developers naturally see standards as barriers to getting the job done, though this is often because:
  - The implementation is done wrong.
  - The processes are too restrictive or too heavy.
  - They were not properly communicated.
  - All of the above.

  It will be up to you and the transition team to explain to the development community in your organization why you are implementing ISO 9001. Be clear and be honest. ISO 9001 is usually implemented for two reasons: (1) having ISO 9001 certification is a market differentiator (or even a market requirement) for a manufacturer, and (2) ISO 9001 helps to produce consistent quality—this makes the manufacturing process (or, in our case, the development process) more predictable and enables better planning. Your teams will have lots of arguments, particularly about creating and signing records and other items that they will see as waste. As the ISO 9001 standard is implemented, you will need to begin training that will be repeated on a frequent basis to ensure that all employees affected by the standard are aware of how to do their jobs based on your organization's processes.
- *Monitor*: Once you have everything ready, you will need to ensure two things: (1) that your processes are being followed and (2) that your processes are working. Quality managers should always be working to improve processes that require improvement, improve training when the training is not sufficient, and completely remove policies that are proving to be counterproductive or do not add value and are unable to be improved.

Creating Your Policy and Process Documentation

If you recall from earlier, the first part of the mantra concerning ISO 9001 is to say what you are going to do. That's what the documentation step is all about—putting into writing how you develop your application. In this section, we'll identify what needs to be documented. However, don't forget that your organization may have additional requirements and standards (e.g., ISO 13485, Sarbanes-Oxley, etc.) that also need to be factored into this outline of processes.

To get started, you'll need to create some basic policies.[2] You can do this in a very agile way by defining the basic policies and then reviewing the impact of each policy during the next sprint retrospective meeting. Changes and additions to the policies can be discussed in the retrospective and then the policy documents can be updated.

- Quality policy: Think of this document as the top of your quality management system. It sets the stage and provides an entry point for the rest of your system. You can either document your entire QMS in this single document, or modify this document to provide the location of all of the other significant documents that will make up your quality management system.
    - Involve all roles in the creation of the quality policy.
    - What's your goal? Why are you doing this?
    - How will you manage your documented policies, keep them up-to-date, and communicate them to new and current employees alike?
    - Write it up and explain your commitment.
        - "Our policy is that we develop only the highest-quality products."
        - "Our policy is that we partner with our customers to build the best custom software."
- Audit policy: An active internal auditing policy helps your organization do an excellent job during the compliance audits that are required at regular intervals to maintain certification.
    - Who will do the audit? Who is trained to do audits? How will they be done (all policies or focused, surprise or scheduled, both/all)? Who enforces the outcomes (corrective actions)?
        - Surprise audits can be problematic. How will you account for the potential loss in velocity when the audit interrupts the team? Quality managers may need the authority to override the product owner.
    - Who will be engaged to handle formal compliance audits?
- Document control: Where will important artifacts (including documents, records, and source code) be stored?
    - Is there a naming standard?
    - How are they versioned?
    - Archiving: How long are documents saved?

  - Which documents are considered controlled documents? You will definitely want to consider the following documents:
    - DONEness definition
    - Product backlog
    - Design specifications (if applicable)
    - Functional specifications (if applicable)
- Review and approval policy: Many artifacts require review by multiple people within the organization, and some require approval by specific individuals within the organization.
  - Who reviews which artifacts? Who approves them?
  - This will also drive which artifacts must be created during development. Take advantage of this to find out who really needs what information (don't create information that no one wants or needs to read).
  - It is also a good idea to create some kind of template or description so everyone knows what each artifact is supposed to hold (at the same time, make sure that everyone understands which parts of the templates are required and which can be dropped if not useful or applicable).
- Nonconformance policy: How does the organization respond when defects are found at the customer site?
  - How do we confirm the defect? (Do we bring their environment to us? Do we go to them? Do we just take their word for it and hope to re-create?)
  - How do we rate the severity of the defect (routine, annoying, serious, critical)?
  - Which severities are allowed to go directly to a Scrum team? Which severities go to the product backlog for later consideration (based on the prioritization of the item)?
  - How do we assess the impact of the defect on other customers? Which customers are affected? How do we inform the customers? What do they do until it's fixed?
- Corrective and preventative action policy: What does the organization do with defects?
  - Corrective action:
    - How do we fix defects at the customer site (hot fix, patch, complete redelivery, using remote connections to get in and change it)?
    - How do we track which customer has what versions? Fixes? Patches?
  - Preventative action:
    - How do we ensure that defects don't make it to our customers?

Development Processes

You will also need to document your development processes. In an agile environment, you will want to include some or all of the processes (not to mention adding some of your own) shown in Tables 24.1 and 24.2.

Table 24.1 Scrum Processes That Will Require Documentation

Process	Items to Consider (Remember that Scrum defines some of this quite clearly. For example, only the product owner can prioritize the backlog, but everyone should be able to see it and add to it. Don't change the basic rules of Scrum when documenting this.)
Backlog management	• Who changes the product backlog? • Who prioritizes the product backlog? • Who is allowed to view the product backlog? • When an item is added or modified, how do you know who did it?
Sprint planning meeting	• Timing? • Attendance? • Purpose?
Sprint review meeting	• Timing? • Attendance? • Purpose? • Is a record of decisions made during the meeting required?
Daily Scrum meeting	• Timing? • Attendance? • Purpose?
Sprint retrospective meeting	• Timing? • Attendance? • Purpose?

Focusing on Customers

Section 5.2 of the ISO 9001 standard addresses some interesting aspects of customer focus.

How does management ensure that the organization is meeting customer requirements? In an agile project, that's actually fairly easy to do. Customer needs are addressed using the product backlog that is maintained and prioritized by the organization, led by the product owner. To complete the picture, however, you need to consider the following:

Table 24.2 Other Processes That Will Require Documentation

Process	Items to Consider
Release planning workshop	This is the workshop held when we are getting an initial sizing and arrangement of the release backlog for a project. • Timing? • Attendance? • Purpose? • T-shirt sizing practice?
Scrum team staffing	How do we define our teams? Are there guidelines for the types of expertise needed on each team? • 5 to 9 people per team • Who is the Scrum master? • Who is the product owner? • Who is on the team?
Application testing	• What type of testing is required? • Who is supposed to do it and how often? • What happens when a test breaks? • Who writes the tests? • Who validates the tests?

- How do you prove that every item that the Scrum teams work on came from the product backlog?
- How do you ensure that Scrum teams only take their work from the product backlog?
- How do you keep Scrum teams focused only on product backlog items?

Resource Management

Resource management is likely where many of your problems will begin to occur. Many organizations try to "do more with less" to the extent that they often lack enough of the proper skills to get the job done. But this is exactly what Section 6 of the ISO 9001 standard is all about—Do you have enough money and people to test your software, audit your processes, and keep the entire QMS up-to-date and effective? If your organization is unwilling to commit the proper resources, stop now—ISO 9001 isn't for you.

Whenever you introduce an employee (newly hired or otherwise) to one or more roles that he or she has never handled in your development organization, you will want to be sure that the employee has received the appropriate training and that the training was effective. You will also need to be able to prove that the employee has had the proper training through some form of training record.

Infrastructure and Work Environment

Infrastructure and work environment considerations in an agile development can be very fluid. A lot depends on how many teams you will have, how complex your product runtime and development environments are, and how you plan to test your products. For ISO 9001, your infrastructure and work environment must reflect what is genuinely necessary to meet your product quality goals. While this certainly includes computer hardware and software (Scrum teams need to have hardware and software environments that support development and testing and enough environments to properly support high quality development), it also includes what might end up being significant facility modifications to create team rooms, white boards for brainstorming, tables and chairs for the team rooms, in-house wireless phones, white noise generators to reduce team room noise, wireless laptops for developers, extensive reworking of your internal wireless access point capacity, software for continuous build and test servers, etc. There can be quite a lot to worry about here.

For ISO 9001, your goal is to document what your teams and your products need in order to develop a quality product. In general, you should be clear about the software and hardware requirements that every team must meet, while you can be a lot less specific in the definition and content of the team room. This is because, while a significant problem can develop because two different versions of a particular software tool might be in use, the exact size and shape of a team room is much more flexible. However, be careful not to cut corners here. It will seem like everything you do is going to produce little to no tangible benefit. However, everything you do here will improve the work environment of your developers, and that will result in a high-quality product.

Measurement, Analysis, and Improvement

ISO 9001 will also require you to define how you plan to measure, analyze, and improve your processes in order to reduce failure (any outcomes that do not meet your quality standards) to zero. In this section, you will need to consider issues presented in Figure 24.1.

Review and Revise

The same forces that drive the emergence of the product backlog—market needs, customer needs, business needs—also drive changes in the organization's quality management system. What is important today may be of secondary concern tomorrow.

How will you ensure that you are actually meeting customer requirements?

Are your customers still reporting defects?

Are customers reporting that your product isn't meeting their needs?

Monitoring and measurement of processes: Are they resulting in consistent quality? Is the resulting quality good enough?

Continuous Improvement

Sprint retrospectives: Results will need to be saved as a record. How the team uses the information will also need to be recorded.

Look for ways to improve system-wide processes (continuous integration, configuration management, etc.).

How do you define a major/critical defect? How does one product's defects compare with the organization's other products?

Tracking Defects and Customer Complaints

Handle customer complaints and fix defects. How can you ensure that defects don't make it to the customer again? How can you ensure that defects can't escape the sprint? How does management review your major defects? What caused them? How much time was lost as a result of rework/redelivery?

More than fixing, though, how do you make sure that your system documentation reflects the corrections? How do your test suites get updated?

How do you handle informing your customer base when a major/critical defect is found in your product?

What should your customers do until the defect is fixed?

How do you get critical fixes to all of the right customers quickly?

Can your customers back off their fix patches or releases?

How are they added to the backlog and prioritized with other work?

Use risk management tools to help prioritize defects.

Defects that linger for a long period of time without updates/comments can draw the attention of auditors.

Are defects being resolved quickly enough? Are they prioritized properly?

Figure 24.1   Measurement concerns.

The focus of today's development activity may be quite different tomorrow. Taiichi Ohno,[3] considered the father of Toyota's groundbreaking Toyota Production System, suggested that proper standards change fairly constantly (at least once a month). In the complex world of software development, we need to build the capability for review and revision of our quality management system into our daily lives.

Leveraging Scrum to Improve Process

Scrum, by definition, provides opportunities on a daily basis to identify obstacles. These obstacles can be as simple as a basic hardware failure (e.g., "My mouse doesn't work anymore") and as complex as a significant process failure (e.g., "I can't finish my task because no one will give me access to the proper database tables"). We can learn from these obstacles and create improvements in our processes that mitigate or altogether eliminate the possibility of the same problems in the future. We can leverage Scrum to make it happen by:

- Using the DONEness definition to capture development policies
- Using sprint planning to review the DONEness definition and building its requirements directly into the sprint backlog
- Using sprint review to accomplish the requirements of the organization's review and approval policies
- Using sprint retrospectives to identify ineffective policies and correct them

Using the DONEness Definition

Build applicable development policies right into the organizational definition of DONEness. Some examples of this are:

- Document control
  - "By the end of the Sprint, all PBI-related artifacts must be updated (their change description tables updated), and checked in to the project source repository."
  - Change logs should include the date and name of the person who made the changes.
- Review and approval policy
  - "Before the end of the sprint, completed source code must be reviewed by two senior team members." Make sure that you have some kind of proof that a review was done.
- Preventative action policy
  - "Root causes for critical defects should be determined and reviewed during sprint retrospective for potential policy or DONEness definition changes."

Using Sprint Planning

When any Scrum team does sprint planning, they can use the current DONEness definition to ensure that the latest policy changes make it into their planning.

- Always make sure you have the latest version of the DONEness definition!
- Convert those DONEness needs into tasks:
    - "Update story narrative document and change log."
    - "Ensure all artifacts are checked into project repository."
    - "John to review source code for correctness and coding standards."
    - "George to review source code for correctness and coding standards."
- Of course, more experienced teams can create fewer tasks, but there needs to be proof of any reviews (what was reviewed, who reviewed, and for what).

Using Sprint Reviews

You may also want to consider the creation of a sprint review record that is completed at every sprint review meeting and helps to ensure that there is recorded proof of the periodic software review and all documentation modified during the course of the sprint. The record will need to be saved according to your document control policies, can be quite simple in structure, and can help to provide information regarding:

- What was reviewed (can refer to PBI ID if applicable)?
- Final status of each item (DONE or NOT DONE)?
    - This must be tested against the DONEness definition; review as much as possible—be prepared to offer proof of documentation, tests successfully run, internal reviews, etc.
- Who approved? Collect their signature as well.

Using Sprint Retrospectives

Just as with the formal policies, use your sprint retrospective meetings to review the effectiveness of the documented processes and decide on changes and improvements to make. Scrum teams should alert the quality manager whenever:

1. A policy is unclear or incorrect.
2. A policy had to be deviated from during the sprint and why.
3. The team finds an improvement to the policy
4. The DONEness definition is missing something

The findings of all retrospective meetings should be documented and saved as a project artifact (per your organization's document control policy). Quality managers should be held responsible for periodically reviewing all retrospective findings in order to locate trends and common problems.

Formal Reviews

Even though sprint retrospective meetings provide excellent opportunities to reassess policies and processes on a regular basis, you may still find it useful to hold a periodic, detailed review of your collective quality management system. Scrum teams will often question processes, but a management review needs to go deeper. Management reviews periodically assess the quality management system to ensure that it is meeting its stated objectives. In an agile project, this can be easily managed by adding a step to the project planning process to review the QMS and its impact on previous projects. While a once-a-project review is usually sufficient, your organization may want additional reviews, in which case you could:

- Review at a predetermined midpoint during the project
- Review during sprint retrospection every one, two, three, or even four sprints during the project

If doing a review once during a project is too often, you could also schedule quarterly reviews, biannual reviews, yearly reviews, etc. How often you review your QMS should be driven by how well the system is working for you and how often you have to deviate from it during the course of your project. However, even a solid, proven QMS should be reviewed no less often than once a year.

The review itself should include an examination of the following:

- Objectives of the QMS: Are they still applicable?
- Deviations from the QMS during recent projects (completed and ongoing): Do those deviations indicate processes that are obsolete or ineffective?
- Results of audits.
- Corrective and preventative actions (CAPA) status: Do your defects indicate possible failures in the development process?
- Results from previous changes to the QMS: Did your changes better enable the QMS to meet its objectives? Are your customers more satisfied?

Reviews of the QMS should include all roles from the development community (coders, testers, analysts, etc.) to ensure that all relevant perspectives are brought into the discussion.

Summary

ISO 9001 was written to establish consistency in product quality. Agile development creates improved product quality by fostering more collaboration between team members and establishing a closer connection to the customer. Implementing ISO 9001 and agile development are not mutually exclusive activities.

To implement ISO 9001 in an agile development environment, one needs only to learn the basic rules of the standard (either by attending the proper training or by hiring someone who has) and then following these steps:

1. *Create a starter set of policies*: Your organization will need to document its initial quality policies (i.e., quality, auditing, document control, review and approval, nonconformance, and corrective and preventative action) and development processes (e.g., sprint planning, sprint review, sprint retrospectives, backlog grooming, etc.).

2. *Teach the policies*: Anytime that a new policy is created or an existing one is changed, the users of the policies (primarily management and the developers) must be informed of the change, taught how the change affects them, and taught how to follow the policy. This can take place in a classroom setting for a significant change, or just an email for a minor change.

3. *Execute the policies*: Build your code. Follow the policies unless you discover you can't, and then make sure you can justify why you couldn't when the organization assesses the policies again.

4. *Assess and correct*: Review your policies. What worked? What didn't? Fix what didn't.

5. *Repeat*: Go back to step 2. Teach your organization about the policy changes (if any) arising from step 4 and do the steps again.

By following these steps, your organization will create a quality management system that works, rather than a system that gets in the way of actually getting work done. By involving your entire organization in the creation of the system, instead of just a select few, you will achieve better buy-in and better understanding of the policies and processes, why they exist, and how to use and follow them.

Lastly, of course, should your quality management system get in the way, be prepared to scrap the pieces that don't work and try again. As Dr. Ohno suggested, standards that don't change every month are a waste. Don't waste your time and energy on useless policies.

Endnotes

1. This is really important. ISO 9001 will not help you deliver high-quality code. If you have poor processes and deliver poor code, all ISO 9001 will do is help you deliver poor code all of the time. Make sure you can deliver code that meets your quality standard when applying ISO 9001. Otherwise, you'll find yourself in a constant state of process revision that will cause breakdowns all throughout your organization.

2. You can find more information at http://www.bigagiledevelopment.com/qualitymanagement.

3. Ohno, Taiichi. *Workplace Management*, trans. Jon Miller. Mukilteo, WA: Gemba Press, 2007.

Index